CHRIS

ANTI-CAPITALISM

The
Social Economy
Alternative

SPOKESMAN

First published in 2002 by
Spokesman
Russell House
Bulwell Lane, Nottingham NG6 0BT
Phone 0115 9708318
Fax 0115 9420433
e-mail elfeuro@compuserve.com
© 2002 Chris Hill

ISBN 0 85124 658 3

A CIP catalogue record is available from the British Library

COVER
Aubade II by David Platts (1997). Some of David's work can be viewed at www.artifexlondon.com.

Printed by the Russell Press Ltd. (phone 0115 9784505)

FOREWORD

The final draft of 'Anti Capitalism' was completed a few days before the terrorist attack on the World Trade Centre. I thought of furiously scattering topical references throughout the text, so as not to seem out of date, but decided against it. Recent events have only served to bring forward the recession anticipated in the book, and the instability of the global economy has been confirmed. The measures of poverty and dissatisfaction contained here were collected at the top of a long economic boom. For at least two years, social conditions are likely to worsen, reinforcing the case for change.

When you read this, you may wonder where I have been the last few months, but it will not be because the arguments have weakened. The need for an economic alternative grows ever more urgent. The anti-capitalist movement may have been forced to draw breath, but its significance has not diminished.

Chris Hill, November 2001

ACKNOWLEDGEMENTS

My first thanks should go to all those Militants and activists, who, over the years, have put up with me discussing economics, when they would rather have been talking about something else. More recently I would like to thank Bill Hopwood, Mike Campbell, Janie Percy Smith, Michael Barratt Brown, Andrew Glyn and Dave Sellars for their wisdom and advice. John Wallace for taking the time to whip me in to grammatical shape (against all his political instincts!) and Helen Seymour for performing the double feat of proof-reading and living with my bad moods. Also David Platts for his beautiful picture that forms the cover.

CONTENTS

INTRODUCTION

Draws a sketch of capitalist development world-wide, analysing why the benefits of growth have by-passed so many.

Traces the relative decline in the British economy from after the war until the nineties.

Analyses the growth of poverty in the eighties and the unevenness of employment growth over the recent cycle.

Shows the growth in inequality and explains why this is likely to be a continuing trend.

Britain's fastest growing city economy. Shows how poverty has grown despite the successes.

Suggests that if we do not relate economics to what makes us happy, economic policy is meaningless. Cites psychiatric research evidence to back up the argument that modern capitalism tends to undermine our self-esteem and break down supportive social bonds.

Notes the lengthening of the business cycle and suggests reasons why. Rejects determinist capitalist crisis theories that foresee inevitable collapse. Introduces discussion of economic and financial instability.

Dissects reality from hype in the new economy debate, concludes that the main effect will be to intensify competition and analyses increasing divisions in the labour market.

Describes the make up of the public company. Looks at the ownership and power of the corporation and how they have become socially owned without being socially controlled. Recognises that public ownership is more a political than a technical problem. Challenges the assumption that corporate governance is effective – examines underinvestment and the misallocation of profits. Breaks down the meaning of globalisation. What is necessary and what is not?

Identifies the 'wall of money' building up internationally from pension and insurance funds. Explains how stock, derivative and exchange markets have become little more than casinos and examines the consequences of this.

3. THE FAILURE OF CENTRAL PLANNING 147

Contradictions of Central Planning

Discusses why the allocation economy is unworkable

Market Socialism Communist Style

Examines what the experiences of Hungary, China and Yugoslavia have to teach us. The first two are examples of centrally planned economies in transition to the free market. Yugoslavia, with all its distortions, represented a new form of economic organisation.

Other Planning Variants

Examines attempts to plan capitalism. Concludes that they can only be effective in exceptional political circumstances e.g. war. Why the politics of globalisation virtually rules out social democratic state intervention for the future.

Planning – Some conclusions

Discusses how some elements of the Yugoslavian self-management system could be enhanced to become a model for a socialised economy.

4. THE GREENING OF SOCIALISM 176

Talks of the contribution of green economics to developing a people-centred analysis. Examines their economic policies. Argues that their politics (as presented by Green Parties) ignore the realities of economic power and builds in the inevitability of splits between reformist and fundamentalist wings, the latter retreating to a form of lifestyle politics. Talks of the need for the coming together of socialists and anti capitalist greens.

5. OUTLINES OF A SOCIALIST ECONOMY 192

Core of the argument is that major corporations should be run by a combination of worker, consumer and state representatives. Develops the idea of professional consumer networks. Explains how social ownership is technically easy to achieve. Examines how shared information between socially owned enterprises will allow both planning and competition to co-exist in a networked economy.

Runs through what socialism could achieve, emphasising how the knowledge economy lends itself to the exercise of social control, and then tackles all the arguments against socialisation (lack of incentives, inefficiency, soft budgeting etc.).

Rebuffs the arguments of the free traders and explains the need for exchange and import controls, particularly in a transitional period. Emphasises the need for a European and international dimension and suggests how socialisation could avoid trade deficits between regions and countries.

How the number of employee owned enterprises could be increased under the socialised sector. Reviews the advantages of co-ops.

Argues that the small business sector must be supported within an improved framework of workers' rights.

Tackles the fundamentalist argument that the above would change little. Expresses a belief in the long-term aim of the non-money economy. Sees the socialised economy as a transition - the breakpoint where we cease to be victims of market forces and take control of the world we are creating.

Argues that the Labour Party has become similar to the US Democrat Party and that radical movements are forced to build outside it. Recognises the weakness of the left and the absence of activists in general. Discusses the shortcomings of anarchist style politics. Points to indications that the political pendulum may again be moving back to the left. Suggests that there is scope for alliances seeking to rebuild working class representation in an economic downturn. Expresses the belief that, in the face of a world plagued by economic uncertainties and unaccountable oligarchies, the struggle for a democratic economy will re-emerge.

INTRODUCTION

Dancing in the streets was not a feature of Tony Blair's re-election. When the privatisation of the Welfare State became a central plank of the campaign, it is not surprising that over forty per cent of us found something better to do than vote on June 7th. With Labour's landslide, it looked as though we were set for another term of leave-them-to-it politics.

However, after a decade of relative political quiet, **something** is clearly going on. The political current that jumped from the developing to the developed world in Seattle in 1999, attracted three hundred thousand people on to the streets of Genoa at the G8 demonstration in July 2001. Far from fading away, the rolling anti-capitalist protests appear to be building in strength, just as the three main capitalist countries, the US, Germany and Japan are synchronising a global downturn. With the media concentrating on violent clashes and the force used by massive police mobilisations, the significance of the anti capitalist protests is often missed. For the first time, arguably for a generation, young people can see an attractive entry point in to general politics, rather than limiting themselves to single-issue campaigns. Parallels could be drawn with the engaging effects of the Vietnam war protests in the sixties, but two differences are immediately obvious:

Firstly, today's activist is much more focussed on where the problem lies (capitalism) and who is responsible (corporations) compared to the often confusing idealism of thirty years ago, and secondly, those who became politicised in the sixties and early seventies tended to gravitate naturally towards socialist (and feminist) ideas. Not so today.

There is a witty banner that keeps reappearing on anti-capitalist demonstrations:

Overthrow capitalism. Replace it with something nicer

Tongue-in-cheek though it is, it highlights the central dilemma. If the system is to be overthrown, what is to be put in its place? There is an urgent need to engage with a new generation of activists about what socialism means in the modern context and how we can achieve it. That is what this book is about - the need to replace the capitalist economy with a social economy and just what this means.

I have spoken on economics enough times to dread the glazed looks and silences that can follow what I thought was a fascinating and animated delivery. In one of his more perceptive remarks, US President Lyndon Johnson once said, "Speaking about economics is like pissing down your leg. You feel it's hot but nobody else does". It has to be accepted that waves of statistics about money and desperately dull institutions like banks and corporations are unlikely to touch people's spirit. It can all be knuckle-chewingly boring.

Hopefully, this will not be the case here. Economics, or more accurately political economy, touches and forms every aspect of our lives. Keep asking 'why?' to any statement on the human condition and you eventually end up back at genetics, psychology or political economy (more than likely a combination of all three). Not just poverty and wealth, but the way we bring up children, associate with each other, absorb outlook and culture and so on, are to a great extent determined by the way the economy is organised and power is distributed. For those wanting to understand and change the world, coming to grips with economics is compulsory and can be interesting!

No one is likely to suggest that capitalism has solved all the problems of economic society. Poverty, inequality and attendant ethnic strife and civil war can be observed throughout most of the world. But is there any better way of organising the economy? The book seeks to tackle the question in relation to the advanced capitalist countries in general, and Britain in particular. The reason for this emphasis is that, in a global economy, the fate of the smaller, developing economies, is to a great extent in the hands of the larger ones. Also, it is easy to pronounce that there has to be a better way in the poorest countries in the world. The case is harder to argue in the richest.

This book's analysis of poverty, inequality and the labour market draws on the British experience, as does the political conclusion at the end. Discussion of corporate and financial power, the history of planning, alternative ways of organising the economy and green economics, is applicable to and uses examples from most of the advanced capitalist countries. These countries share a number of features. The most important point of difference, in economic terms, is between the Anglo-Saxon economies, chiefly Britain and the USA, and the rest. The American elite has led the world in tearing down barriers to the free market, while in Europe and Japan corporate hierarchies are more stable and social protection measures are still in place. From an analysis point of view, this is not a major problem. All the movement is in one direction; towards the Anglo-Saxon model. For European economies, the introduction of 'flexible labour' and 'improved capital markets' is only a matter of timing and degree (1).

The book has been arranged to encourage skipping and dipping. We all have different fields of knowledge and I have tried to structure the chapters in such a way that the thread will not be lost if the reader moves to what they consider controversial and interesting.

'Anti capitalism' has an immodest aim. It starts by defining what the problems of the free market political economy are, goes on to discuss the solution and ends with how we politically set about implementing that solution. I see this broad synthesis as strength, though there is a price to pay in the level of generalisation that has to be employed.

The general thesis is this: the virtuous circles that combined in the post war economic boom to lift investment, profits, employment and incomes broke down in the mid nineteen seventies. In their place, an era of intensified competition began, of which globalisation is a symptom. Ever-larger companies and financial institutions strain to obtain a global reach and penetrate every potential market. If governments seek to control these global markets, they are punished by investment being taken elsewhere.

The system is not staggering towards an apocalyptic conclusion; capitalism remains dynamic, but as the free market becomes more uncontrolled, tensions increase within it. The free market creates 'winner takes all' economies in which poverty and inequality tend to grow. Divisions widen between those with plenty of money and no time, and those with no money and the time of the under-employed.

A tendency towards global overcapacity in manufacturing limits the possibilities of profitable activity and reinforces the shift to service industry in the advanced economies. As a consequence there is a need for corporations to continually generate demand for new services. Marketing budgets rise inexorably. Individual consumption is everywhere, promoted in preference to collective effort and enjoyment. The local football team is wound up, the corporate football club prospers. Increased consumption bears little relationship to happiness, while the social support networks so important to well-being, continue to corrode. And these are the good times.

The majority of the large economies prospered in the nineties with the help of the boom in the American economy. US growth has proved to be unsustainable and there is a strong possibility of the world being tipped into recession, sending rising jobs figures into reverse and writing down the value of savings. The chances of economic disruption have been magnified by the concentration of international finance. The scale and mobility of investment funds is now such that if panic takes hold amongst financiers, an economy can be laid to waste within weeks. The Asian currency crisis of '97 showed as much.

For all its large organisations and institutional trappings, the free market is anarchy. We have control over our individual consumption but little else. Employment, work patterns, hours, wages, investment, housing, local development, what we are offered in the supermarket or on TV: all these things are delivered through the invisible hand of the market, without any conscious social control other than the odd planning permission.

The negative aspects of the free market can only be combated by the socialisation of the large corporations. There can be no return to a more egalitarian social democracy that depended on the social consensus of the post war boom for its existence. The undermining of the structures that drive globalisation is now necessary to achieve a more equal and socially supportive society.

At the same time socialists have to recognise that in any transitional society the role of the market remains crucial in allowing choice and as an indicator of business underperformance. The failure of Soviet type central planning was not only due to lack of democracy but to the abolition of the market in the allocation of goods and services.

State ownership versus private ownership is the wrong way to pose the socialist case. It is rather this: should public corporations be run in the social interest or should they be run to maximise profits? Production is organised at a social scale within huge organisations, but is run according to the primitive rules of private ownership and increasing shareholder value. Instead of being run by part time directors recruited from the old boy network, corporations should be run by trained representatives of the workforce, consumers and the state. To end the destructive effects of profit maximisation, the power of shareholders would have to be broken. This has to be done through public ownership. Regulatory measures only increase the level of aggravation in the system, as business seeks to avoid increasing state interference. Taking over the financial institutions that own the majority of company shares would virtually achieve this on its own. Such a move would involve guaranteeing the value of people's pensions, insurance and savings policies. Future financial turmoil is likely to make this politically popular.

Total state control of enterprises is to be avoided. The economy would be guided by a fusion of market and planning principles. A comprehensive economic plan would exist, built up with the participation of all active agents in the economy, but representatives of the state would not dominate any enterprise. If both consumer and workers representatives opposed proposals in the plan, they would not be implemented. Enterprises would still exist in the marketplace. All goods would be priced and enterprises would be free to buy and sell to whom they wished. However, the nature of the market would be radically different.

Commercial secrecy would be abolished. Socialised companies would be obliged to make all standard management information available on the net, from Board minutes to raw material prices. Their charges and performance could be analysed by anyone who cared to look. When everyone knows everything about everyone else, the tendency to co-operate becomes stronger than the tendency to compete. Open information will again avoid the abuse of monopoly. Private industry has already realised the potential in collaboration and networks, but the nature of competitive capitalism limits its development.

A patent system for new inventions may still be necessary but anyone would be allowed to exploit an idea; the creator would only have a right to royalties. Further to this, trained consumer representatives would be part of a national system committed to ensuring that industry meets our needs. Universities could become centres of expertise for different sectors gathering information, sharing best practice and training consumer representatives in what to look for and improve.

Underneath the socialised sector, the role of independent co-operatives would be expanded. Private enterprise would be unequivocally supported but within an improved framework of workers rights. Entrepreneurship would be encouraged, but not at the expense of exploiting other people.

The book moves to a conclusion by considering what green economics, with its human and environment-centred approach, can add to our understanding, and whether all the above is just superficial froth that would retain all the inequalities and exploitation of the free market system.

Finally, if this all makes sense, how do we fight for it to become a reality in Britain? The argument is made that it is no longer possible to consider the

Labour Party a potential vehicle for radical ideas. Despite the historically negative experience, possibilities are opening up of building new left parties in Britain and internationally – some are already in existence. Many lessons need to be learnt from the failures of the left in the past and a culture of openness and organisational flexibility will be required, but there is definitely the political space for a movement based on the ideas of a socialised economy - a movement that will draw on both red and green constituencies. Whether any new party will have the political commitment to see these ideas through to their revolutionary conclusion, future battles will tell.

If that is what is in the book, it seems to me almost as important to say what is not. Throughout its writing I have been aware of dealing with the grey and cold blocks of economic structure. This is not an angry book, though there is much to be angry about. I have tried to give recognition to the human values that lie underneath economics but my main task is to lay out the argument for an alternative economic system that is successful even on the terms of a Financial Times writer. It is not about how we will get there and the struggle and commitment that will involve. Trade unions, for instance, barely rate a mention, yet they will play a key role in arguing for and building a movement for socialist change. 'Anti Capitalism' is, in a way, a utopia. Not in the sense that it is unrealistic, but because reality is unlikely to turn out this way. That does not matter. The important thing is that a practical alternative is shown. We can alter it on the way.

Another major exclusion (I am sure there are many), is that very few divisions beyond rich and poor are dealt with. The book is virtually blind to differences related to race, gender, disability or nation. This is not to belittle their importance. The text is already dense with statistics; to further subdivide any line of analysis into its constituent parts would have made it unreadable. It is important to be aware of this though. Take the discussion of the 'time-rich' and 'time-poor' households. To reflect reality, we should really talk of time-rich men and time-poor women in almost all households because women still do the overwhelming majority of domestic and caring duties (2). As another example of the complexities underlying a simple rich / poor division, we could note that fully 50% of the ethnic minority population in Britain live in the 44 poorest local authority areas (3). The economic changes called for here will not be a solution to much of the institutional discrimination and cultural prejudice that exists in society, but they form a necessary underpinning for any lasting solution.

Statistics are untrustworthy assistants, but they are all we have, and I am afraid I have used them in bucket loads. Without statistics we are reduced to making prejudiced assertions (largely what economics consists of!). Take one of the most commonly used set of statistics, the unemployment rate, and it is easy to see that one statistic just begs another. By unemployed do we mean those claiming benefit, those looking for work or those of working age not working? If the latter, before we can judge whether there is a non-working problem, we need to know why people are not working. If they are on invalidity benefit, is that because they really cannot work at all or because the work they might be able to do is not available? And so on. Doubtless, I will be guilty of statistical gloss on occasions, but I have tried to draw evidence from sources that are unlikely to support my arguments and only ask for them to be believed in as far as they illuminate a general trend. Ultimately, all statistics have to be held up against common sense and personal experience.

I am acutely aware of the parody of socialists as substitutes on the touchline of events, cheering at disaster in the hope they will be called back into the game. The establishment parties can afford to be smug in many of the advanced capitalist countries. What does poverty, inequality and free market hypertension matter if you can deliver more consumption to the majority every year? I do not believe in imminent economic collapse. The American economy could even return rapidly to health if sufficient foreign capital pours in (though it's very unlikely). But neither do I believe in the reassurances of leaders that worship the accomplished fact. We can already see that the Anglo Saxon economic miracle was overstated. It is impossible to tell when and why economic quakes might occur but we can at least map out the fault lines. What is certain is that when those quakes arrive, the free market parties will have no response.

All very well, but can an economic programme that suggests we should be bringing the world's major corporations into public ownership be treated seriously? It does sound shockingly ambitious. Most of us mere mortals are likely to opt for 'being realistic'. Some sense of history is needed to steady the nerves. The public corporation is only a passing form of capitalist organisation, one that is falling increasingly into disrepute. It will take a political movement of immense proportions to democratise those organisations, but no one should be so lacking in hope or imagination to think we are saddled with the corporation or capitalism for all time.

I have tried to show here why major corporations need to be taken into social ownership, how they could operate, and how it could be achieved, in a technical sense, with minimum disruption and disadvantage. Political rhetoric about individual freedom is empty without the access to resources, time and the social networks that social ownership can begin to open up. A new generation of radical activists is being formed who do not cleave to socialism as their natural inheritance. This book argues that the call for the socialisation of major companies should be a cornerstone of any new political movement. The restraints on that ambition are not objective reality but our own lack of political confidence. As the saying goes, the powerful only seem so when we are on our knees.

CHAPTER 1.

WHAT'S THE PROBLEM?

For the last thirty years the average annual growth rate for countries with a gross domestic product of more than $50bn. was 2.8%.. Now, in compound interest, anything that increases by 2.8% a year will double every 25 years. Let us take the gross world product of 2000 and project it forward:

Year	Estimated human wealth in billions of dollars
2000	17,000
2030	40,000
2060	91,000
2090	209,000

From Adrian Berry, The Next Five Hundred Years. (1)

In spite of periodic falls, the Stock Market always goes up over the long run. Not because of speculation or greed, but because the progress of capitalism is relentless. Persistent innovation, technological achievement and plain human endeavour establish new ways of making things happen and create new and better products and services that people want to buy. Higher demand for those products and services fuels higher profits: higher profits fuel higher share prices. It's really that simple.

Jeremy Utton, the Analyst Oct. '98

The above maths suggests there will be a fifteen-fold increase in our living standards by the end of the 21st century. Not exactly a call to arms for revolutionaries - the only problem should be distributing the wealth fairly. In the first section of the book I will be trying to show why such rave reviews of capitalist progress are misplaced.

The arguments address the entire advanced capitalist world but there is only room to dissect one economy and that will be Britain. Still one of the advanced countries, it should be possible to muster a case for capitalism's defence. First though, to put the discussion in context, it is necessary to have the briefest look at what has happened in the undeveloped world. An average growth rate of almost 3% over the last thirty years may be true of most countries, but for some, particularly those in sub-Saharan Africa, social and economic collapse has been a more common experience.

THE GLOBALLY EXCLUDED

There is no intention here to make out that in all places and at all times capitalism causes misery, though in some parts of the globe you could be forgiven for thinking so. The picture of unending increases in living standards does not apply around the world. Capitalism is a tremendously innovative system that destroys to create. Traditional cultures and social systems are torn down and replaced by market systems, often with disastrous results.

The first imperial forays into the Americas, Africa and Asia were driven by interrelated factors of politics and profits but as the 20th century progressed imperialism took on increasingly economic forms. Political empires have retreated only to leave the economic grip of the USA, Europe and Japan on the Southern Hemisphere even tighter. Now the squeeze is that of the international corporations and financial institutions, not governments. Government's role is reduced to guaranteeing companies freedom to operate in a profit maximising manner.

Oversimplifying for the sake of clarity, the developing countries we are talking about were used to produce raw materials and cash crops for the advanced countries. Poor but stable peasant communities were broken up and land put over to produce cotton, beef, bananas etc. Foreign capitalists did not develop the internal market. Other than some processing facilities, little industry or infrastructure of roads, communication systems or education were developed. Displaced peasants moved to the towns in search of work but few found jobs. No jobs, no wages, no demand for goods that would sustain industrial growth. The virtuous economic circle never started. Worse than that, the countries' agricultural produce became bound for export, so requiring the importation of basic foodstuffs and declining self-sufficiency.

Some advances were made during the prolonged world boom that followed the Second World War and lasted until the mid-seventies. Growth was such that commodity prices were sustained and there was a trickle of local benefit, but since that time commodity prices have collapsed. On a world index of all non-oil commodities (the produce of the undeveloped countries) an amount that cost $110 dollars in 1980, could be bought for just $75 in 1999 (2). At the same time that these countries were receiving less money for their produce, the dollar price of goods that had to be imported was continually rising.

Inevitably, country after country had to borrow from the west. At first, in the early seventies, it was for expansion. Developing countries accepted the loans that were being sold by the banks, desparate to recycle the huge surpluses being generated by oil-rich countries. Then, when commodity prices plunged, loans were needed to bail the developing countries out. Enter the IMF and World Bank with their 'stabilisation' policies. They would lend more money only on condition that management of the economy was tightened in a way that invariably increased unemployment and destroyed what existed of a welfare state. Two such 'structural adjustments' were implemented before the Rwandan massacres and the election of fundamentalists in Algeria. So loans to the developing world that stood at $600 billion in 1980, amounted to $2.2 trillion by 1996 (3). Nigeria, not untypically, has a foreign debt of $29bn., equivalent to almost 100% of its annual gross domestic product. Servicing that debt became impossible.(4)

No resistance was to be tolerated in the American-led free market world. If you wanted to be in the game, you played by the rules. Open up markets, deregulate the financial system, privatise industry, remove subsidies and balance the budget.

After 1989 the communist bloc could be added to the victim list of the free marketeers. The West's determination to force through 'shock therapy' on Russia - immediate tight budgets and privatisation - led to a 50% drop in industrial production and a massive increase in poverty. At the same

Fact Box

Indices of global poverty

1.3 billion people live in absolute poverty (earning less than $1 a day), a greater number than 25 years ago. In sub-Saharan Africa and south Asia more than 40% of the population is this poor.

Half the world's population lives on less than $2 a day.

Ratio of incomes of the top 20 richest countries to the 20 poorest:

1820	2:1
1900	5:1
1960	20:1
2000	40:1

A third of adults in the developing world have no access to safe drinking water or regular paid work.

One third of the world's children are undernourished

time, it created a form of gangster capitalism that pours money in to speculative ventures and foreign bank accounts, but invests little in the real economy.

A thumbnail sketch like this hides many differences. There was a clutch of developing countries that entered the growth cycle, in particular the Asian Tigers, and the development route of South America was very different from Africa, chiefly because of the almost complete absence of foreign investment in the latter. However, the pattern is clear. The operation of capitalism has pauperised great swathes of the world, not just relatively, but absolutely. Inequality has increased both between the advanced and emerging economies and between the rich and poor within those countries (5).

As the economies of some countries sunk, so internal tensions, often ethnically based, increased. Military governments threatened by internal revolt increased spending on arms for internal security and military adventures against neighbouring states. The advanced and over 12 million die every year under the age of 5 - 95% of them from poverty related diseases.

One million women between 14 and 55 die each year from the preventable disease of tuberculosis.

In Africa real per capita incomes, at 1987 prices, have fallen from $670 in 1975 to an estimated $520 in 1999

Eliminating World Poverty. Department for International Development. Dec 2001.

World Labour Report 2000. International Labour Organisation (6)

countries - particularly Britain, that sends 80% of its massive arms production to the third world, were only too happy to supply both sides of any conflict.

The history of armed conflict provides a damning indictment of the political economy of capitalism (and Stalinism) in the twentieth century. It is not just the carnage of the great wars that scar the century, but the generalisation of conflict **within** states, most of it inflamed by desperate poverty (see box). So in Africa today we are left with the appalling reality of 12 war zones existing simultaneously

In the words of the Wall Street Journal "Who cares if Africa has fallen off the edge of the global marketplace? With the end of the cold war it has lost its strategic significance....it is too poor to matter.....Africans do not have the money to buy Coca-Cola. They lack the education and the use of Windows. The continent cannot pay its debts...Save for the beacon at its southern tip, it is best left to mercenaries and missionaries" (7).

Statistics of suffering can be produced ad nauseam. It is at its worst in Africa but it is not only Africa. Yet against this, the United Nations Development Programme (8) estimates that just $40 bn. spent over the next ten years would be sufficient to meet the basic nutritional, health, education and sanitation needs of the 1.3 billion people living in absolute poverty. That represents only 6% of what the industrial countries spend on arms each year.

The point to be made here is that the global triumph of capitalism is more mirage than reality. Even before we examine capitalism's prospects it is evident that, in the twenty-first century, millions are more likely to continue experiencing war, famine and displacement than a fifteen-times increase in living standards.

Defenders of capitalism would have us believe that third world poverty is due to the incapable and corrupt governments that took over when direct imperial rule came to an end. But in the last century of wealth extraction, what have the multinational companies (and their reflections in government) done about developing infrastructure, increasing the productivity of domestic agricultural producers and building up indigenous industry in the undeveloped world? Very little - their job was to make profits for shareholders back home. There is nothing inevitable about what has happened in Africa; much of it has productive agricultural

Fact Box

Armed conflict

Of the 160 largest states in the world, 55 were involved in armed conflict by 1991. Overwhelmingly this armed conflict was internal and not between states.

Only 10 states were engaged in war in 1947. The number increased continually through to 1991. Though the figure has dropped substantially since the collapse of the Soviet Union, the basis for peace is often fragile, and ethnic struggle is becoming more common.

Peace and Conflict 2001 Center for International Development and Conflict Management.

land as well as being rich in raw materials. Dictators are normally the result, not the cause, of poverty.

No one wanted the continent to face economic collapse. In fact we would all be better off if the African states had been able to participate in the growth of world trade. Multinational profits could have been invested locally, minimum prices guaranteed for commodities, non-arms development loans extended in a planned way, bartered increases in trade agreed, profit-sharing technical investments made etc. What made decline inevitable is that free market capitalism does not allow for any conscious social control, whether those involved have an interest in broader human development or not. Profit maximisation and the market dictate. The poor countries of the world were not given the resources to build up their own economies, and because of that, are unattractive to international capital today. Their fate is sealed.

Back to the capitalist heartland and a look at Britain.

BRITAIN AFTER THE BOOM

Before proposing an alternative economy, we first need to understand the present one. Only when we have understood the problems can we discuss whether an alternative system is necessary or capable of solving them. In the following sections, we will trace how the British economy has fared since the '70s and how far it is meeting human need. The chosen yardsticks of performance are poverty, unemployment, the nature of work and inequality. Interestingly, it is possible for all these facets of life to deteriorate, while total wealth goes on increasing. Having established some general trends, the specific example of boomtown Leeds illustrates what they mean for daily life.

The performance of an economy however, should not be judged only through the eyes of the poor. How is it experienced by those doing quite well - the celebrated middle-Englander? The final part of the chapter asks the most difficult, but important question: what do we all need from an economy to make us happy, and is it delivering? This section should carry a mental health warning – it is thick with statistics and not a light read. However, it is divided into subject areas and can be usefully dipped into.

The United States emerged from the Second World War an economic colossus. It became the holding company for Global Economy plc. While its own economy had boomed during the war and suffered no material damage, those of its fading imperial competitors in Europe emerged war damaged and indebted. Under the Bretton Woods agreement, the dollar became the currency of international trade, and the US was generous in the loans it gave to European states to help them rebuild and, of course, purchase American goods.

A unique set of circumstances laid the basis for the twenty-five year boom. There was high demand from post war reconstruction with plentiful and cheap labour ensuring high profitability (weak unions and agricultural labour moving to the towns). New techniques, often developed in the war, were spun out in the electrical, chemical and electronic industries, producing new consumer goods. Everyone began to aspire to owning a TV, car and a range of 'white' goods like fridges and washing machines.

International politics was similarly reconstructed in a way that encouraged the boom, as European rulers learnt lessons from the inter-war experience. Economic collapse had released a virulent fascism that had moved beyond the control of the ruling class, and there was now a determination that economies should be managed in such a way as ensured near full employment. Keynesianism, the use of budget deficits and devaluation to smooth out the business cycle, was adopted everywhere.

Further, the economic hegemony of the United States was so complete, it was as though the laws of capitalist competition had been partly suspended. Instead of one country benefiting at the expense of another, Europe and Japan held on to the ropes of the US balloon and all rose together. The process was reinforced by the cold war: military expenditure remained high, pumping demand into the economy. The USA was also determined, through political pressure and material support, to keep the likes of Germany and Japan in its sphere of influence and not allow recession to produce fertile soil for the growth of communism.

So, after a deflationary stumble in the late '40s, European devaluations, the military build up for the Korean War and the credit extended to Europe through the Marshall Plan, the foundations were laid for the long boom in which more goods were produced than in the entire previous history of mankind.

Long term growth in the advanced capitalist countries 1820 - 1973 (1)

	Output	Output per head of population	Stock of fixed capital	Exports
1820-1870	2.2	1.0	n.a.	4.0
1870-1913	2.5	1.4	2.9	3.9
1913-1950	1.9	1.2	1.7	1.0
1950-1973	4.9	3.8	5.5	8.6

Average annual percentage growth rates

Compare these figures to performance at the top of the boom in 1998-2000 when, in the UK, output grew by an average of 2.4% a year and the level of investment did not grow at all. Manufacturing output in 1998 was the same as it was ten years earlier. (2)

The reasons for the collapse of the boom need not concern us here. It was triggered by the oil crisis, but the background was a decline in profitability and high government borrowing. The point is that the 1975 world-wide recession marked a return to more traditional capitalist ways. The significance of Margaret Thatcher leading the Tories to power in 1979 was not that she shook up a tired state dominated and corporate-ridden economy, as she told us, (the real economy was never again to show the vigour of the boom years). Her intention and success, was that she restored power to the boardroom and strengthened capital against labour. The powerful corporate forces that were gathering behind the move to financial globalisation in the UK and US were the main supporters and beneficiaries of her project (3).

By 1975, the world was a very different place from 25 years earlier. The economic dominance of the US was under threat from Japan and the emerging Asian tigers (S. Korea, Hong Kong, Singapore, Taiwan etc), as well as from successful economies like Germany. International competition from high productivity/low wage economies was fierce and now there was not enough demand to go round.

On a capitalist basis, the only response that a weak economy like the UK's could make, was to force up productivity by having fewer people produce more goods for less money. The 'more' never really happened but the 'fewer' certainly did.

When the Tories came to power, the economy was growing strongly and inflation rising to over 15%. Instead of applying the traditional methods of slowing an economy by making the banks lend less to people, Thatcher deregulated the finance industry and lifted exchange controls - the banks could borrow and lend from and to whom they wanted. That meant the only economic weapon left with the government was the level of interest rates (the famous 'one club' policy). If interest rates were raised, fewer people would want to borrow. The economy would slow and inflation drop. Unfortunately, higher interest rates also meant that people and companies could not afford to service their loans, whilst, at the same time, money poured into the country to take advantage of high interest rates, forcing up the value of the pound. Inevitably, manufacturers became unable to export, as their goods became more expensive relative to foreign products. Factories closed at an alarming rate. Between April and November 1979 British interest rates, already high by international standards, were raised from 12 to 17% (Germany's interest rate averaged 6.7% at the time).(4)

The 1980 - 1982 recession was traumatic for the working class of Britain in its speed and severity. One fifth of all factories shut, manufacturing production fell by 14% and unemployment quadrupled to three million. By 1983 two million fewer people had jobs than in 1979.(5)

If the creation of a healthy economy had been the Tories' sole objective, their actions would have been illogical. By early 1980, it was evident that ·the economy was nose-diving, but as late as Oct 1981 the bank base rate was still 16% and the pound sky-high. More strategic issues were at stake. The government was determined to increase the profitability of business and shift the balance of power from the workforce to the boardroom. In its way stood a powerful trade union movement, and one of the key ways of weakening the unions was the creation of mass unemployment, so that behind everyone with a job was someone else willing to take it. The political gamble of allowing unemployment to rise so high almost didn't come off. At the worst point of the recession, the government was only supported by 20% of the population. However, the jingoism of the Falklands War and the slice of the vote taken by the new Social Democratic Party assured Thatcher of her '83 election victory.

She emerged from this period enormously strengthened. Sections of workers had already been defeated - steelworkers, dockers, printers etc. Much of the rest of the official trade union movement cowered before the legislation that banned secondary picketing and made unions financially liable for unofficial action. The heroic exception was of course the year-long struggle of the miners, but the Tories had prepared and little action was taken in support of the miners by other trade unions. The forcing back to work of the NUM in March 1985, was a terrible blow to the confidence of the organised working class.

In the modest economic upturn that followed, the government was able to stay in power by offering the majority of workers an increase in their take-home pay, while continuing with an economic restructuring that never had popular support. Between 1982 and 1992, £60bn. pounds of state assets were sold off, mostly at knockdown prices, in a wholesale privatisation process that had the benefit to the government of further weakening public sector trade unions. It also meant that £3.5bn in revenues to the state each year were lost (6). The proceeds of privatisation, along with North Sea oil revenues, were not invested in the economy but paid the social security bill for the growing numbers of unemployed. The welfare state was weakened and benefits were cut. The rights of the consumer were trumpeted but the ability of civic institutions like local government and the trade unions to oppose the central state were continually attacked.

By the time the Tory cabinet slid the stiletto between Mrs Thatcher's ribs in 1990, the day to day experience of capitalism in Britain had become a very different one from the mid 1970s. The wealth produced was undoubtedly greater, but where the caricature of working class life had been the stability of an apprenticed working life and jokes of Jaguars on council estates, those same estates had become workless and crime-ridden. Those who could, moved out. For the luckier ones, life still seemed less secure. The early '90s recession hit the service and financial sectors of the south hard. Even the red-braced storm-troopers of the City of London had their confidence knocked. The sixteen years of the Tories left a richer but much more socially divided country and poverty now existed on a massive scale.

POVERTY AND UNEMPLOYMENT – ARE THEY BEING ERADICATED?

It is of little use to just describe poverty - the reply is simply, it was ever thus. What is important is the cause of poverty, whether it is increasing and the ways and consequences of eliminating it. If the section is thick with figures, it is because the received wisdom of the age is that poverty in advanced countries like Britain is a marginal problem. It isn't. Those that take no convincing can move quickly through.

Fact Box

The number of children living in poverty went up by 100,000, to 4.5 million, in the first two years of the Labour government.

Joseph Rowntree Foundation Aug 2000

Poverty

Poverty is not **just** about having no money, but the draining daily struggle to get by must surely be its central mark. Nor is it a matter of only being concerned about 'absolute' poverty. Welfare benefits are higher today than 50 years ago but what is considered essential for a decent life has expanded enormously. TVs, fridges and phones are to be expected in any home, but ask any 13 year-old, and a pair of fashionable trainers is also essential to life! Poverty can only be viewed in relation to the general expectations of society. The benefits system is increasingly constructed to ensure that claimants have most of their housing costs paid and enough to eat but have no money for anything else. The gap between what the poor and the better off can expect from life grows wider.

The majority in Britain are not poor, but it is a massive problem that cripples millions of lives. The people who suffer most from poverty are single parents, the unemployed (including older workers who have dropped out of the labour market), pensioners, disabled and the low-paid. Women and people

Fact Box

Large increase in relative poverty

The number of people living on less than 40% of the average wage:

1979	1.7m.
1991	7.7m
1998	8m

John Hills, The Future of Welfare, London School of Economics plus Joseph Rowntree Foundation Nov '99

35

from ethnic minorities suffer disproportionately. Poverty, particularly relative poverty, increased massively under the Tories. Under the first New Labour government the position changed little. Only in the third year of office did the Party start to take steps to tackle the problem.

Poverty wages

For the working poor a minimum wage of £3-60 an hour for the over 21s was introduced in '98. It is a terrible reflection on the level of wages that such a modest minimum still raised the pay of 1.3 million people. The minimum wage is half of average earnings, and future increases will not raise it above that level (2). The rates are in fact little different from those set by the old Wage Councils in industries like hairdressing and tailoring, before the Tories abolished the Councils.

In line with its 'making work pay' policies, Labour has made an impact with

> ## Fact Box
>
> ### Benefit claimants
>
> In Oct '00, an unemployed single person over 25 received benefit of £52-20 plus the majority of their housing costs. That is £7-45 a day for bills, food and clothing, never mind enjoyment. In all some 5 million people are wholly dependent on benefits and one in five children are growing up in totally benefit dependent households (1)

the recently introduced Working Families Tax Credit. The credit has increased the take-home pay of the lowest paid families. From April 2001, any family with a full time worker was guaranteed an income of £214 a week. That meant that single-earner families with two children were £30-40 better off over quite a range of weekly earnings (£120 – 280 per week), compared to the old Family Credit scheme. However the scheme is not as generous as the government makes out when the effects on Housing Benefit are taken into account. It does not end the poverty trap, nor help those without children (3).

Pensioners

Poverty amongst pensioners in Britain is a national disgrace. In Denmark, a pensioner can expect a state pension equivalent to 77% of average earnings. For Britain, the figure is less than 20% (4). It is estimated that two thirds live off an income of less than £100 a week (the single pension was £75 in 2001) (5). In 1980 the Tories cut the link between pensions and average earnings; instead they were only to rise in line with prices. If the previous formula had still been in operation, a pensioner couple would be £37 a week better off today (6). Labour has refused to re-link pensions to earnings, instead choosing to target the worst-off pensioners with a minimum income guarantee that will rise to £100. Like all means-tested benefits, this will have the effect of creating a trap where pensioners are crowded around a level just above absolute poverty.

Disabled

Enormous numbers of people are poor because they are disabled; 6.5 million claim some sort of disability benefit and 2.97 million people of working age are wholly dependent on sickness or disability benefit (7). Reasons for the large increase over the last twenty years are complex. For one thing, during the boom, many of the disabled, males in particular, were able to stay in work in more sheltered jobs such as storesman. The great manufacturing shakeout of the early '80s, combined with productivity drives, put many on the dole and subsequently on to Incapacity Benefit.

Single Parents

The growth in the number of single parent households (currently 1.3m.) is a long-term social trend, which no amount of moralising is going to reverse. This is not the place to discuss why this need not be seen as a problem. What is clear though, is that without a revolution in childcare provision and the availability of work that fits with it, these (overwhelmingly) women will be trapped on benefits.

With 14 million people living at less than half of average earnings, the scale of the problem is clear, but are things getting better or worse? We have seen above that the minimum wage, the working families tax credit and the minimum income for pensioners might improve the lot of the poorest, but the reality is that the numbers existing on only slightly more than social security levels keeps on growing. For those left on benefits only linked to prices, their relative poverty will continue to worsen.

Most would agree that, central to the elimination of poverty, are full employment, a decent minimum wage, access to decent public services and an adequate child care and benefits system. Full employment and the minimum wage

---

Fact Box

Poverty rates have risen sharply

The following percentage of households lacked three or more necessities because they could not afford them:

1983	14%
1990	21%
1999	24%

Items defined as necessities are those that more than 50% of the population believes that 'all adults should be able to afford and which they should not have to do without'

Poverty and Social Exclusion in Britain. Joseph Rowntree Foundation. Sept. 2000 will be discussed later, but the outlook for the welfare state is gloomy. It should not be easy to summarise the condition and trajectory of the welfare state in a couple of paragraphs, but the clarity of the government's strategy is only matched by its mastery of public deception.

Government spending, as a percentage of National Income, has been broadly constant for many years, but the percentage taken up by Social Security payments has tended to increase and now accounts for around one third of all spending. Thirty four per cent of that goes on pensions, a declining share and a sum that, on present trends, will grow little in the next century. However, the government is determined to reduce the social security bill by making benefits hard to come by and 'encouraging' people back to work. The former tactic is embodied in the removal of the lone parent supplement or the conditions imposed on those wanting to claim incapacity benefit (8). In a different guise, there is the generalisation of means tested benefits over universal benefits - e.g. all incapacity benefit is lost if you earn more than £9,500. There is only talk at the moment of taxing child benefit or means testing pensions but the direction is towards a single level of means tested income support, with all other benefits having to come from private provision.

Helping people back in to work is entirely laudable, and some of the training or childcare measures that have been introduced are to be welcomed, but behind the press releases is the stealthy move towards workfare. If you are capable of work you have to take whatever is on offer. The principle of having to take work if it is there commands much popular support but the 'firm but fair' policies of the government avoid talking about the **nature** of the work. It is often badly paid and temporary. And what happens if it ends or you leave - will you be able to return to claiming benefit?

Ministers, and the Tory leadership even more so, have shown great interest in workfare in America. Take one such scheme introduced in Fairfax County, Virginia in April '96. "Welfare recipients have 90 days to find employment or they are placed in unpaid community work experience during which they keep some benefits. After 24 months however, they are expected to be almost entirely self-sufficient. At that point their family benefit.....stops altogether. Under some circumstances free health care and food may continue for a year longer." (9). Such brutal withdrawal of benefit is not yet politically feasible in Britain, though few would any longer be surprised if it were raised. Pilots schemes are already being run that dock benefit if clients do not attend numeracy and literacy classes.

Another important aspect of poverty is whether the poor are benefiting from the non-cash elements of the welfare state through better schools, health services, housing and so on. The list is mantra-like. In any interview, a minister will pronounce that improvements in these services are what the government should be judged on. But if there are improvements, it is not clear that they are feeding through to the poorest sections of society.

Fact Box

Housing spend has fallen

Government Spending on Housing:

Tories '92-'97 £7.8bn
Labour '97-'02 £3.3bn

Shelter's 'Roof' magazine, July / Aug 2000

Council housing used to be cheap because it was subsidised. Over the years, the subsidies have been eliminated with the direct consequence that the amount paid out in Housing Benefit has risen along with rents. This has intensified the poverty trap in the process. What is the point in working if you face paying rent of £60 a week? Even under the Working Families Tax Credit, you loose 85p in Housing Benefit for every extra pound earned.

Education is moving to a geographical grammar school system, whereby those parents who can afford it move in to the catchment area of academically successful schools, leaving those in the inner city with falling rolls and income. Changes in the Health Service are harder to distinguish. There may be an improvement in services overall, but what is clear is that increasing numbers have moved to private health care to buy their place at the front of the queue. The NHS is becoming a second tier service for those unable to pay (see below) (10).

After implementing Tory budget cuts in its first two years of office, Labour started to increase expenditure. In the July 2000 Spending Review an extra £43bn. a year spending was announced through to 2004. In 2001 this was increased again (for the last time),to take spending increases to 3.6% a year through to 2004, concentrated on Health and Education which are to receive increases of 8% a year.

> **Fact Box**
>
> **... as has capital investment**
>
> Government capital investment in schools, hospitals etc. (including the Private Finance Initiative) as a percentage of gross domestic product:
>
> | | |
> |------|------------------|
> | 92/3 | 4% |
> | '96/7 | 2.6% |
> | '99/00 | 2.1% |
> | '03/04 | 4% (projected) |
>
> Ed Crooks. Financial Times. 21/11/00

Again though, all is not what it seems. The years of relative spending decline have to be taken into account. Total expenditure as a percentage of national income will be less in 2004 than in all but three of the eighteen

Fact Box

Overall government expenditure falls as well

Government spending as a % of GDP.

1982	47
1992	44
1999	37
2004	40

HM Treasury May 2001

years of Tory government up to 1997, and public investment will have only returned to the level it was in 1993. A further danger is that the social security budget is projected as virtually static (increase of 0.7% a year). Any economic downturn and an increase in unemployment would destroy the calculation (11).

Where Labour has differed from the Tories is that, to date, they have put most of the money from extra tax (overall tax up from 37.6% to 40.5% over the first parliament) and a growing economy into health and education rather than tax cuts. Sustaining real budget increases to 2004 and beyond will depend on the health of the economy. We have already been warned that extra taxes will be needed.

Unemployment

The headline unemployment figure for the number of claimants fell from over 3 million at its peak in the early '80s to under 1 million at the start of 2001 - the lowest for 21 years. Is there a problem any more?

First of all, ever since the Tories came to power in '79, the number of claimants has been manipulated downwards through exclusions and rule tightening. Not being able to claim Job Seekers Allowance for six months after you leave a job voluntarily, and only being able to claim the benefit for six months instead of two years are perhaps the most significant changes. It means that someone with a working partner is unlikely to be able to claim benefit. A more reliable guide to the real unemployment level is the Labour Force Survey. In a sample of 40,000 people, they count how many have been out of work for four weeks and have done something about finding a job in the last two weeks (so those that have given up are still not counted). The survey gives us an estimated unemployment figure of around 1.5 million.

Even at the top of the business cycle, the system fails to provide paid employment to those who want it. True, employment prospects have improved greatly since '97; one million full time workers have been added to the payrolls. Though it was only in that year the numbers in employment (both part and full time) returned to the pre recession level of 1989, despite the increase in the working age population.

What hits you when you examine the figures is that the proportion of the working age population that is economically active (in work, a student or in training), is much the same now as it was when unemployment was over three million (see chart). All things being equal, there should still be three

Fact Box

Growth in numbers not working but not counted as unemployed.

Twenty years ago 400,000 men of working age were 'economically inactive' (not counting students). That figure is now 2.3 million.

Twenty years ago one in six men over fifty were not working. That figure is now one in three.

In Aug '96, for the first time there were more people on long term sick / incapacity benefit than there were on the dole.

Welfare to Work - Where Next? Ed. Max Nathan. Centre for Local Economic Strategies. 2000 + Centre Piece Summer 2001.

million unemployed. In fact you could argue that with the increased entry of women into the labour market, there should be more than three million unemployed. So where have they all gone? The truth appears to be that there has been a massive drop out of men from the workforce, principally from the shrinking manufacturing sector in the north (though coastal towns have also suffered badly). The unemployment is largely hidden. Many people have been forced to retire early or ended up on Incapacity Benefit (claimed by 1.5 million people in 2001) (12).

The regional disparities are alarming. In the three most prosperous regions of Britain the percentage of the working age population actually in work is about **twenty percentage points** higher than in the least prosperous areas. In Merseyside, Clydeside, the Welsh Valleys and parts of the North East, employment rates struggle to reach sixty per cent of the available workforce. Overall it has been estimated that another 1.75 million jobs would be needed in the north to bring the working age employment rate up to the same as in the south (13).

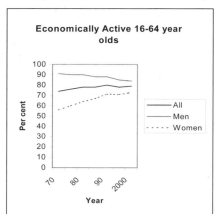

Economically Active 16-64 year olds

'Economically active' includes students. In the last twenty years, the overall activity rate has stayed static, around 78% of the working age population, while the proportion of women in the labour force has risen from 64 to 73%. In contrast, the proportion of economically active males has dropped from 90 to 84% over the same period. A large exit from the labour market.

Source ONS

44

So more people would like to work than unemployment figures suggest. These are by no means all older men in the north. The New Deal for instance statistically abolished long term youth unemployment. Yet a study in 1999 estimated that there were 600,000 under 24 year olds who were unemployed, not in education and training and not claiming benefit. So for every person claiming in that age group, there is another out of the system (14).

Most of the jobs boom has been in areas that did not have a severe unemployment problem in the first place (15). In some parts of the country there is a real shortage of labour at all skill levels (we will ignore for the moment that 'shortage' is often related to how low the wage is). In Milton Keynes for instance, (unemployment rate 1.5%) bars have shut in the evening for lack of staff and one warehouse recently recruited the twenty new workers it needed from Grimsby! (16). Currently some fifty-five local authority areas have a claimant rate less than 1%. Levels not even experienced in the sixties.

Of course most urban areas have their pockets of unemployment and, as we will see later, all conurbations have lost jobs. But it is important to counter the government's general line that it is all about providing people with the skills to occupy existing jobs. Skills are essential, but in many towns and cities there is still an absolute job shortage even at the top of the boom.

What about the areas that seem to have both a large number of vacancies and fairly high levels of unemployment? Is this the result of the demonised scrounger, committed to staying on the dole at all costs? First there is the skills issue. The unemployed do not have many of the skills the available jobs demand. The importance of improving technical, personal and IT skills cannot be denied. Condemnable then, that companies play so small a part in the process, expecting parents and the state to provide them with a work-ready member of staff. (17)

There is the other end of the equation to consider though, – the sort of jobs on offer. Manchester Low Pay Unit did a survey of the vacancies on offer at Lancashire Jobcentres (see box). It is hard to be morally outraged that they are not snapped up. The findings matched my own visit to the Huddersfield Jobcentre in the spring of 2000. Sixty per cent of the 344 vacancies on the board, paid £4 an hour or less.

Fact Box

Vacancies in Lancashire Jobcentres.

Part time	50%
Temporary	25%
Minimum pay rates	30%

'Behind the Figures' Financial Times 22/8/00

So how many people would want work if they could reasonably expect to be trained up for the job, were helped with child care responsibilities (nursery or school hour jobs), paid a minimum wage of £7 an hour, and the job existed not too far from their home? An accurate answer is impossible, but the Labour Force Survey does ask the simple question 'would you like to work?'. At the top of the business cycle, the survey still indicates there are over three and a half million people who would want a job.

THE GROWTH IN INEQUALITY

The gap between rich and poor continued to widen during Labour's first two years in office, government statistics showed yesterday.

Financial Times 14/7/00

I understand the class war is over. Who won?

Letter to Radio 4's P.M. programme after Tony Blair's conference speech (28/9/99)

Fact Box

Large increase in inequality under Thatcher

The percentage of the national income that went to these households (3)

	'79	'91
Poorest 10%	4.1	2.5
Richest 10%	20	26
Poorest 20%	10	6
Richest 20%	36	43

The British post war social democratic settlement ended with the boom. In the place of full employment and narrowing differentials came polarisation - the rich started to get richer and the poor became poorer. The process was part market driven, part politically driven (1). Of the advanced countries only New Zealand experienced a comparable growth in inequality over the eighties, and for similar political reasons.

The principal signals for a return to Victorian standards were the lowering of top tax rates to 40%, the deregulation of the money markets and privatisation. Later the Tories went on to abolish the Wages Councils that fixed minimum wages. The upshot was not just a widening of the gap between rich

47

and poor, but the creation of a superclass, largely based around the City of London, who were just silly rich.

The process has not gone unnoticed. The population at large has drawn the opposite conclusion to John Major and Tony Blair's belief that society is becoming classless. Since the '60s the Gallup polling organisation has been asking the question "Do you think there is a class struggle in this country or not?" In the 1960s around 60% answered yes, 70% in the 1980s and in 1995, 81% said yes. In the 1996 Social Attitudes survey 87% said they thought the gap between rich and poor was too great. While we are discussing the move towards a class-less society it is worth noting that in a MORI poll of 1949, 43% of people identified themselves as working class. When the same poll was done in 1991 the figure came out at 61%! (2).

Under the Tories, the transfer of national income from the poor to the rich was dramatic (see box above) and the figures represent large amounts of money. If the division of wealth had remained the same between 1979 and 1991, the poorest 20% of families would have been £3,000 a year better off (3). The growth in inequality has slowed since 1999, but until the third year of the

Fact Box

Growth in inequality not reversed in the nineties

In 1977 the top ten percent of earners received 2.75 times the amount of the bottom ten per cent.

By 1997 they received almost 4 times as much

"The findings also suggest that mobility (up the pay scales) actually fell over the period inequality increased"

Welfare Abigail McKnight. DTI. Employment Relations Research. 2000.
www.dti.gov.uk/er/emar/errs8.pdf

Labour government, it was still in the same direction. Changes since then are likely to have temporarily halted the growth in inequality, but modest redistribution policies will not reverse the pressures of the free market to widen the gap (4).

The drivers behind growing inequality have been the lowering of higher rates of income tax and corporation tax, the shift from wages to profit in the national income and the increasing proportion of those profits being paid out as dividends (5). The increase in dividends over the 1979-1991 period was equal to the fall in the proportion of GDP going into investment. Putting it crudely, the rich were shifting the balance of the economy towards profits, pocketing those profits and being taxed less on their winnings.

Is this all just the politics of envy? Does it matter if people get rich as long as the economy moves forward and everyone receives some benefit? The point should not be dismissed lightly. It is the 'trickle-down' position. Allow the rich to become richer and they will invest more, expanding the whole economy and giving everyone the opportunity to earn more. The theory is very popular with the well off, but is hard to sustain.

The booming USA of the 1990s is often cited as a case study. Two landmarks were the cutting of capital gains tax on unearned income from 49% to 28% at the end of the 1970s, followed by President Reagan cutting the maximum rate of income tax to a similar level in 1986. Supporters go on to argue that these measures led to a massive increase in venture capital funds (high-risk finance for businesses) and prevented the technology industry migrating to Japan (because big incomes could be made in Silicon Valley), thereby helping unemployment to drop to below 4%.

It would be perverse to argue that letting the rich become richer has no effect on the level of investment funds available, but whether those funds actually **are** invested is dependent on other factors. There were in fact recessions shortly after both the above tax cuts were introduced and taxes were **increased** at the start of the nineties before the boom kicked in. Rich people may have been providing the money for dot.coms two years ago, but now investment in the US is tumbling. In a recessionary environment those investment opportunities no longer look very profitable.

Overall there appears to be little or no link between the concentration of wealth and the success of an economy. Many other cultural, historic and economic forces are at work. One of the most unequal societies in the world, Brazil, is not likely to be cited as an economic success story. Yet a pound invested in every stock market in the world at the turn of the century produced its largest returns, not in the USA, but in traditionally social democratic Sweden.

The rich accumulating wealth, yet failing to invest in the real economy, is precisely one of Britain's economic problems. The idea of a fair day's pay for a fair day's work is deeply ingrained in working class psyche. Few object to someone earning a good wage for skill and hard work. But with the super-rich, any idea of 'earning' their money was abandoned long ago, if it ever existed in the first place.

Anecdote is a poor means of analysis, but an example may help. I recently came across a young banker in his late twenties who occupied what didn't seem to me a very powerful position in the City. He was deputy team leader of a group of six working for a foreign bank. They analysed the global telecommunications industry and advised on what shares to buy etc. He was honest enough to reveal that his wage the previous year was made up of £100,000 basic salary, £250,000 bonus and a £50,000 golden chain to encourage him not to leave!

MINIMUM WAGE

In a global economy, we are constantly under pressure to keep costs down.... we can only pay what the company can afford... if people aren't happy, they can always move.

MAXIMUM WAGE

In a global economy, we are constantly under pressure to keep our top staff..... we have to pay them whatever is necessary to stop them moving.

The media encourage us to be outraged at the relatively small amounts involved in benefit fraud, but have little to say about the growth in top salaries and widespread tax evasion. These salaries are **always** someone else's higher price or lower wage. They have to be paid from somewhere. Appeals to increased productivity ignore the fact that it is the rich who decide how the gains from productivity are divided.

You don't have to believe that property is theft to think that things have spun out of control. One of the problems in looking at inequality is tracking the rich. The Inland Revenue base their wealth statistics on a sample of people who have just died and the value of their estates. Ignoring the fact that wealth can be hidden away to avoid appearing in any taxable estate, this measure will not grasp the relatively recent phenomenon of share options that, until the stock market crashed, stuffed executive mouths with gold.

Fact Box

Failure pays well at the top

One of the most lucrative occupations for a company boss is to get the sack for doing a lousy job. The top five pay-offs for sacked company directors in year 2000 amounted to £13.5m.

Something of a record was set a year later, when Marconi's Chief Executive was paid off with £1m. for reducing the value of the company by 97% in one year!

The wealth-creaming that occurred with privatisation even made the press agitated. It took place in all industries - water, gas, electricity and rail, but reached its most obscene level in power generation, where £23 million of share options were offered to directors and senior executives at National Power and PowerGen (6). No justification can be offered that any of that was earned. Jan Lechley, the recently retired Chief Executive of Smith Kline Beecham, was paid a basic salary of £2.15m. a year, but his real wealth was in his share options, a package worth £80 million (7).

The super class has emerged from four sources - top professionals, entrepreneurs, entertainers and the silver spoon brigade. There is a town's worth of millionaires in Britain today – 74,000 - and in case we are carried away with the idea that inequality became unfashionable in the '90s, this is an increase from 6,600 seven years ago (8).

We cannot measure wealth but rather just glimpse the signs of it. We do know that, as money makes money, the seemingly endless rise in the stock market over the last twenty years shifted further resources towards the 'haves'. One band of emergent millionaires is the elite of the professions. The earnings profile for the **majority** of solicitors and accountants is much the same as it was in the 1950s (too much!), but in the last two decades the front runners have left the pack. In 1995 the average wage for an accountant and solicitor was in the £30 - 45,000 bracket. However, a partner in City solicitors could expect to earn £200,000, a commercial barrister £350,000, and a partner in a large accounting firm £190,000. 10,000 City brokers and consultants earn more than £150,000 and in the year before the stock market bubble burst, one thousand of them were thought to have earned over £1m. in bonuses (9).

Back in the corporations, wages have been pretty perky as well. The average wage of the Chief Executives of the top 100 corporations in 2000 (before any share options are included) was £717,000, a handy £216,000 increase on five years before. In the same year, a survey found that 110 directors of top companies were paid more than a million pounds. And so it goes on. In February 1997, there were reckoned to be 140,000 people earning more than £100,000 a year, a sevenfold increase over the previous ten years(10).

To anyone who argues for a more egalitarian wage structure comes the argument that if you don't pay the international rate for the job, these entrepreneurial giants will export themselves. This raises an interesting point. Top dog wages appear to be the only corner of the capitalist system that belief in markets breaks down. Rather than keep lowering the wage until you run out of decent applicants, the system is that you fix your own wage alongside the highest international comparison you can make convincing.

It is a system that is working well for the private sector participants. In 1981 a Whitehall Permanent Secretary earned 45% of the average salary of a Chief Executive. By '95 that was down to 19%, though without a noticeable flood abroad of Permanent Secretaries (11).

As we have already noted, looking at salaries only shows some of the picture. With the help of the stock market, money breeds money. Perhaps a better way to trace the growing wealth at the top is to look at luxury spending. A few examples:

760,000 households report a second home (12)

Estimates put the number of foreign au pairs at 170,000

In the mid-eighties Mintel, the market researchers, estimated that £524m. a year was spent on cooks, childminders, cleaners and gardeners. By 1997 the figure was thought to be £4bn. (13)

From a point of near extinction, domestic service has returned with a vengeance. On the Today programme (Radio 4 14/9/99), the Nat West Bank representative explained that this sort of work had mushroomed, and that over the last year 20% of all start up businesses opening accounts with the bank had been in domestic service. Once again the have-nots are looking after the haves.

It might be thought that Inheritance Tax could tackle inequality. At least it gives the government the chance to capture some of the wealth pouring down the generations (and what a nonsense inheritance makes of equal opportunities). Unfortunately the tax is now something of a joke, only paid by those who chose to. In 1950 the tax netted the equivalent to 1.4% of GDP. By 1990, that was down to 0.3%, or 0.1% of marketable wealth (14).

It is sometimes argued that, however offensive large incomes may seem, they are not large enough to make a difference if shared around the population as a whole. I'm not so sure. One man, Labour-supporting Bernie

Ecclestone, picked up £617m. in the year to Nov. 2000 (this is **income**, not wealth). This is more than would have been paid to 80,000 people on the minimum wage. One man, in other words, earned more than a city of fast food workers, the size of St. Albans.

After narrowing since the Second World War, inequalities in wealth and income have been growing since the eighties. A privatised and deregulated market reinforces such a trend. Governments supporting the basic mechanisms of such a system are forced to abandon the politics of redistribution, notwithstanding some minor changes to the benefit system. In the whirl of figures, it is important to keep stressing that it is not just a matter of there being rich and poor people, but that the divisions are becoming wider and, because of the media, more visible. It would be strange indeed if, at some stage, this process did not produce a political reaction.

Inequality is not a matter of income alone however; it permeates every facet of life. Let us briefly look at two such areas.

Education

According to the Labour Government, the problems of our inner city schools can be reduced to a lack of aspiration among the pupils. Teachers are blamed for accepting failure as inevitable. Such wilful ignorance of reality is not only an insult to the intelligence, but to the thousands of teachers who struggle to carve out opportunities for their children against all odds.

Class divisions within education are not new, but in recent years, the move towards funding based on the number of pupils in a school and the increasing geographical concentration of poverty, have intensified the divide. For the better comprehensives, it is now selection by postcode rather than the eleven plus. The Independent on Sunday (8/12/96) calculated that house prices bore a 30% premium if they were near a good school.

Tory education reforms were intended to introduce market mechanisms into education and reduce the power of Local Education Authorities. The shift to self-management of schools was sold under the politically popular slogan of 'parent power', but the market logic employed was similar to that applied to sausages. The idea was that successful schools, as revealed in the exam result league tables, would expand and become renowned for various specialisms. Not surprisingly the tendency has rather been for the successful schools to expand up to their existing physical capacity and then become ever more selective, while still conforming to the dominant academic model (15). The reconstruction of the grammar school system, by any other name, is well under way.

The tragedy of this is that Britain has always had an education system that has catered well for the top 20% achievers, but by international comparisons has miserably failed the intermediate level of student (leaving aside a more radical analysis of what education is meant to be doing). Studies continually show that academic achievement is the best predictor of prospects and that qualifications are still closely associated with parents' social status (16).

Fact Box

Private health and education spending continue to increase

Private spending as a percentage of total spending.

	1980	1995
Education	8%	18%
Health	11%	18%

Nicholas Timmins. Financial Times. 28/2/00

Inner city schools are experiencing falling numbers and income as parents keenest for their children to succeed, try to enrol them in suburban schools. This, in turn, reduces resources and choice and creates a non-academic environment. The schools also bear the brunt of the infrastructure cuts that the Tories implemented, with no wealthy parents to appeal to (17). How stark the difference is in Leeds, will be shown below.

There is little doubt that the total number of qualifications is rising, despite suspicion that GCSE standards have been watered down. Equally, numbers in higher education have increased enormously. The problem is the class-based distribution. On the announcement of the 1999 'A' level results the Financial Times ran with the headline "Increase in A-level pass rate linked to changing social mix". It went on to say "The inexorable rise in the A-level pass rate can be attributed to the growing number of middle class children sitting the examinations" (18). In 1994 less children were entered for A-level in Islington - seventy nine - than Eton sent to Oxford or Cambridge.

This brings us on to the other traditional scar of British education - the private school. The middle class, in steadily increasing numbers, chooses to abandon what it sees as a crisis-ridden state sector when it can afford to (see box).

Average annual fees are between £6,000 for a day pupil, up to £11,000 for a boarder. This compares to £2,300 spent on each pupil in the state sector. In 1996, all but 22 of the top 200 schools, by A-level results, were in the private sector (19). 90% of private school pupils go on to university (20).

The removal of such a large slice of motivated middle class children to academic crammers is obviously to the detriment of the remainder of the state system. It is on a scale unique to Britain and is a glaring reinforcement of our class system. Nor is there any sign of its presence diminishing, thanks to the increasing incomes of the better off. Indeed, despite various democratisation drives, the percentage of students from private school at Oxford or Cambridge actually went up between 1969 and 1992 from 35% to around 50% (21).

Health

Shortly after coming to power Labour charged Sir Donald Acheson to chair an inquiry into inequalities in health. The Inequalities in Health Report was published in Sept. '98 (22) and the first paragraph of the preface read as follows:

"This report addresses an issue which is fundamentally a matter of social justice; namely, that although the last 20 years have brought a marked increase in prosperity and substantial reductions in mortality to the people of this country as a whole, the gap in health between those at the top and bottom of the social scale has widened. Yet there is convincing evidence that, provided an appropriate agenda of policies can be defined and given priority, many of these inequalities are remediable."

To someone not involved in the health world, both the class differences and extent of illness are shocking. It is also not just the health divide but the cure divide that is becoming worse. Labour is clearly putting additional resources into the Health Service and yet, in many cases, shorter waiting lists for operations appear to be the mirror image of longer waiting lists to see consultants in the first place. In the first year of the Labour government 160,000 people paid for private operations so they could move to the front of the waiting list, a 50,000 increase on the year

Fact Box

Health and class are related

The mortality rate amongst unskilled men of working age in 1970 was twice as high as that of professionals. By the early '90s it was three times as high.

In 1996 17% of professional men reported a limiting long standing illness compared to 48% of unskilled men. Among women the proportions were 25% and 45%.

Acheson Report '98

before (23). Not an option open to the hard up.

So it goes on. There is a danger of statistical overload. The case is made that inequality has grown significantly over the last twenty years - and with Labour's policy perspective, it is unlikely to be reversed. It should also be emphasised that inequality **is** a problem, not just morally undesirable. As we shall see later, studies have shown that mental health is more susceptible to relative poverty than to absolute poverty. It is easier be poor when everyone around you is poor, than to have no money to spend in a rich society.

It is now appropriate to see how the trends we have discussed in poverty, unemployment and inequality reveal themselves in a particular place.

LEEDS - NEW BRITAIN IN ACTION

Leeds is a city in West Yorkshire, northern England, numbering around half a million people. No one but a complete misery would deny that there have been major improvements over the last 20 years. When I moved here in 1980, the M1 had completed its journey into the centre of the city like some inter-galactic highway, flattening swathes of working class Hunslet in the process. 'Big' engineering in the area – Hunslet Engines (rail), British Leyland (car engines), Doncaster Monkbridge (aircraft parts), Vickers (printing machinery) – was being clobbered by the deep recession of that year. Many factories were closing, leaving empty shells or derelict land.

The once massive tailoring industry that employed 30,000 people in East Leeds, was in its death throes. The household names of Burtons and Hepworths converted their factories to warehouses for foreign goods. The unemployment rate was heading for 10% and more.

The Centre itself sported great bald patches. Civic enthusiasts of the '60s had cleared old buildings, but often no investors had come forward to replace them (at least this saved Leeds from some of the concrete eyesores that plague other cities). Beautiful buildings, and even major town centre streets like Boar Lane, lay blackened and semi-derelict. 'Prosperous' was not the feeling it gave. Then it all began to change.

Two factors were central to the Leeds boom. It was in the geographical centre of Britain and at the apex of the M1 and M62 motorways. In the decade of booming financial services, it also won the unspoken competition with Manchester, across the border in Lancashire, to be finance capital of the north. The net result was that the city became a distribution centre and regional office base for national organisations. All sorts of virtuous circles were set in train, much of it property-led.

Demand for property rose and rents rose with it. Developers found it profitable to invest, the building industry flourished and the jobs poured into the new offices. There were more wages to be spent in the city and so it was worth putting money into the town centre.

Between '81 and '97, 36,500 additional jobs were created in Leeds, an increase of almost 10% (total number employed 330,000) (2). Accountants and solicitors arrived in droves. In 1980, there were just 50 independent accountants operating. Five years later there were 2000.

Hundreds of millions of pounds went into improving the city centre: pedestrianisation, renovated Victorian arcades, new theatres, warehouses turned into flats, more clubs and wine bars than you would have thought possible. The hype about turning Leeds into a continental twenty-four hour city began to look a reality, particularly when sufficient people seemed prepared to brave the northern climate to populate the street cafés!

Fact Box

The amount of office space and level of rents boomed

New office space let in Leeds each year and the average rent per square foot.(1)

1982	70,000	£5
1984	225,000	
1986	300,000	£6-50
1988	400,000	£10-50

The student population at the two universities and colleges beyond, exploded to over 40,000. This came in handy as many of them worked in the new nightlife venues to keep their student loans under control

Symbolically, the top retailer, Harvey Nichols, opened its first store outside of London in 1997 and if any more proof was needed that Leeds was a coming city, Railtrack decided to spend £167 million on renovating the train station, laying down extra tracks and platforms. It was hard keeping pace with the demand to come here.

So Leeds has become a good place to be. There are plenty of jobs, it's a shopper's paradise, it looks good, and manages to support three 'what's on' magazines. It is important to recognise and appreciate these improvements, but what may impact on the visitor does not tell the whole story. Four-wheel-drive city is also home to entrenched and widespread poverty.

What makes the contrast starker is that many of the poorest areas butt straight on to the town centre. One of the problems for the 5,000 tenants on the Little London estate is that, from 8am onwards, commuters swarm on to the estate, parking up before walking the last 200yds into town.

Since the seventies, poverty has become concentrated on the council estates and wards still made up of 19th century terraced housing. The scale of the problem is alarming. Leeds City Council submitted a bid for European Funding in '99 for what it called the Inner Area. The patch covered a population of 227,000 – itself the size of a large town. Within the Inner Area are pockets of extreme deprivation, but even aggregated up to a large geographical area covering 12 wards, statistics offer a chilling testimony.

Unemployment	'98 – 11.7%. compared to 3.5% in the rest of Leeds
Housing	1 in 5 homes classified as unfit to live in.
Income	1 in 3 households living in poverty (less than 50% of average earnings). 43% of household income from benefits, compared to 22% nationally
Health	Hospital admissions for mental health and respiratory diseases more than 40% higher than the rest of Leeds

| Education | 12.3% of students achieving grades A-C at GCSE, compared to 45.1% nationally |
| Crime | Domestic burglaries seven times the national rate. 74 per 1000 households per year compared to 10. |

Big money Leeds moves upward in virtuous circles. In the Inner Areas the circles tend to be vicious and downward. Many of the estates, when they were relatively new and there was full employment were seen as desirable places to live. Life may not have been ideal, but there was a waiting list to move on, people had money in their pocket and took a pride in the place.

Fact Box

Large growth in office jobs and commuters to fill them (2)

	'91	'97
Workers in Finance Sector	54,000	69,000
Workers in Manufacturing	59,000	56,000
Number of commuters coming in to Leeds, minus the number going out	50,000	63,000

Now most that have the chance to leave. The ones who stay are those that cannot afford to buy. Without the purchasing power, the few shops decline or close. The number of empty properties grows with the inevitable accompanying vandalism. Reduced housing budgets fail to keep up with maintenance and repairs. An air of demoralisation sets in.

But why is it that the prosperity and jobs growth of Leeds has bypassed these areas? Crudely speaking, many of the Inner Area residents used to work in the declining manufacturing sector. Instead of the new office jobs going to them, people living outside Leeds are filling them.

Leeds would seem to be calling out for Labour's skills revolution, a drive to put the unemployed on the estates into the call centres and finance houses (though where would the displaced commuters find new jobs?). Before addressing that, we must just note in passing the profound absurdity of having 69,000 (80,000 according to year 2000 estimates)(3) people in one city involved in nothing more productive than sorting out our access to purchasing power; the finance sector.

In a job-rich city like Leeds, every effort has to be put into retraining. Lives can be transformed as a result, but a sense of reality is needed. A huge number of people, concentrated in the inner city, have experienced years of stress, demoralisation and loss of confidence. A quick fix training course may not be an option or a solution.

Nick Davies wrote a powerful book in 1998 called Dark Heart (4), subtitled 'the shocking truth about hidden Britain'. It was a piece of investigative journalism into the state of people's lives in inner city areas of Nottingham, London and Leeds. Even allowing for the fact

Fact Box

How the population of Hyde Park live

25% unemployed or on training schemes
34% households completely dependent on benefits
58% of those of working age not working
33% had not had a holiday longer than a weekend in the last three years
30% reported that they felt seriously depressed
35% had been a victim of crime in the last 12 months

that he had a vested interest in making conditions appear shocking, it was depressing reading.

The area he chose in Leeds was Hyde Park, a mixed area of council and terraced housing close to the University. The area had hit the national news about a year before Davies arrived, when the local pub was burnt down in a riot. Drawing on a 1995 survey of almost 600 households in the area, he first presented the statistical catalogue of poverty (see box).

Then came the background. "During the 1980s this community had been shaken to its foundations by a series of massive quakes as the underlying structure of work shifted and splintered. New electronic technology which cut away some jobs forever; the deregulation of finance and markets, which allowed British companies to use cheap labour in the developing world; the stripping away of union power and labour laws, which allowed employers to shed workers in order to improve their productivity. George Brays, the engineering firm that had employed several generations of men and women from Hyde Park and Burley, cut its workforce from hundreds to dozens. The British Screw Company on Kirkstall Rd., the forge, the brewery, all the old textile plants and engineering firms were either cut or closed forever. It was as if someone had drilled a hole in the underside of Hyde Park and drained away the jobs. This was the beginning, the key ingredient in the chemistry of despair which now overwhelmed the place."

After taking us through 70 pages of the anxieties and troubles faced by those he interviewed, he ends with this description of poverty:

"….beyond the small minority who lack even the basic necessities of life, it turns out that there are numerous people in the community who live in real need and who avoid disaster only by living in the social equivalent of an iron lung, surviving only because they allow themselves to be encased in rigid self-discipline – to control themselves and their instincts, to measure every penny and plan every action, so that they never give in to temptation by spending the evening in the pub or giving their children new toys or buying new clothes or going out to the cinema. If they control every detail of their lives and strap themselves down within strict limits, then they can cling to the four essentials of life (food, fuel, shelter and clothing). But these lives of quiet desperation are always on the edge of disaster. One mistake, one weakness or one extra problem: that is all it takes to plunge them into trouble. An unexpected bill, a crime, a physical sickness, a mental illness, a violent partner, an aggressive neighbour, an accident at home, a bereavement or an addiction. Some stumble over the edge accidentally, like the old lady with her phone bill. Some deliberately jump, like the ones who drink, knowing they are blowing an entire week's money in a single night but preferring six days of trouble to a lifetime without laughter."

And what was it that the residents told the council would improve their lives most? A list that is repeated time and again around the country:

Play schemes	
An organised baby sitting service	
More full time nurseries	
Outreach workers for young people	
Playing fields	

Youth clubs	
Home helps	
More doctors	
Better housing repairs, damp proofing and insulation	
More police	
Funding for college courses	
Better public transport	
More streetlights	
Clean up campaign	
Local supermarket and cashpoints	
Pub with a garden	
Council gardener	
Better street cleaning	
Cooking and laundry facilities	
Community centre	
Traffic control measures	

And above all, money and jobs. (4)

Leeds is a success story of the last twenty years, by most traditional forms of measurement. It is not a Liverpool or Sunderland or even a Sheffield, where there is an absolute job shortage, and yet huge bands of poverty persist. Labour is pledged to tackle poverty while giving succour to the market forces that have intensified inequality. They hope that a combination of a steadily growing jobs market, combined with training, in-work benefits, and an element of work compulsion, will put people in these communities into jobs. The American experience would suggest that, even if that happens, it would be substituting in-work poverty for out of work poverty.

What is interesting in the list above is that the jobs requested to improve people's lives do not involve office and I.T. skills. Many could be taken up immediately by members of the community. The jobs would, wholly or in part, have to be publicly funded, but there would be short-term savings on benefit payments and longer-term paybacks in the reduction of crime, improvement in health etc.

The option of tackling poverty through decently waged, state-funded employment has been closed down as too expensive. Yet those on benefits, if it was combined with a raft of childcare choices, could be offered the chance of taking meaningful employment to improve their area. It would be one way back to rebuilding self-confidence. We will look later at how it could be afforded.

What about all those people working in the Leeds finance industry though? How do they feel about the economic system we live under?

BUT ARE THE BETTER OFF HAPPIER?

If the ideas of an alternative economic system are ever to reach out to the majority of the population, then they must be addressing the concerns of those that do not consider themselves poor. The elimination of poverty will always be the starting point for socialism, but it is not a creed for the poor alone.

The starting point for any analysis has to be an acceptance that the **majority** in Britain has become materially better off over the last 20 years (1):

	1979	1999
Consumer spending per year per person at 1999 prices	£5,600	£8,700
Number of people taking foreign holidays	9.8m	29.1m
Households with: washing machine	74%	90%
Telephone	67%	94%
Central heating	55%	88%
2 or more cars	11%	24%
Colour TV	66%	97%
Home computer	0%	27%

In 1999 the National Statistical Office announced that, for the first time, the average family had spent as much on leisure as on housing and food – all about £60 per week (though the purchase of a computer is classified as leisure). Two questions then need to be asked about this increased wealth. Was it bought at a price and is it making people happier?

Life at Work

The first is easier to tackle – we can still talk in the economist's language of statistics. Evidence abounds that while our position as consumers has strengthened, as producers and workers we are increasingly exploited, and we spend much more time at work than we do going round the shops. The form of the exploitation is that we are being worked harder for longer at more inconvenient times, with greater insecurity.

The 'downsizing' of the eighties went all the way up the ladder. Shop floor and management, public and private sectors were expected to produce the same amount with fewer people. Productivity drives tended to emphasise sweating labour rather than investing in the latest equipment. The inevitable result was an increase in hours worked. Britain is the only country in Europe where the number of hours worked has gone up over the last decade.

In the decade from 1988, the average hours of overtime worked by full time males increased from four to seven - and for women, from three to six (2). The change has hit women particularly hard and over the same period the number of full time women working more than 40 hours a week has grown from 27% to 45%.

In terms of hours worked the greatest increase is amongst lower and middle management. As the years pass, an ever greater proportion of the workforce becomes defined as professional, technical or managerial (up from about 1/5th in 1971 to 1/3rd in 1991). It would be a mistake to see these people as cigar-toting hirers and firers. Responsibilities are continually pushed downwards, often with little financial reward. Managers in the retail or service sector may earn little more than £13,000 a year for running their shop or burger bar, but are expected to deal with everything that happens.

A Britain at Work survey that interviewed 30,000 employees in 1999 reported that one in three managers were working more than 48 hours a week. "Only 56% of managers said that they felt secure in the position they slave so hard to maintain...... and many of those questioned insisted that the extra hours were expected as part of the job, and were not put in out of choice" (3). One in two working men and one in three women work some or most Sundays.

Long hours amongst the wealthier professionals is leading to the development of the 'work-rich, time-poor' strata that was mentioned before. This group is increasingly employing women who are excluded from the full time jobs market because they cannot afford the childcare costs. Instead, they clean the houses and look after the children of their wealthier neighbours.

The pressure to deliver, with overworked managers passing on their frustrations, has made stress the biggest occupational health problem. The Department of Health claim that up to 6 million days a year are lost from people being off work with stress related mental conditions (4).

It is not just a matter of working longer and harder. The changing structure of work has meant that an increasing number of workers have to work in the evenings or at weekends. One person's consumer convenience is another's evening shift at Tesco. The traditional interpretation of a job meaning full time work, Monday to Friday, is out of date. It never was the case for women, but now only 51% of men work to the old pattern. In one in four two-parent households, at least one parent now regularly works in the evening and the number of people with two jobs has almost doubled since 1984 to 1.2 million (5).

Shift workers in manufacturing are disappearing along with the factories, but similar jobs are re-emerging in the factories of the new millennium, the call centres. The TUC report on the industry (April '01), told not only of poor wages but unendurable surveillance. Employees can be expected to be on the phone for eighty five percent of the time - time that can be monitored exactly. They are told not to spend long with each customer, and sometimes have to put up their hands to ask to go to the toilet.

If the intensification of labour wasn't bad enough, the contractual context has worsened. With docile union leaderships, management continually seek to use labour more flexibly. There are now more than one third more temporary employees than in 1992 -1.7 million (6) – and they are not just working in seasonal industries. Let the Financial Times set the scene: "our study has revealed a 67.5% increase in five years in the number of manufacturing employees on temporary contracts. These can be for as little as a day, though typically last from three to six months.

The use of such workers has become critical to many manufacturers, which are switching to just-in-time practices, in which stocks are minimised and companies turn out goods quickly to fulfil orders.

Several companies – including the UK divisions of Black and Decker , Proctor and Gamble, the Raleigh bicycle company and chocolate makers Bendicks of Mayfair, say temporary workers have helped them improve competitiveness" (7).

In general, employers have sought to make their core workforce more flexible by expecting staff to undertake a wider variety of work and be able to stand in for workmates. In addition, flexibility has been introduced to working hours on the employers' terms. At its most draconian, this may be the zero hour contract when the employee does not know whether they will be working unless they receive a phone call. Otherwise, it could be the annual hours contract whereby, as long as you do not work more than the agreed hours in a year, the employer can make you do unpaid overtime in busy periods.

Beyond the core workforce, contract and part time workers are used to cope with peaks and troughs. One of the major reasons for the growth in self-employment under Thatcher and an explanation of why it has fallen slightly in the '90s, is that much of it was involuntary. Big business decided to employ only those staff directly involved in producing the goods and services. All other functions, typically cleaning, catering, building mainte-nance etc., were put out to contract. The Financial Times again:

"Executives forecast that their use of contract workers would increase further...

Of the executives surveyed, 87% reported restructuring in their organisations over the past 4 years....While this had increased produc-tivity and profitability, it had made employees feel less secure.

Employers are also using contract workers to fill the skill gaps. More than half the executives expected to use non core staff to meet skills short-ages." (8).

The new contract staff are always going to find their margins scrutinised and squeezed, but we have been passing through the good times. Many contract staff may be earning a decent living and taking advantage of south-eastern skill shortages to keep up their charges. They are fully aware though, that any drop in demand, any retraction to the core workforce, will put them first in the firing line.

Fact Box

Numbers of part time workers (millions)

1980	4.79
1998	6.84
2010	8.73 (projected)

Cambridge Econometrics (9)

There is no reason to suspect that the drive for flexibility will ease up. A report by Cambridge Econometrics in '99 suggested that **all** employment creation of the next ten years would be accounted for by part time jobs. By that time, part time jobs would account for a third of all jobs.

Those workers will be able to keep shops open late, staff the call centres and distribution depots, and serve food and drink around the clock in the café bars. The labour market is tending to become more stratified between high-fliers and low-fliers, the ones who can take advantage of the constant flux and those that cannot. "For not all the young are well equipped for this brave new world of economic insecurity; not all can strike a hard bargain with employers. The new work ethic can only help a quarter or a fifth of the population to advance. Those leaving school with few or no qualifications cannot demand anything from employers, and the insecurity of the labour market is, to them, a threat, not an opportunity"(10)

So households may be materially better off than they were 20 years ago but there has been a high price to pay. Work is likely to be more stressful and those pressures will be brought home. Long hours and shift work are also likely to affect the quality of relationships and childcare. "The pressures on families are huge – one reason why Britain has one of Europe's highest divorce rates. A recent survey by the organisation Parents at Work revealed that parents feel exhausted after a long day, relationships are put under pressure, and there is no time or energy for the children. Some 64% said they did not see enough of their children and nearly three quarters of women say they do not have enough time for themselves"(11).

Happiness

Let's consider further the situation of those who have enough money to have choices and move into that dangerous world of feelings. Humankind is a frighteningly adaptable species after all. Maybe we can get used to the intensity of work (it can be interesting), spending much of our life in a car (12), moving away from our friends and family for the sake of a job, and never having enough time. There's at least enough money to buy a bottle of something, get out to a club or indulge in a bit of shopping.

The trouble is that the evidence shows we are more miserable than we ever were. This is a difficult area, we are on to feelings that can only be measured by what people say about themselves. Yet if a discussion on the need to reorganise society does not engage with what makes us happy, it is almost irrelevant. However wet it may sound, the political economy we want is that which maximises the chance of people feeling good about themselves and the people and world around them.

Once we have attained the basic requirements of life – food, warmth, shelter, clothing etc. – what makes us happy becomes a subtle and complex matter. No one is likely to suggest that happiness is related to the growth of National Income. If proof were needed, a form of contentment survey was undertaken in Japan in 1958 and 1987. It showed no shift in feelings of well being, and yet in the intervening years, per capita income had grown by five times. Similarly, while genes and chemicals must play a role in the contentment levels of individuals, they will not account for the growth of discontentment across the population as a whole.

I am indebted to Oliver James and his book Britain on the Couch (13) for tackling the crucial question 'Why we are unhappier than we were in the 1950s – despite being richer'. Much of what he says reinforces the prejudices many of us hold as self evident, but it is reassuring that his opinions are backed up by references to over 500 pieces of psychiatric research. It is not necessary to share his enthusiasm for Prozac or even New Labour to see the line of analysis as vital to an examination of capitalism. With all the caveats that psychiatric survey evidence may only be relied on to reveal trends, or that the causes of mental states are hard to isolate, the reasoning is powerful.

James' thesis is that the structures of late capitalism have undermined our self-esteem and emotional attachments – both vital to contentment. This has led to a drop in the serotonin in our bodies, which in turn has produced an increase in depressed and aggressive behaviour (opposite sides of the same coin). While he produces evidence to back his arguments, it is not important here to be convinced of the chemical bridge to depression through serotonin levels.

First of all, he presents the data that indicates an increase in violence and depression. Reported crimes of violence in Britain have increased from 6,000 a year in 1950 to 239,000 in 1996. Maybe the traditional punch-up was rarely reported, but we can probably conclude that there has been an increase in aggressive behaviour.

He calls on various surveys to support his position on increased cases of depression. The largest involved 39,000 people in eight countries, including Britain, surveyed in the mid eighties. There are real problems about the reliability of people's memories and the words people use to analyse their feelings (depression was a less acceptable condition in the '30s), nonetheless the differences between the generations is so big, it is likely to indicate a trend. People who were 25 after the second world war were 3 to 10 times more likely to have suffered from depression than those who were 25 before it.

Self-esteem has been under attack on several fronts. We have a need to feel useful, valued and in control of our lives. We also need to feel we are doing OK in comparison to the people around us. In the past the majority lived a more collectivist working experience, in factories, mills, mines and so on. Most of the people around you would be doing similar things and earning similar amounts. Back home, the bonds of community were much stronger. How many of us have heard pensioners regret the loss of friendliness today with "we all used to be hard up in those days, but we looked out for one another"?

In the absence of the mass media, personal progress would be measured against people around you in these residential and work communities. It was not a golden era, conditions were harsh, and women in particular must often have felt trapped, but in terms of self esteem, you were likely to be achieving all that could be expected. Compare that to today.

Communities of interest have tended to replace geographical communities. Social life exists at a more intense level than it used to, but it usually costs and is chosen rather than just being there. With mass ownership of cars and the decline of local shops, opportunities for casual social engagement have diminished. Increasingly our community is the TV. Unlike the real world this community is full of well off beautiful people doing interesting things. Their activities are interspersed with adverts designed to make us feel inadequate if we do not buy something. One study estimated that the average American child sees 200,000 adverts by the time they are 12 (14). In Britain £4,000m. is spent on TV advertising alone.(15)

Selling involves generating a need in individuals by increasing their anxiety (how can I possibly impress women if I buy shirts from Marks and Spencer?). The emphasis on individuality encourages us to continually compare ourselves to others, particularly media images. We are told everything is possible and yet it so clearly is not. There is an increasing crisis of expectation.

Millions will feel they are unaffected by the media, that they enjoy the entertainment but do not feel it impinges on their own world. But, as one example, evidence exists to suggest that continual exposure to same sex beauty lowers our self-esteem. The lotions and potions industry certainly relies on us making desperate attempts to improve our looks.

Feelings of inadequacy and failure are not just generated through the TV. Education is again being remodelled to intensify competition, and mark out failure. In every league table there is a bottom as well as top. As for our working lives, the most common workplace – the office - tends to be hierarchically organised with continual selection for positions and individually determined salaries. There is plenty of scope for negative self-evaluation and feelings of anxiety.

James' comments as to why our need for emotional attachment is less fulfilled are more controversial. His main concerns are childcare, divorce and old age. In 1950 one in eight marriages ended in divorce. The figure is now one in three. Of those people under 40, almost half have been touched by divorce, either as parents or children. He does not hit out at single parenthood but rather sees the hurt to all parties in the divorce itself.

The reasons for increased divorce rates are complex but link back to the crisis of expectation. Relationships have become much more intense, we expect much more from them, and consequently are more disappointed when they do not meet our needs. Personal fulfilment has become a high priority as against marriages 'for better or worse'. Combined with women's demands for equality in relationships and greater financial independence, the net result is an increase in single parents and single householders. (16)

There is a danger of reaching glib conclusions here. It is easy to accept that we expect too much from relationships and now find it easier to extract ourselves. It is equally easy to see that divorce is a painful experience for all involved. Does that necessarily mean though that everyone sticking in and making the best of it would increase the sum of human happiness? Is it worse for a child to be with parents who are unhappy together, or for someone to live alone rather than put up with an unsatisfactory relationship? These are not easy questions.

The second category of broken emotional bonds lies with old people. Sadly, evidence of the increasing isolation is clear and accelerating. The proportion of over 85s living with relatives fell from 31% to 19% between '71 and '91. If they were moving in to nearby sheltered housing (too rarely the case), this may have been a good thing. More disturbing is that in 1962 survey evidence showed that 75% of over 65s had children living under 15 minutes away. By 1986 this was down to 40%.

It may be thought that these issues have little to do with a discussion of economic structure, but that would be far from the truth. The pain of being human will always be with us, to fall in and out of love, to lose people, grow old and die. The priorities of economic organisation however would be turned around under social ownership. Support to families and relationships would be given through childcare options, allowing more time away from work and rebuilding **local** social networks that would allow fulfilment beyond the household. Let us be clear: such words could be read in any liberal leaning pamphlet. The key to making them a reality is turning the need for profit into just one objective in the functioning of the economy, a lesser one to developing human solidarity.

Many would accept the analysis that capitalism only recognises one relationship, the individual to the market, and that this has an eroding affect on collective activity. Our increasing power as individual consumers is not matched by the satisfaction of our social needs. Such a critique is sometimes interpreted as socialists having something against individual enjoyment. If you are not marching around in a collective, then life has no meaning. The truth is that there can still be plenty of opportunity to shop until you drop in the society envisaged here, but alongside the developed markets of capitalism, strenuous efforts would be made to build and rebuild social links. The ways would be multifarious and would need to be organised by people. They will not just emerge through the natural play of market forces.

A Demos survey, which interviewed over 1,000 tenants in 1999 (17), showed that "people are generally not interested in getting to know their neighbours". This is surely sad, though not surprising. In the residential context we now have a deeply individual and isolationist culture. There is little that brings us together, and in these communities of strangers the fear of crime and violence grows. Yet no one chose this pattern. The market operates in a deeply conservative way, duplicating off the shelf estates around the country. They sell, so why bother doing anything else?

What about building some houses for people who want to spend some of their time living collectively? Housing which contains both personal living space and some communal facilities. This is commonplace in Nordic countries and is surely a common-sense response to a society made up increasingly of single householders. Experiment with community owned local shops. Give local resident associations control over surrounding land to establish their own ventures. Offer them a small budget for social events - anything that brings people together in an unpressurised way and offers the possibilities of friendship and mutual support. Experimentation, local control and unbureaucratic support are the key. It is not a matter of one solution fits all. Nor does it imply a belief that we should all be living on each other's doorsteps. Privacy is not incompatible with a friendly and safe neighbourhood. It is something we all want but little is being done to naturally create it.

Housing is just one area of life where action could be taken to strengthen the bonds of affection and self esteem that James talks about. The rebalancing of our social needs with our needs as individual consumers would require a new focus across the board. Business management for instance would need to concentrate more on staff welfare and putting something into the surrounding community.

Social involvement requires time, it often requires having a little money and regularly poses the question of what the kids are going to do. A high minimum wage, putting resources into childcare and reducing the working week will not bankrupt the economy, but neither will it maximise profits. Again and again we face the choice of either breaking with profit maximising logic or being locked into a pattern of development that is not of our choosing.

Is this all crass social engineering? Who wants to suffer the tedium of endless organising meetings anyway? The libertarian argument is that increased wealth has opened up choices for the majority and it is up to the individual to seize their share. The existence of (unfulfilled) opportunities can cause unhappiness. So what? That's life and there is nothing we can do about it.

But if opportunity can be combined with more supportive social bonds, unhappiness might be minimised. Even if we accept that the majority are happier than they were 50 years ago (and a powerful case could be made that this is so for women), there is widespread unease that we are losing something along the way. The old securities and certainties, particularly organised religion, have disintegrated without anything replacing them. We are being thrown forward to acquire and perform (economically, socially and sexually) increasingly as lone individuals. Holding on to friends, let alone being part of any 'community', is difficult. It is surely not dewy-eyed sentimentality to think that society needs reorganising to better address **social** satisfaction, and the way we can support each other.

It is interesting to note that twelve years after the fall of the Berlin Wall, the majority of East Germans still mourn the passing of the solidarity that was part of that society. For all that communist East Germany was an oppressive, centralised and backward state, much of the population still expressed support for a democratic form of socialism.

A word of warning before leaving the discussion of happiness. 'I feel stressed at work, depressed at home and I've got no friends' does not translate easily to seeing the need to become an active socialist. In general, people will be defensive of their lifestyle even if they are critical of its content (particular job, particular partner etc.). To call to people from what can appear a parallel existence of socialist consciousness, will not win much support. The battle for the minds of the (slightly) better off is a challenging one. It is one that must be won and we will return to it in the final chapter.

WILL THINGS IMPROVE? - THE SPECTRE OF THE BUSINESS CYCLE

The collapse of the global marketplace would be a traumatic event with unimaginable consequence. Yet I find it easier to imagine than the continuation of the present regime.

George Soros, one of the world's leading speculators, in 1995 (1)

I have attempted to establish that, at this stage of capitalist development in Britain, unemployment and poverty are endemic. There is little prospect of improvement because the main causes (low growth and investment, combined with a continuous shake-out of the manufacturing workforce and fierce international competition) are here to stay. This remains a static view though. If we are examining the problems of capitalism, the tendency towards boom and slump cannot be ignored.

The scope of this small book is already over ambitious. To enter a discussion of capitalist crisis theory would be foolish. Nonetheless, for the sake of synthesis, a few general points need to be made. The first is that there will be no 'final crisis' of capitalism. It was unfortunate that some socialists around the turn of the century interpreted Marx's theory of the falling rate of profit (2) in a way that suggested the system would grind to a halt and all they had to do was wait for it to fall into their laps.

Tracking the tendency of the rate of profit to fall in real life is a complex business. There are counter-tendencies such as the lowering of the value of capital, but the important point here is that the short-run battles between capital and labour over the share of profit and wages in the economy are of much more significance. At the end of the Second World War when there was widespread poverty, unemployment and a lack of union power, there was a massive shift from wages to profit internationally. The same thing happened under the Thatcher / Reagan offensive of the 1980s, when the profit rate in Britain was pushed up from 3% in 1979 to 8% in 1989 (net rate of return of British manufacturing industry). (3)

Capitalism has become a form of ordered chaos. It is no longer the primeval swamp of cotton and coal magnates in head to head class conflict with their workers, but is manipulated by huge sophisticated organisations. Yet in determining the outcomes of the system, today's capitalists are as helpless as their forebears. Take just one instance - the collapse of the Indonesian economy in 1997 that led to the overthrow of President Suharto.

In 1996 the World Bank delivered an upbeat report on Indonesia called 'Sustaining High Growth with Equity' (4). You had to look hard for any blemishes. Growth steady at 7.8%, inflation down to 6.6%, a budget surplus, increasing foreign exchange reserves, foreign and domestic investment buoyant. Six months later the economy was in tatters.

The background was the general turmoil in Asian financial markets. Indonesian interest rates had been raised to avoid overheating the economy and, as a result, speculative money had poured in and caused the value of the currency (the rupiah) to rise. The same speculators, who are often respectable financial institutions trading not directly but through derivatives (more later), decided it was time the currency was 'corrected' downwards. Unfortunately in true free market fashion, the correction turned in to a dive.

The rupiah fell by 36% in 4 months. Companies and banks who had borrowed dollars abroad found they had 'non-performing loans' on their hands - the financial world is full of euphemisms - as the cost of their dollar loans had just exploded. The stock market fell by 40%, 250 banks were closed, investment halted and the economy slowed to nil growth.

No capitalist, or few anyway, had an interest in crashing the Indonesian economy. Events had an alarming and anarchic profit-maximising logic to them. The human cost or long term consequences were not considered. In an unstable world such speculative visitations can come to any country, detonated either internally or externally. Britain is no more protected than Japan was, now in its tenth year of 'bust' in the boom and bust cycle.

Anarchy is not the only feature of capitalism. The system remains dynamic, but tensions and contradictions are continually building up within it and have to be resolved. The tensions can be of different sorts at different times. In the late sixties pressure on profits caused the investment rate to fall and economies to slow. The seventies were typified by inflationary troubles as credit, extended to keep economies moving, went in to speculative property and asset deals rather than production. Today the mountain of cash from profits, pensions, mutual and insurance companies that took the American stock markets up to unsustainable levels, is likely to take the world in to recession on the rebound.

Capitalism is continually losing its balance. The economy can move forward steadily if conditions exist to make profits and if those profits, along with savings, are reinvested back into production. However, unplanned as it is, the system is dogged by its failure to maintain a balance between the level of wages and investment (demand), and the level of production of goods and services (supply). The classic business cycle, starting at the bottom, used to be that potential for profitable activity was spotted in a particular sector. Investment would be made, workers taken on and paid wages, some of which would be spent on the goods being produced. Investment and production would move up again, further increasing demand, and so on. The virtuous circle would continue until supply outstripped demand. Prices would then fall, companies go bust, and workers be laid off. The cycle didn't go back to where it had started. On the way, many companies would have invested in more modern productive equipment and it would be the low productivity companies that would go to the wall.

The four or five yearly business cycle roller coaster is no longer apparent. Big business has become more strategic and forward thinking. If the upwave inevitably turns into a downwave, why invest in new machinery that will be underused in the next recession? Longer periods of slow growth can replace the boom and bust cycle, and this typifies the British economy in the 1990s at least up to 1997. However, continuous slow growth is not an option under capitalism. The search for greater profits is the primary driver of the system and, if profits and savings are increasing but not going back into investment, they must inevitably end up in speculation. We have had South Sea Bubbles and Dutch bulbs in the past; this time it is the turn of the American stock market.

The Business Cycle in the US

The only surprising thing about the end of the US boom was the number of people who appeared to be surprised. But then, as international economists have an amazing record of failure to predict downturns, that too is unsurprising. (5)

The writing of this book has covered a fascinating period of capitalist development in the USA. These paragraphs were first written at the turn of the millennium, when the dot.com revolution was still driving share prices to new heights and the air was hot with enthusiasm for the transforming effects of the 'new economy'. I tried to be suitably delphic in my pronouncements at the time – 'Economic leaders are shutting their eyes, holding hands and talking the market ever upwards. It is all alarmingly similar to the year before the 1929 Wall Street crash.'

Then came March 2000. Technology stock prices collapsed and pulled consumer confidence down with them. Investors rediscovered that share prices have to be related to future profits, and that technology companies did not seem too good at producing them. The

Fact Box

The US boom had to go bust

	As a % of GDP	
	'91	'97
Stock market valuation	45	147
Private saving	18	13
Private investment	13	18
Current account deficit	$48bn	435bn

Thompson Financial Datastream

speculative bubble burst with all its classic features. Talk was no longer of eradication of the business cycle, but how long and how deep the recession would be. Journalists abandoned the jargon of the new economy for more immediate concerns.

The exact global repercussions of these events will still be the subject of debate when this book is published. The optimists are holding on to the possibility of an early recovery and I do not consider myself any more capable of six monthly projections than the average economist soothsayer. What is important is that the boom has created stresses that have to be resolved in some way and at some time.

The pieces of the jigsaw are relatively easy to put together and are familiar pieces. The cycle began with improved profits and investment leading to higher employment and greater confidence in the future. Being capitalism, confidence then moved on to speculative exuberance. The money making machine called the stock market was delivering returns of 30% a year for the five years after 1995. The personal sector reduced savings and went on a spending spree, relying on the value of their rising stocks to pay for retirement. Demand over this period rose faster than production and created a huge deficit in the balance of trade, which was financed by the US attracting a phenomenal 70% of the world's capital account surpluses into the country (6). The growth was unsustainable and virtuous circles were bound to turn into the opposite.

The unwinding will look like this. Investment goes down as growth rates fall. Managers of foreign capital become reluctant to finance the trade deficit as profits fall, causing the dollar to drop and inflation rise. Investors become a downward drag on demand as they save more to recoup their losses on the stock market. Workers are laid off, further reducing demand and confidence… and so on. All the arrows that pointed upwards begin to swivel around. Talk of a soft landing is merely the hope that the problems of an overvalued stock market, the trade deficit, and low savings will be dealt with over time, rather than in a crash. While the timing of adjustments is always difficult to predict, the outcome is less so. The whole experience has shown that the business cycle is very much alive.

INFORMATION TECHNOLOGY, THE 'NEW ECONOMY' AND JOBS

In bringing to a close this analysis of the problems of advanced capitalism, a final dimension needs addressing – the future. We hear much of the technological restructuring of the labour market. What does it mean and what does the future hold for us?

Leave aside business cycles and possible crisis points in capitalism. If we just project forward what is happening, what changes can we expect over the next twenty years or so?

Information technology and genetics are subject to an enormous amount of hype. Without in any way belittling the significance of completing the human DNA map or the increasing sophistication of computer communication, there is usually a determination by the media to see present developments as **the** mould breaking ones. In reality, the development of technology has continued at break-neck speed through much of the last century. It would be an interesting discussion, with no foregone conclusion, to consider which of the following is likely to have had the biggest social and economic impact:

1) Water wheel
2) Three mast sailing ship
3) Steam engine
4) Electricity
5) Cars
6) Electrical goods after the Second World War (including TV)
7) The potential of the internet and electronic commerce

There are admittedly some big ones on the horizon. Developments that do not so much bear on the social and economic, but call into question what it means to be human. The ability to genetically clone a child with chosen characteristics is all but here. Our knowledge of the human make up is such that we are likely to be able to buy drugs to make us the sort of character we want to be (an anti shyness pill is on its way). Then there is the interesting medium term prospect of computer implants in the brain. As the essence of thinking is to connect one thought to all other thoughts, and to consider all possible alternatives, some scientists believe there is no barrier to the creation of super intelligence. Such super charged brains would be able to think so fast that half a minute would seem like a year! (1).

Most technical developments are incremental. The miniaturisation of machines (nano technology) continually opens up possibilities. Similarly, the increasing ability to make computers that can learn from experience and programme themselves pushes back the limitations on robotics. However, advances in genetic and molecular engineering, along with the internet, have commanded the most public attention. They represent the front line of the never-ending (western) human quest to control nature, with all the dangers associated with that. We are offered the glimpse of a world where is seems possible to make almost anything out of anything. Already, man made chemical substitutes are replacing raw materials like rubber and sugar cane, and the equivalent to plastic can be grown as a crop.

A recent report from an architectural college (2) describes the bio-house, most of it already technically feasible, made of flexible protein-based materials, smart glass, 'frozen smoke' insulation material, wholly solar-powered and containing a fridge programmed to order more of the food you like when it is running out. It is all interesting stuff but does not say much about the important things of life – jobs, money, health and what time we have to get up in the morning.

Undoubtedly, some technological breakthroughs will be transforming. If real progress is made in, say, nuclear fusion, to make it safer (the main problem is intense heat) and more economic to produce, or in our ability to extract fresh water from seawater, serious long-term sustainability problems might be avoided. The significance of the leap that has been made in communication technology, lies somewhere between the life-transforming and baseless hype.

Clearly everything that can be digitised will be accessible instantly, anywhere, whether it is a film, music or a currency transaction. There are consumer goods implications. An example is that instead of mobile phones (and only slightly less irritatingly), people will be walking around with their micro-earpieces and watch transmitters / computers. More significant are the outcomes of e-commerce, ordering goods and services over the computer or on TV. Such changes add impetus towards the 24-hour society (see below). The number of jobs will also grow in the creative and information processing industries, but the revolutionising effect is often overdrawn. Here is a typical piece of technological hyperventilation from a review of the 1999 Institution of Economic Development conference. (3)

"The world is changing faster than ever before. Our economic development thinking is being challenged. Services can be provided virtually anywhere – Gibraltar-based telephone betting, which avoids UK taxes, is a case in point......

The new century will be very different. What commentators are calling a 'new economy' is dawning. It is characterised by:

➤ Intelligent use of technology
➤ Communications technology creating competition
➤ Innovation having greater importance than mass production
➤ Investment in concepts or the means to create them, rather than new machines
➤ Rapid change as a constant feature

The key to the new economy is working with information. We talk now about knowledge based industries, but what matters is how the knowledge is transmitted and used."

Nothing above is wrong, there is just a need to calm down. We live in a manufactured world and enjoy services delivered by people. Read some of the hype and it would seem that the economy will be entirely made up of people thinking up concepts and zapping them to each other, but the internet will not deliver your Argos order, nor does it make a good job of doing your hair.

Ideas of the 'new economy' sit uneasily with the fact that the fastest growing sector of the international economy is tourism, possibly accounting for 10% of world Gross Domestic Product (4). The jobs created in this sector are not generally knowledge based but rather the opposite, poorly paid part timers in hotels and restaurants. Much the same can be said of most job creating service industries. They may have a knowledge-based core that sells brand names rather than the product, but most of the jobs in these companies are concerned with delivering the designer economy to the market place.

The most profound effect of the communications revolution may be on organisations and the market itself. Management theorists suggest a shift from hierarchical organisations modelled on armies, to geographically scattered networks (5). This is still the stuff of business schools. What is certain is that, as the majority come on line and start to use the net for consumer information, competition will intensify.

I recently did a web search on a particular piece of kitchen equipment. Response to the key words came from around the globe, including a supplier in inland China. An e-mail through to Molly Ling from their website was instantly replied to, offering me a machine at rock-bottom price (NB average wages £1 a day) with a three week delivery schedule and the ability to order without leaving my chair. The internet is becoming a powerful tool to the consumer, but it will tend to increase instability, as loyalties, habits and attachment to locality are broken in favour of global price competition. The fact that I went off and bought my machine at Argos only shows how instantly gratified modern day consumers need to be!

Technological advance and the way it is exploited has always shaped society. Underneath the hype, how is it shaping Britain? New technology, stiffer competition and consumer demands are rapidly restructuring the nature of work. Some aspects (flexibility, part time working etc.) have been discussed earlier in the Life at Work section, but other trends are visible.

At the centre of the process in Britain is the decline in the number of people employed in manufacturing. 1998 was a landmark year in the scissors effect, when the rising numbers employed in finance on its way up, passed the numbers employed in manufacturing on its way down. In fact three sectors employed approximately 4.1million each – manufacturing, finance and wholesale and retail.

Employment in manufacturing is on trend to employ a similar amount to agriculture by the middle of the century. If shopping and other leisure services are the major growth areas it is not surprising that part time jobs are those which are most in demand.

Far from organisations becoming networks, as the internet theorists might have us believe, current trends appear to be in a centralist direction. Take Tesco as an example. Prior to the mid-eighties, their supermarkets had a fair amount of leeway in where they ordered from, and goods were often delivered direct to the supermarket. Over the next few years the company created a network of just nine warehouses nationally, which receive instant point-of-sale information from all the regional supermarkets. The information is translated into renewal orders and the food supplier given a two day delivery deadline (down from 10 days in 1983), with an accompanying ½ hour wagon delivery slot at the warehouse. The net result is that Tescos hold 30% less stock than their competitors (6).

The same centralising trend and a desire to cut overheads, while offering a round the clock service, has driven the call centre explosion. When I ring my local bank manager 300yds down the road, I am routed there via a receptionist in Wales. It is estimated that by 2002 there will be 480,000 call centre workers (2.35% of the working population) based in 5,000 centres (7).

Teleworking, working from home using communications equipment, is growing but perhaps not as rapidly as was anticipated 10 years ago. Almost 1 million people count themselves as teleworkers but the figures have to be treated with care as it counts anyone who works one day a week or more from home. Even so, the numbers are projected to grow by 200,000 a year (8).

A crucial question arising from all this is: what sort of skills are required for the future? The workforce is constantly moving away from the manual towards the managerial. In 2000, there were roughly 10.5m managerial and technical workers and 7m. manual workers, the reverse of what it was 20 years ago (9). Interestingly though the number of skilled trade workers is set to decline by 0.5% a year (10). The skills that are needed in greater quantities are not in the main 'hard' skills, in terms of knowing a body of knowledge (though the number of legal, financial and health professionals is likely to go on increasing). Rather, they are skills of communication (personal and computer) and generalised thinking.

The commentary contained in a recent labour market assessment of the Huddersfield and Halifax area of West Yorkshire, could be repeated for most of the country (11). After noting the long term growth in female, part time, self employed and temporary workers within the context of a gradual shift from manufacturing to services, the report had this to say about growing skill shortages:

"With the exception of shortages in new and high tech occupations and industries, most or all of the occupations identified in the area would have appeared in any local skill shortage list at almost any time over the last 15 years. This is further evidence that, although some shortages are due to cyclical pressure in the labour market, they are also symptoms of deep-seated skills deficiencies."

In an accompanying survey, employers were clearly aware of the generalist nature of the skill shortage. They identified computer literacy, management, marketing, selling and problem solving skills as the ones that would need to be improved most in the next few years. These are the skills held by a literate, self confident, integrated society. There is no demand for us all to become physicists and systems analysts.

As it is, in the most comprehensive survey of its kind (12), the Basic Skills Agency estimated that fifteen per cent of all working age adults had a low / very low literary capability (the definition of low capability is complicated but relates to everyday reading demands like using the phone book or reading labels). Thirty three per cent found basic numerical tasks difficult. Not surprisingly, there was a strong link between lacking these skills and being out of work.

The employment market of the future is a product of technological advance in its class setting. The divide between the two job camps of low skill, low wage and high skill, high wage is likely to grow wider. Increasing skill levels is vital, but the rhetoric of the government sits uncomfortably with widening class divisions in education. It is also important to recognise that increasing skill levels may solve the problem of certain individuals and company staff shortages, and may enhance economic growth, but they do not alter the structure of the labour market. It is not only a matter of job creation often being in the wrong place. The economy is generating hundreds of thousands of service jobs where employers want good communication skills, but only pay unskilled wages. A first at Oxford will still not earn you more than £4 an hour as a waiter.

SOME CONCLUSIONS

To return to the original question. If taken over time the economies of the advanced capitalist countries are tending to grow by 2.5% a year, is there really a problem with capitalism, or are the difficulties just a product of continual and necessary restructuring? Condensing this section produces the following conclusions:

1) The average **is** just for the advanced capitalist countries. Large parts of Africa and the ex-communist countries are economically devastated. The world's second largest economy, Japan, has suffered a decade of stagnation. Much of Asia has experienced a severe recession at the hands of speculators and numerous South and Central American countries are, again, facing economic difficulties.

2) We conducted a health check on Anglo Saxon capitalism after a nine year growth cycle pulled along by the US economy. That economy has now reached a point of having a record trade deficit, no net savings and a stock market that in July 2001 still bore no relation to the future generation of company profits. Despite the discovery of a new growth era by some politicians and theorists, there is every likelihood the house of cards will fall in the coming period. If it does, the impact will have global repercussions and much more benign looking economies like Britain will be dragged into recession.

3) In Britain over the last twenty years, absolute poverty may have been slightly reduced, but the numbers facing relative poverty, by being forced to live on less than half the average wage, has increased enormously. Evidence would suggest that it is precisely relative poverty that causes the most psychological damage.

4) Even the majority who have experienced growing purchasing power as consumers face a shrinking welfare state, weakening social bonds and unachievable expectations. Added to this can be a marked decline in a range of quality of life measures that we have not had the space to deal with (1).

5) At a high level of generalisation, the labour market of the future will be characterised by two great blocks of workers: those that manage services and those that deliver them. The latter will need more personal and IT skills than were ever needed in manufacturing but are unlikely to be rewarded any higher. In addition they will face the brunt of 'flexible working practices' that offer ever-increasing choice to the consumer.

6) Developments in computer and communications technology strengthen the free market by increasing consumer knowledge and making consumption more global and competitive. The technologies have also brought to completion the globalisation of financial markets with the economic power that vests in fund managers. Acquiescent governments have allowed the free market to tighten its grip through bodies such as the IMF and the World Trade Organisation by knocking down barriers to free trade. This has had the effect of increasing inequality within and between countries, a trend likely to continue.

7) Third Way politics is the provision of the welfare state that the free market can afford. Wedded to this logic, the Labour government is only able to increase expenditure or redistribute incomes at the margins. It would not claim to be able to do anything about the business cycle other than making a commitment to stability, which means low inflation / low growth in a low productivity economy like Britain. However many measures are taken to increase training and the 'entrepreneurial spirit', unless investment levels and demand are tackled, Britain's productivity growth is likely to remain poor.

8) Successive governments have set about turning the welfare state from a social insurance system to a safety net system. Assistance is targeted at the poorest and universal provision either ended or delivered at a low standard. The process will intensify the drift to private provision and support for the Welfare State will tend to wither. People will not be prepared to pay taxes for services that do not benefit them.

9) Labour are probably the most effective managers of a capitalist economy seen in Britain. Many of their reforms will help the market system function more efficiently ('supply side' economics) but it is very unlikely that they will impact on the major trends outlined above.

I was determined when starting this opening section, not to make out that life in Britain was some sort of hell on earth. Such a gloomy picture might back up socialist arguments but will not chime with reality for the majority of people. Many things have improved over the last twenty years. Millions are better off in material terms, and having enough money to move into a better house, go out, or take an extra holiday is clearly important. Despite the Tories' best efforts, tolerance of different lifestyles has increased. Further steps have been taken on the road to female equality. The centres of large towns and cities have become better places to be, and so on.

Yet over the last twenty years there has been a growing awareness of the spoils being divided unfairly, of the division between the insiders and outsiders growing. What is improving for the people on the Little London estate? The schools, hospitals, buses, housing, benefits, pensions, the position of the low paid, conditions at work? Yes, some additional money has come through since '99 (2) that will last as long as economic growth and the budget surplus does. But no one is claiming to be reigning in the power of the free market. Quite the opposite. Labour is installing profit maximising firms at the heart of the welfare state, in schools and in hospitals. It is the free market that generates inequality and yet New Labour politically sells poverty as a matter of inadequacy, of 'they' the poor and 'us' the normal ones. It is as though just a few people were falling off the edge of a fundamentally healthy economy. The reality is that between a quarter and a third of the population struggle with poverty, a divide that moves upwards in times of recession.

It seems that the future is better grasped through the science fiction of Robocop than through the pen of political pundits. In films of that ilk, society is divided between the pampered managerial classes and the dispossessed. They live in different zones and experience different realities. The privileged are never moved to change anything because the suffering never touches them. For their part the dispossessed can only be heard through riot and revolution. They are only films, yet today 10% of the population of the USA live in privately guarded buildings, while 2 million are in prison at any one time (3). The same features of inequality and separation are growing in Britain.

On top of the growing inequalities of wealth and power can be laid the problems of materialism. There is nothing New Age about such a critique. It is merely to understand that an economic system is not embedded in social relations, but rather that social relations are embedded in the economic system. In other words turbo-capitalism, as it is sometimes called now that the communist brakes have been removed, only recognises the individual and the market. We are encouraged to believe that all our needs can be met through consumption, and of course they cannot. Whether you prefer to call them spiritual or social needs does not matter, they are not being fulfilled. Mental health is going to be easier to achieve if we create an economy that, after the elimination of poverty, has as its primary function the development of relationships between people and between people and the earth we inhabit. Just what that means, we will examine later.

In an inevitably dry statistical manner this section has tried to draw a picture of economic life in Britain today and over the next few years. Before going on to see how things could be improved, it is necessary to examine where the power to change things lies.

CHAPTER 2.

CORPORATE POWER, BIG MONEY AND THE NEED FOR SOCIAL CONTROL

THE PUBLIC CORPORATION

This chapter will attempt to show that the power to shape economies lies in the boardrooms of global industrial and financial corporations, not with private entrepreneurs and governments. I will argue that to tackle the problems outlined in Chapter One, corporations will need to be brought under social control. That this need not be a repeat of Soviet type centralism or nationalisation of the past, will be discussed in following chapters. Socialisation is rather the first practical step on the road to an economy that combines social co-ordination of large-scale production, with local control over the rest.

Support for the existing economic order is always argued in the same way. There are only two ways to run an economy it is suggested. One is through private enterprise (efficient, responsive to consumers, exciting) and the other is through public ownership (statist, bureaucratic, grey, and costly). We have already seen that while the free market may be efficient at producing things cheaply, it is grossly inefficient at meeting overall human need. The other crucial flaw in this argument is, of course, that the economy is not dominated by private enterprise, it is dominated by **public** corporations operating in a (largely) free market. Let us examine the significance of this.

In a place like Britain corporations are likely to do most things better, or on a bigger scale, than their small business counterparts. Better pay, better management and training; more investment and research. As a worker, you are likely to be at an advantage working for a branch of a multinational on a green-field industrial estate than for the small business supplying them.

As so often in life though, this is the right answer to the wrong question. The significance of the large corporations is not that they are necessarily terrible employers (though they often are in less developed countries) (1), but that along with the financial institutions, they control much of our lives. They exercise that control without any reference to people affected by their decisions. A complete lack of democracy could possibly be forgiven if they contributed to solving some of the problems identified previously, but they are the source, rather than the solution, of many of those problems.

Reflect on the nature of private enterprise for a moment. The entrepreneur as depicted by the 19th century capitalist theorist, Adam Smith, was someone who owned his mill or factory, turned up most days to squeeze what he could out of the workforce and, with a thin layer of management, toughed it out in the marketplace to maximise his profits. In contrast, the modern corporation, at least in Britain, are often owned by the millions of people who have pensions and insurance policies - the pension fund managers and insurance companies holding the majority of the shares. In theory the representatives of these millions of policyholders, with their power to elect the Board of Directors, can then appoint the Chief Executive to run the company. To all intents the company is socially owned but in no way socially controlled.

The new society does indeed grow within the belly of the old. Future generations are likely to wonder how we allowed such enormously powerful institutions to be guided purely by the need to maximise profits.

The corporate constitution

Once a private owner of a company has cashed in and sold shares to external shareholders, there have to be rules about how a company is run. Thus company law governs public companies. It has to be said that the rules are not that tight and are mostly about accounting and information practices and the responsibilities of Boards of Directors. Whether Chile or China, corporate law is notable for its similarities rather than differences.

The Board of Directors runs the company. It will typically consist of executive directors (managers) and non-executive directors (independent outsiders) in equal proportion, though the pressure is on to have more independents (2). The existing company Chairman (and it nearly always is a man), often still recruits new independent directors on the old boys' network. They will probably be directors of several companies already, and will be rewarded handsomely for attending between 6 and 11 board meetings a year – perhaps receiving £10-20,000. Once on the Board it is difficult to remove a non-executive director unless they fail to attend. The Board will be about 16-20 strong (3).

Appointments to the Board and several other key decisions have to be approved by the ritual of the annual shareholders meeting. This is a chance for campaigners who own a few pounds worth of shares to try and gain some publicity for their cause. The large institutional investors who actually own the company sit on their hands or ignore the whole process. There are rarely any surprises.

As a way of exercising external control over management, the Board system seems peculiarly ineffective. The independent directors devote insufficient time to the job to do more than endorse management decisions. One interview survey produced this comment by a Chief Executive Officer as being typical of how non-executive directors view their job (4):

"The Board are responsible for the strategy....To me it is, of course, clear that there is a limit to what a Board member can do. After all, we have eight meetings a year, which last a day or a day and a half. I think it is wrong to assume they can do more....They are reactive in essence, less proactive, at least typically."

And from another non executive director:

"The job is do-able – but the key question is how much time. As a non-executive myself I could not accept a requirement of 25% involvement. But it is not satisfying to be a nominal director"

It would be reasonable to conclude that public corporations, with budgets the sizes of countries, are run by ill-informed part timers. The non executive directors give a few days a year, often know little about the business (British Airways slid into quiet decline with over half its Board of Directors being diplomats!) and have personal relationships with the leaders of the company that make a questioning attitude unlikely. The reality is of course that senior management runs the company. They are likely to be much more responsive to the vagaries of the stock market, than any director control and will not be above concealing information from the Board. The only effective control exercised by the Board is its power to hire and fire the Chief Executive.

This need not be. It is a function of old time capitalist traditions. Dispersed individual share ownership of the past has meant no real voice for the owners of the company on the boards of directors. However, as ownership becomes concentrated in the hands of financial institutions, an interesting form of capitalist social ownership is evolving.

Corporate Ownership

Despite the bonanza stock market conditions of the late nineties and the arrival of the internet day trader, individual share ownership is in historical decline internationally. To be sure, more people own shares than before, but they do it through intermediary financial institutions. The driving force behind rising stock market values has come from pension funds investing our savings. In most advanced capitalist countries individuals only own between 16 and 24% of the value of shares. In the UK individual ownership has declined from 50 to 16% since the 1950s. Domestic financial institutions now own over 50% of British company shares (5).

Fact Box

Share ownership

Total London Stock Exchange Value £1500bn. Owned by:

Financial Institutions	52%
Individuals	16%
Foreign owned	27%
Others	5%

Share Registry Survey 1/1/99

Potentially, the financial institutions wield enormous power, but there is an international split as to how they exercise it between what are called the banking and capital systems. The first is associated with Germany and Japan, the latter with the UK and USA. There is no need to go deeply into the differences, but there are implications for how corporations could be socially controlled.

In the capital system that dominates in the UK, large shareholders play little role in running the company. Disciplines on management come from the threat of shareholders selling company shares (reducing the value of management's stock options in the process), or the possibility of a hostile take-over bid from another company. While a take-over might produce redundancies, it is worth noting that it is also likely to **increase** the value of management stock options, a fattened redundancy package not available to the workforce.

The ownership concentration in Britain is truly remarkable. Citywatch, the market research company, estimate that the top five fund managers (companies like Mercury and Prudential and Schroder) control 26% of the shares of the top 100 companies on the Financial Times Stock Exchange listing, while the top ten fund managers control 36% (6). Yet a Financial Times interview survey of 74 Financial Directors out of the same 100 companies would indicate that these fund managers do not become involved in company affairs. They often do not put people on the Board and almost half of those interviewed felt that their main shareholders "rarely or never" offered useful comments about the business.

Opposite characteristics exist under the banking system. Here, either banks in the case of Germany or other companies in Japan (the keiretsu alliances) are fully involved long-term shareholders. In return for their commercial or financial support they will expect a greater say in managing the company. Evidence would suggest that this results in higher investment, as a result of the investors not expecting such a large rate of return. Hostile take-overs are also rare because the major shareholders work with management to improve the company (7).

The defenders of the capital market are stretching a point to claim that take-overs improve company performance. A 1999 OECD study of what sort of corporate management systems produce the best results first of all concluded that take-overs have no great effect (8):

"The vast majority of studies find no significant improvement in firm performance following a merger. In fact most suffer a negative impact....On the other hand, hostile take-overs do not exhibit the same deterioration in performance as mergers. While some studies show small, but significant, post hostile take-over returns, others find no significant efficiency gains." (9)

The report then added:

"Since efficiency gains of take-overs are at best quite low and target shareholders are receiving average premia of around 30-40%, take-overs seem to be primarily motivated by other objectives rather than the disciplining of management. Target shareholder gains come primarily at the expense of other stakeholders, labour in particular." (10)

To shed the delicate phrasing of international reports, they are saying that when a company is taken over and its shareholders make an instant profit of 30-40% on their shares, that has to be paid for. As it is not normally paid for by increased profits, it comes from reduced costs and it is the workers who take the brunt of that. Redundancies are the most common response. In recent bank mergers the promised level of redundancies seem to have been the proudest boast of the predator company. But the report found more insidious ways of making workers pay. For instance in 10% of take-overs, the pension funds were raided to pay for the profits of the shareholders.

The failure of the German / Japanese system is said to be that it takes the edge off competition, fostering too cosy relationships between large firms. It is true that both these capitalist economies, particularly Japan, have faced intense problems over the last decade. However their history still refutes the argument that free capital markets and the existence of corporate raiders improves the productivity of an economy. The fact that corporate management focussed on long term growth and not short-term shareholder gain, has given those countries an enormous productivity advantage over the UK.

The case for the ending the dictatorship of shareholder value is argued in a book that won the Financial Times prize for innovative management writing (Arie de Geus, Living Company, 1997). Written from a corporate perspective, it starts by showing that the most successful companies are often the oldest, companies that have never been taken over by other companies. The book then goes on to develop an argument with radical implications. Shareholder power, he says, is a remnant of days when capital was both scarce and critical to the success of a business (imagine the finance needed to build cotton mills, steamships and mines). This is no longer the case. The companies that are coming to the top today have very little asset value (e.g.Microsoft) and the assets provided by capital play an ever-decreasing role. "Giving capital close to total power seems to be in total contradiction to the times". Even using capitalist logic, the case for the shareholder is disintegrating.

The main thrust of 'Anti Capitalism' is that the first step of socialist economic change has to be the bringing of major corporations under social control. Three related conclusions flow from the above:

1) Evidence would suggest that external interference, through major shareholders and banks exercising monitoring and control, has a beneficial effect on increasing productivity. This of course is not social control, but it gives the lie to propositions that a company could not be externally guided.

2) At the corporate level 'private enterprise' has lost its meaning. In purely technical and not political terms, all you would need to do to socialise corporations is amend company law. It could be specified that boards of directors should be made up of say worker, consumer and state representatives in equal proportion. Management would be there in an advisory capacity.

3) As things stand however, even if this was politically feasible, the institutional investors would use their votes at annual general meeting to ensure that any director who did not pursue the maximising of share value was removed. But we have shown that there is increasing concentration of control in the hands of pension, insurance and saving institutions. Take those bodies into public ownership and the socialisation process would almost be complete.

This is not to argue that public ownership equals socialism, nor that public ownership is an easy political event to achieve. We will return to these fundamentals later. The point to be made here is that commentators would have us believe that socialism made sense decades ago but is now hopelessly irrelevant. The opposite is actually the case. When the capitalist world was populated by thousands of individual owner managers, the socialisation of the economy would have been difficult if not completely utopian. Conversely in today's corporate world the technical steps required to bring these giants under popular control are relatively simple. You would not have to take anything off anyone (though you might want to). It is a political, not a practical problem. But why do corporations need controlling anyway?

Corporate Power

One reason why political abstention continues to grow in Britain is that politicians / the state appear irrelevant. The resources of the government, particularly when it controlled great slabs of the economy through the nationalised industries, used to dwarf those of individual companies. Though governments were linked to and absorbed the wishes of the leaders of industry and finance, they were at least seen to have the final say on directing the economy. Talk of state planning was (almost) treated seriously. After years of endless mergers, acquisitions and privatisations concentrating ever more economic power in fewer hands, the balance of power has shifted decisively away from government. We live in a huge and sophisticated consumer economy that none of the major parties can affect because they choose to accept the rules of the free market.

Perhaps the symbolic end of the domination of state over company in Britain came in 1974. Ted Heath as Prime Minister, locked in struggle

Fact Box

The economic power of transnational corporations is enormous (13):

Fifty one of the largest one hundred economies in the world are corporations

The three hundred largest transnationals account for one quarter of the world's productive assets.

Transnational corporations hold 90% of the world's technology and product patents.

with the miners and the country working a 3-day week, called in the Chairman of British Petroleum to help him out. He asked that BP deliver more oil to the electricity generating stations to loosen the grip of the miners on power production. Knowing that Heath would not dare to issue anti- competitive emergency legislation when taking Britain into the Common Market, the Chairman simply informed him that it was not in BP's commercial interest and left the prime minister whimpering about lack of patriotism (11). Global arrogance is not confined to oil companies. In the words of the Chief Executive of NCR "National Cash Register is not a US corporation. It is a world corporation that happens to be headquartered in the US." (12)

It is not the purpose of this section to catalogue the wrong doings of transnationals. A great deal of literature now exists that does just that. Much of it can be traced through websites like www.corpwatch.org or through publishers such as Zed Books. The intention here is rather to register the financial power that these corporations wield and how they misuse it.

The number of corporations operating internationally has grown steadily over the years, but power is still concentrated in the largest (see box). In the recession at the beginning of the '90s there was speculation that the trend towards huge corporations was moving into reverse and that de-merging would become the fashion. It was not to be. As soon as the US economy started to move forward, the frenzy started again (see box). The last year of the US boom ('00) saw all records broken. More than $3,495bn. worth of deals were announced world wide (14). It is worth pausing to reflect on the sheer scale of the money being poured into shareholders pockets, rather than being put into productive investment.

Fact Box

There has been a large rise in the value of mergers and acquisitions

Billions spent annually

	'92	'98
US	$400	$1600
UK	£10	£30

Tony Jackson. Financial Times. 13/7/99

The new century dawned appropriately with a celebration of corporate power. On the 10th Jan 2000 the world's largest merger was announced between America On Line (AOL) and Time Warner that valued the new company at $327bn. There is nothing wrong with organisations combining to bring together the potential of cable media and the internet, but the transfer of wealth from consumers and workers to shareholders in these mergers is at a truly staggering level. Ted Turner, the Vice Chairman of Time Warner apparently promised his 9% stake in Time Warner to the deal "with as much or more excitement than on that night when I first made love 42 years ago" (15). Possibly no surprise since the value of his shares had gone up by $3.2 **billion** over the weekend. But then how exciting is that amount of money when you had $6.8bn to start with?

Similar less dramatic tales can be told for Britain. When BT merged with the American phone company MCI in 1996 they paid out £4.5bn. to the shareholders (16). The level of mergers and acquisitions in the UK in the second half of the '90s probably resulted in a premium to shareholders of around £10bn. a year. Some of the biggest individual shareholders are of course senior management, which goes some way to explain their enthusiasm for mergers and acquisitions. If all these figures have ceased to have meaning, it is worth reminding ourselves that £10bn. a year represents 300,000 home care workers plus 300,000 child care workers at decent rates of pay.

Over time these mergers and acquisitions have resulted in major industrial sectors of the world economy being carved up between just a few firms. In consumer durables the top five firms control almost 70% of the world market. In automotive, airline, aerospace, electronic components, electrical and electronics and steel, the top five control more than 50% and in oil, personal computers and media industries they control over 40% (17)

Globalisation

Corporate driven globalisation dominates our lives. Hardly a political speech passes without reference to it, but as with the internet, the realities of the process differ from the hype. The concept is politically highly charged. The leadership of the Labour Party are keen to use it as a justification for their free market policies, as globalisation appears like an external force, like gravity, rather than a product of human activity. Unless we pull in the boundaries of the welfare state, reduce production costs and make labour more flexible, our economic base will leak away to other parts of the globe. Entirely true if the political premise is global free trade and free movement of capital. This is what the 'race to the bottom' is all about. Countries line up in front of the global corporations to compete on who can offer the cheapest and most compliant labour, the largest market potential, local suppliers, the most developed state subsidised infrastructure and of course the best golf courses and private schools.

Globalisation is best understood as much as a political movement as a reorganisation of productive forces. Some myth puncturing before moving on. In terms of the movement of capital and the importance of trade, there is no more globalisation today than at the beginning of the century. In Britain the value of exports and imports as a percentage of gross domestic product has barely shifted from 45% (the same is true of Germany and France. Japan's percentage has actually declined). The flow of capital abroad and investment in other countries was also at as high a level as it is now.(18).

What has changed is that **production** has been globalised. At the turn of the century you may have had great trading companies and capitalists investing in Argentinian railways, but you did not have branches of John Brights yarn spinners dotted around the globe. Now some seventy thousand companies have overseas branches. Even here though, it is important to keep a clear understanding of the process. The image is often produced of the global assembly line. Car seats produced in one country, axles in another and the final assembly undertaken in a third. After all, one third of world trade is intra firm i.e. between one branch of a multinational to another. However the US Commerce Department calculates that all but 10% of America's intra firm trade consists of transfers of finished or near finished products from US makers to their foreign sales affiliates or vice versa (19). They may be multinational but even the world's largest companies still have the majority of their assets in their home country (20).

If you are searching for the truth, seek out an insider that thinks they are writing a secret memo. In the same 1991 memo in which he argued that 'Africa was vastly under-polluted', World Bank Chief Economist Lawrence Summers had something more profound to say about the global revolution that is worth quoting at length:

"What's new? Throughout the outline (he was commenting on a draft report – CH) I struggle with the evidence showing what exactly the proclaimed revolution in production has revolutionised. Foreign direct investment i.e. multinational business has always existed and many of the world's largest firms have been transnational from birth. The globalisation of production has happened sure, but has the telecommunication revolution really had a major impact? I would guess the invention of relatively simple things, like steamship transport, did more for world trade than digitised data transmission. How exactly has the nature of manufacturing been 'fundamentally altered'? Aren't people just incrementally better at doing things that they have always done, like locate production in the lowest cost location for delivery to markets (now 'globalisation of production'), like manage inventories in a least cost way (now 'just in time inventory management'), like choose the appropriate level of vertical integration depending on the production process (now 'critical buyer-seller links'), like match production to demand (now 'short product cycles'). Is a revolution really the appropriate metaphor for these changes?"

Over the last ten years the technology has moved on and the jargon changed, but the insight remains valid. The pace of globalisation has increased, but it is not a new phenomenon. It is part of a process identified by Marx 150 years ago in his work on the centralisation of capital. Business will forever seek to expand, to eliminate competition and increase its profit base. We are encouraged to believe that the transnational company is organisationally necessary but this is rarely the case.

The exceptions are those that require a massive research or investment base in industries such as car and aircraft manufacture, pharmaceuticals etc. For instance between 1992 and 1999 Chrysler invested $6bn. in car manufacturing facilities in the Detroit area alone (21). The new drugs company formed by the merger of Glaxo Wellcome and SmithKline Beecham will have a research budget of $4bn. a year (22). If research and investment is to be funded from profits then the size of the business needed to generate them is larger than could be supported by any single country, even the USA. This is no shock to socialists who have always argued for the international co-ordination of production, and recognise in certain circumstances the advantages of concentration. The bulk of globalisation however is completely 'unnecessary'.

The recent history of Coca Cola is typical. To maintain its 50% control of the world's soft drinks market, the company invaded the former communist block in military fashion. Marketing and distribution were everything. Independent bottling plants were contracted by Atlanta to achieve immediate delivery capability over the whole area ($500m. spent on infrastructure over three years). Salesmen then marched in to achieve vending machine coverage and exclusive sales deals, armed with a dispenser budget of $100m. a year (23).

So what? There is surely nothing wrong with taking Coca-Cola to people who want to drink it. The market is always right ('Always Coca-Cola'). People don't **have** to buy it.

117

This is true only if the measurement of social well being is the amount of product you sell. By using their financial muscle Coca Cola eliminated much of the competition and the choice that goes with it (what a pity that their distribution system does not carry other people's drinks as well as their own). It has also converted a large proportion of the world's children to a drink that dissolves teeth. The history of Coca-Cola also demonstrates that, for some transnationals, the end of achieving total global coverage for their goods and services is coming close (24).

In terms of money coming in and money going out, Britain gains little from globalisation. Major investors have been the United States and prior to their recession, Japan. The investment came chiefly to take advantage of low cost labour to attack the markets of Europe, but despite the Nissans and Toyotas, the outflow of investment funds to other countries has always been greater than its inflow by at least $10bn. a year. Furthermore, the image of inward investment being associated with new car plants and the like, is misleading. The majority of inward investment is into the financial and business services sector and a third of it does nothing useful at all. It is just money used to buy existing firms (25). Foreign management techniques have undoubtedly had

Fact Box

UK companies consistently invest more money overseas, than overseas companies invest in the UK.

	£bn	
	'99	'00
Foreign direct investment in UK	52	86
UK direct investment abroad	128	165

NSO www.statistics.gov.uk/pdfdir/bop0301.pdf

an effect on improving productivity in manufacturing but such things are hard to measure.

Globalisation is pushed forward by companies wanting to profit by covering the global market. They can do this best when there are no capital controls or tariff barriers to restrict their activity – hence repeated attempts through the World Trade Organisation and the ill fated Multilateral Agreement on Investment, to give corporations a free hand.

There is little inevitable or necessary about this process. Some countries gain by the foreign investment, particularly China, but how those gains are distributed in the receiving countries is another matter. Overall the effect of foreign direct investment is to increase the gap between winners and losers both between and within countries.

What often drops out of any analysis is an historical perspective. Not only were the strongest economies built under regimes of capital controls and high tariff barriers to protect domestic industry, but growth rates were also much more vigorous during the long boom when these restrictions to free trade were still in place. In addition there is no relationship between foreign ownership and investment, and economic success. Taiwan and South Korea have less than 10% of their industrial production in foreign hands, while less successful economies of Brazil and Colombia have over 40%. (26)

Corporate Failure

It is possible that many corporate directors are urbane characters who think they act in a socially responsible fashion - not all are trying to poison the world with Coca-Cola! Intentions are irrelevant though, they have to act in a fashion that increases profits and shareholder value. The directors approve strategies that may make sense for the company, but not for the society in which it exists.

This logic has led to appalling corporate acts in developing countries involving environmental damage, health and safety and the general treatment of workers (27), but in a less stark form the system is failing in the advanced capitalist countries as well. Let us start the analysis in traditional economic territory – profits and investment.

Most people go to work thinking that what they do pays for their wage, with a modest contribution to profits on top. They might be shocked by how immodest the contribution is. In 1996 the average profits per employee for the 50 largest Yorkshire firms was £20,715 a year – higher than the average wage (28). Profits make up 15% of gross domestic product in Britain – high by international standards - and they shot up during the 1990s. From '91 to '98 they increased by almost 8% a year (unlike wages), before slipping back as manufacturing industry was battered by the high pound. As a result the UK has ceded its position as the most profitable company in the world to Finland (29).

So making profits does not seem to be a problem in the UK. Nothing wrong with that if they can be achieved with decent working conditions; it is what you do with them that is significant. It is here that corporate capitalism, particularly its British variant, stands condemned.

Traditionally growth was seen as dependent on investment. Companies grew by investing in plant and machinery. They then took on extra workers who bought additional goods and also saved more money. Companies would then borrow those savings from the banks, reinvest in more plant and machinery and produce still more goods. It is the virtuous circle that was at the bottom of the Asian Tiger miracle of the '70s and '80s. While British companies invested about 10% of GDP, Singapore and Hong Kong were reinvesting closer to 30% of GDP back into the economy (30). Underinvestment over decades was far more damaging to the British economy than strikes ever were. In our finance dominated economy, with shareholders wanting instant returns, rates of return demanded on any investment are about 5% higher than in most other countries, with the logical consequence that a greater number of investment projects are deemed not to be profitable enough (31).

A government report in '98 (32) started with the minister's comment that it "revealed a worrying picture of underinvestment". The report went on to show that "British investment worked out at £9,000 per worker per year which is about two thirds of the international average."

The large gap between Britain and the likes of Germany is unlikely to be closed. Continually greater investment makes their workers more productive and so living standards higher, but the

Fact Box

The UK has historically under invested and is failing to catch up

Top 500 investing UK companies compared to the top 300 internationally. Figures for '99.

Accumulated capital stock per worker

UK	£109,000
International	£188,000

Annual investment per worker has been similar to the international companies over the last four years.

Capex Annual Scoreboard (DTI). Dec. '00

solution does not lie in trying to become more like Germany. An important point of economic theory arises here. After being low and flat for many years (33) in '97 and '98 British investment moved up sharply, rising 20% in two years. The investment occurred not in manufacturing industry but in the service sector and to some extent construction. "The service sector investment largely reflected spending on IT systems (note Year 2000 problems), including mobile phone and digital TV networks, call centres and the internet." (34). The investment rate has since moved down abruptly despite the favourable economic climate and has the look of a one off surge. In a more sustained way, the same was true of the US. It was the computer and telecommunication sectors that drove the boom. But if the service sector now dominates the economy, will its investment needs ever be as large as those of manufacturing industries? If not, where are all those profits going to go?

At a common sense level it seems unlikely that the businesses of the 'knowledge economy' will ever generate the investment demands of factories filled with machinery. There is a limit to how much office accommodation needs to be built and once in the building, all a company requires is a full suite of communication systems. An office of 30 people can be computer networked for the price of an insignificant piece of machinery in the engineering industry.

Fact Box

....as a result the productivity gap between Britain and the world is not closing

GDP per worker (UK=100)

	'96	'99
US	139	145
France	121	118
Germany	110	111
UK	100	100

Thomson Financial Datastream. OECD. Nov. '00

If this is part of the reason for the international decline in investment rates in the service dominated economies there are severe problems ahead. When a system based on profit maximisation reduces its investment rate, those profits have to find a home. In the 1990s they were clearly ending up in the stock market, causing an unsustainable rise in share prices.

Take some examples from the 1999 last quarter profit returns of some of the biggest corporate hitters in America. 44% of Chase Manhatten Bank's profits came from their dealings on the stock market. Only 8% of their profits came from traditional lending activities. More disturbingly 30% of Microsoft's increased earnings came from share deals - they have a $20bn equity portfolio. That other IT giant Intel also have a $6bn stock market war chest churning out profits(35).

Similar behaviour, revealing an excess of profits over what they deem to be profitable investment opportunities, is the habit of corporations buying back their own shares. For want of anything better to do with their profits, British companies bought back from shareholders £25bn worth of shares between 1994 and 1999 (36). As well as giving shareholders a premium this is an extremely easy way of boosting earnings per share. Other un-productive homes for profits have already been noted in the dramatic rise in dividend payments (37) and activity in the mergers and acquisition market (38).

Since the 1970s large corporations, the drivers of the system, have failed to invest rising profits back into the UK economy, or any other economy for that matter. Much of the money has gone in buying overseas companies. If it is true that we face a low investment future because of the changing structure of the economy, capitalism will be heading for a fall – it needs to accumulate to survive. A high profit / low investment capitalism is unsustainable. The overvaluation of stock markets will be dealt with in the next section, but if anyone wonders what the problem is, if profits are invested in shares, bare in mind that a share value is fiction until it is sold and banked. Unlike productive investment it cannot be used for anything, it is merely electronic digits on a computer, another form of gambling. Profits, the unpaid wages of corporate workers, can disappear overnight if they are put into shares.

The above description of corporate failure is very conservative, written in the tradition of mainstream economics. The problem is not just a matter of the unproductive use of profits and low investment. Corporations are the engine of capitalism; inequality and social dislocation are caused by their delivery of the free market system. We will deploy a more fundamental analysis in the Green Economics section, but for the moment consider two ways in which the corporate world moulds our needs.

Need is always drawn narrowly under capitalism. It is giving the consumer an acceptable quality of product or service at the minimum price. If it sells, it is needed. This logic leads to the argument that if traffic congestion is holding up lorries, increasing distribution costs and ultimately prices in the shops, wider roads will have to be built. This definition of need ignores that we may not want urban motorways carving up our cities.

Perhaps that is too easy an example. Let us take supermarkets. The industry is now extraordinarily concentrated. The top five chains take £50bn. a year and account for three quarters of our grocery spend. Tesco and Sainsbury alone account for almost half of grocery sales (and the top ten retail chains account for two fifths of **all** retail sales in Britain) (39). As in all other sectors, the corporate mission and our needs are defined as the efficient delivery of good quality, low cost products that will sell with the biggest profit margins (they don't mention the last bit). A moment's thought and it is obvious our needs are much broader. What about nutrition value, the promotion of organic food, the nature of supermarket contracts with the farming industry, the minimisation of waste packaging, supporting local suppliers, stopping the development of out-of-town green field sites, fair trade purchases from developing countries, genetically modified foods, keeping local stores and so on?

From a different angle, consider the moulding influence Amazon is starting to have. Already with thirty two million customers, they have started to offer much more than books and music over the internet. Health products, baby goods, garden equipment, kitchenware, PCs - you name it, it's all there. The economic power just keeps on growing.

This is not to suggest the solutions are straightforward, merely that to have no social control over organisations that have such an influence on the way we live is... is what? You would have to say primitive.

It is not only that need is defined too narrowly in the free market, it is also falsely generated.

Marketing

Many corporations were built on selling consumer goods, but over the last few years, at least in the advanced capitalist countries, profits have been harder to make by traditional means. The mass market has become relatively mature and spending is moving towards services rather than consumer goods. Coming up with the new big idea has become harder and new products are quickly copied (40).

The corporate response has been to add value (i.e. make more profits), by concentrating on brand promotion. Rather than competing on quality and price, the company develops a brand loyalty that tolerates higher prices. Pitch and product is replaced by relationship building. This does not just involve a shift of marketing budgets from advertising (information) to promotion (attitude and spiritual identification), but a fundamental re-structuring of corporations, ably mapped in Naomi Klein's best-seller, No Logo.

Companies increasingly abandon production and instead buy in and brand products. The brand itself transcends the company and becomes free standing. Rather than relating to a product it becomes a reputation. So it is that Caterpillar, traditionally known for its earth moving equipment, has a reputation for toughness (literally and emotionally), that can easily be trans-ferred to clothing. Benetton becomes equated with anti racism, Pepsi owns the spirit of youth rebellion and Reebok owns non-conformity. Take this quote from the chair of Polaroid's advertising agency, John Hagarty, to illustrate just how twisted marketing perceptions have become:

"Polaroid's problem was the way they (the company) kept thinking of themselves as a camera. But the vision process taught us something. Polaroid is not a camera – it's a social lubricant" (41).

IBM do not sell computers anymore but 'solutions'. The products of-fered by these companies are increasingly hybrids of goods, services and entertainment and entreat the consumer to be loyal to what the company stands for. No effort is spared to attach human needs for freedom and friendship to the brand image. Companies no longer sponsor culture, they **are** culture, as chosen lifestyles fuse with labels and the companies behind them.

126

Their efforts appear to be bearing fruit. In '96, DMB&Bs, a New York advertising agency, surveyed 27,600 middle class 14 to 18 year olds in forty five countries. They concluded:

"Despite different cultures, middle class youth all over the world seem to live their lives as if in a parallel universe. They get up in the morning, put on their Nikes or Levis, grab their caps, backpacks and Sony personal CD player and head for school. Eighty five per cent of them listened to MTV." (42). They also concluded that the marketing task was to reinforce this global (corporate) consciousness.

From these mental trends fall very material changes. For one, the inexorable rise in marketing budgets will continue with only a pause for breath in recessions. It is difficult to be accurate but global spending on marketing is likely to be well over half that spent on public education (43). Coupled with this is the drawing of ever more labour into the socially useless activity of fashion innovation. What sells a product is increasingly whether it is different, rather than better, than other products.

Secondly corporations are emptying out. Their value may keep on rising but

---

Fact Box

The endless growth in advertising (45).

Worldwide spending (current prices)

	$bn.	
'87	'93	'99
150	200	300

This only measures radio, TV, newspapers and billboards. Add in marketing, public relations and promotions and it would be more than doubled.

The worldwide drug industry now spends more on branding and marketing than on research and development.

the numbers of workers they employ does not. As brand managers the corporations are not interested in direct ownership of production facilities but instead often choose to contract out work, so absolving themselves of the need to maintain minimum conditions for their staff. Levi's for instance chose the same moment that it sacked 16,000 (over half) its workforce, to announce a new $90m. advertising campaign (44).

A final reflection on personal need. Almost one in five of us now work in the

> ## Fact Box
>
> **Transnationals grow in value but not in the numbers they employ.**
>
> Between '91 and '98 the assets of the world's 500 largest companies increased by 288% but their employment only grew by 9%.
>
> 'The Global 500'. Fortune magazine. July '91 and Aug '98.

Financial and Business Services sector. That is the category of employment that takes in banking, insurance, lawyers, accountants, advertisers, market researchers, security firms and so on. No doubt in any sanely organised society there would be a place for these functions. However, their prodigious growth over the last 20 years (45) is a reflection of both social breakdown (the need for more security guards and increasing recourse to litigation) and purchasing power being in corporate rather than individual or public hands.

No one ever asked for enormous marketing budgets. They are not the result of consumer demand. In fact the growing proportion of the economy devoted to such activity must be one of the most wasteful features of twenty-first-century capitalism. It is also difficult to see how the trend can be reversed as long as profit maximisation rather than social need remains the economic driving force.

In this section we have reviewed the economic power held by corporations and the misuse of that power. We will now go on to discuss the antics of the warriors of the New World Order, the cadres of the Financial Services sector. They have been the lions of the world economy in recent years, we will see if they turn out to be the lemmings.

BIG MONEY

We went into Latin America not knowing anything about the place. Now we are leaving without knowing anything about it.

New York financier talking about the Mexican peso crisis of '95. (1)

When the capital development of a country becomes the by-product of a casino, the job is likely to be ill done.

John Maynard Keynes, economist (2)

I admit to having a lurid fascination with big money. It is the key to so much and yet is so little discussed. While politicians and the media argue about a few million pounds public spending at the front door of capitalism, enough money to solve the problem several times over slips out the back. The demonstration that greeted the World Trade Organisations deliberations in Seattle in 1999 was one of the first times that the

Fact Box

Money moves abroad

Foreign direct investment as a percentage of GDP across all OECD (advanced capitalist) countries.

'75	5
'85	5
'95	12
'97	19

Stephen Thompson. Investment patterns in long term perspective. OECD. April 2000. www.oecd.org//daf/investment/working-papers

effects of international trade and finance on people's lives became the subject of daily news bulletins in the west. As a response to the global casino it was the beginning of a trend. In this section we will examine what is happening in the world of finance and what the outcomes are likely to be. As finance is a truly global system our attention will be focussed as much on its world centre, the USA, as on Britain.

The Tidal Wave of Money

The pivotal contradiction of capitalism in its current phase, is that the growing mass of savings and profits are not being sufficiently reinvested in the real economy. Globalisation has untethered these profits and savings from their national boundaries and a tidal wave of money surges around the globe in search of maximum returns. If the money were going into buildings and equipment, a case could be made for the benefit of these flows, but they are not. Fully sixty per cent of the growing foreign direct investment is estimated to go into buying existing companies, mainly in the advanced capitalist countries (OECD Report. See box).

Consider an alternative. If institutions that control all the money just bought existing property and housing with it, there would be a tremendous rise in rents and house prices (to some degree the picture in Britain at the end of the '80s). That would be seen as a bad thing. As it turned out, corporations instead bought up companies while financial managers invested in the stock markets of the world, taking them up to price levels completely out of correspondence with reality (3). This was seen as a good thing.

The fact is the two processes are similar. Most money that heads for the stock market does not go into new companies to help them invest, it goes into buying existing shares off other shareholders (4). Just as house prices rise if an increased amount of money starts to chase a static number of houses, so shares prices rise if institutions have more money to spend and the number of shares available does not increase. This is asset price inflation rather than the consumer price inflation we are familiar with through the Retail Price Index, and it is just as dangerous. Once it can be shown that the future flow of profits to shareholders cannot justify the high price, investors lose confidence and prices collapse. It was such a collapse that brought on the ten year stagnation in Japan. At the time of writing the exact result of the US share collapse is unclear. The seventy per cent fall in the Nasdaq share index, home to most of the US computer and telecommunication stock, in the year following March '00, was both the cause and result of the boom cycle coming to an end. At the very least it is going to cause a global economic slowdown.

Fact Box

The value of UK pension fund assets has risen (6)

	£bn.
'81	66
'97	549
'00	760

Where does all the extra money come from that causes the speculative spiral? The rise of profits and increasing involvement of companies in share dealing have already been discussed, but the most significant trend is the growing assets of pension, life assurance and mutual funds, particularly in America and Britain (5). In these two countries a combination of a growing number of people being members of occupational pension schemes, ageing populations, growing inequality and the need to avoid the poverty of a state pension, has led to an inexorable rise in the value of the funds. By 1997 managed global investment funds had reached $20trillion (twenty thousand thousand million) and a quarter of this amount was controlled by just 12 fund managers(7).

Pension fund management used to be a fairly sleepy business. Most of the money would be put into UK government's bonds, and such things as property (8). As long as returns seemed to be better than sticking the money in a building society, no one was too upset. Like so much in the finance world, all has changed in the last twenty years.

Many pension funds (about £300bn worth) are put in the hands of fund managers who invest them to obtain the highest returns. The big five managers, companies like Mercury Asset Management, Schroders and Morgan Grenfell, look after two thirds of this amount (9). Most of the money is invested in shares and in the case of the UK over one third is invested in foreign shares, though the pressure is now on to raise this to half (10). In 1999 pension funds recorded a bumper 20.6% return on their investments, the second highest return ever (11). The average rate of return over the five years to '99 was 16.2%. Surely this is nothing to complain about? The value of our pensions was swelling magnificently.

Some pensions are linked to salaries and years of service (defined benefit). Other schemes do not tie the pension to salary at all. They just give you the value of what is in your pension pot when you retire (defined contribution). The pension they lead you to expect is based on a return of about 10% a year. But what happens when what has gone up starts to come down? Buying and selling shares on a rising stock market produces great returns. A negative mirror image appears with a falling market. The retirement pot that you thought might deliver a pension of £100 a week suddenly looks worth much less. To maintain a standard of living in retirement under these circumstances you have to start saving more while you are working. A sharp and sustained drop in share prices inevitably leads to a fall in consumption as well as a drop in living standards. Asset deflation becomes economic depression.

Britain has already experienced the process on a small scale. Everyone with an endowment mortgage received a letter from their insuranc company at the end of 1999. The letter often said that if you expected your mortgage to be paid off with the insurance policy then monthly contributions would have to be increased. The reason for the shortfall was that the insurance companies had sold policies by convincing clients returns would be higher than they turned out to be.

This is not an argument to put our savings under a mattress. It is an indictment of a system that directs our savings into a world of fictitious capital and speculation with so little effect on the real economy. The argument that it is logical to seek the maximum return on our savings from wherever it comes has to be nailed. Which is preferable, to earn the wages of a German worker and earn a secure 7% on your savings or the wages of a British worker and earn a speculative 12% that could be wiped out? Who is better off in retirement? While British savings search the world for the highest returns the home economy suffers from underinvestment and deteriorating infrastructure.

Up to the recent past Germany 'suffered' from undeveloped capital markets. Typically businesses expanded using bank loans while savings went into government bonds. Dealings in stocks and shares have never been a significant part of the economy. However, in the chase for maximum returns German capitalism is adopting more of the features of its American counterpart.

If a greater proportion of investment funds, and not just pension funds, were put in to productive investment, starting new businesses, improving transport and so on, living standards could be raised while still guaranteeing a decent income in retirement.

In a diluted form the problem has been recognised even by Tony Blair:

"Tony Blair yesterday called on pension funds to shift more money into venture capital to back new high growth companies. The Prime Minister said British pension funds invested only 1% of their assets in venture capital compared with nearer 5% in the U.S. and demanded an immediate response from the industry"(12)

What are the consequences of our savings entering the stock markets of the world rather than being usefully employed?

The Stock Market

The world's financial markets have become little more than casinos. Their alleged purpose of raising and arranging finance for industry and trade now accounts for a tiny proportion of their activity. The Nick Leeson affair in 1995 may have been exceptional in its scale, but it opened the world's eyes to just how wild international finance had become. In little more than four weeks the 28-year-old dealer based in the Singapore office of Barings Bank bet $29bn. of the firms money on derivatives tied to Japanese Nikkei stock futures and interest rates. The futures fell instead of rising and he lost $1.3bn. Barings were unable to cover the loss and one of the country's oldest banks went bust (13).

Apologists would have us believe that Leeson was a badly managed rogue dealer who represented no general trend. The truth is the volatility and scale of movement in the equity, foreign exchange and derivative markets represents a real threat to the stability of the world economy.

Let us first deal with the stock market. Everyone has heard of the 1929 Wall Street stock market crash and the depression that started shortly after. In the five years before that crash the value of shares trebled. This time around the value of shares rose fourteen times between 1982 and 2000 and two and a half times from 1995 to 2000. Discounting for inflation the US S&P stock market index rose 570% between 1981 and 2000, while the real earnings of the companies measured in the index only rose by 61% (14).

The 'tide of money' effect discussed above has been clear. In the early 1980s only about 10 million Americans held shares with financial investment institutions (called mutuals in America). The figure is now 45 million. In addition there are about 35m. Americans who own shares directly. As a result the percentage of household wealth held in shares has risen (15). The climbing stock market fuelled the consumer boom in America and the level of saving dropped as shareholders basked in the knowledge that the value of their holdings had risen by roughly $5,000bn. since 1995.

The picture is a little more complex than it first looks. Many of the shares of traditional industrial companies stayed fairly flat, but those of technology stocks went through the roof. The rises of these shares can just look crazy to the outside observer. The twenty best performing technology companies saw their share price rise by between 933% and 2,700% in one year! This of course includes the 'dot.com' companies that were yet to make any profits (17). A speculative bubble was blown up every bit as delicate as the ones preceding it.

Fact Box

Money piled into technology stocks

Value of US technology sector shares and their percentage of total stock market value (16)

'92	'00
$300bn	$4,500bn
(10%)	(33%)

It is worth pausing to look back on the dot.com explosion. Thousands of millions of dollars have been flushed away in failed companies, yet we have always been told that the free market is the best distributor of capital, that it is the investor rather than the business organisation that knows best where to put money. The short history of Boo.com demonstrated how ludicrous speculative capitalism can become. If it were not so expensive it would be humorous.

By the time the company had to shut its doors in June 2000 it had consumed £91 million of investors' money in fifteen months. The original aim of the company was ambitious – to sell trendy sports gear over the internet in eighteen countries simultaneously. The first thing that the senior executives did was to pay themselves £100,000 a year with all the trimmings of limos and first class travel. The place was brimming with PR and Creative directors, but technology and finance officers seemed harder to find (at its peak Boo employed 450). Investors set no performance targets and costs were completely out of control - £500,000 a month was spent just taking 3-D photos of its products to put on the site. Sales were never going to catch up with such a cash guzzling organisation and the investors eventually pulled the plug. It is an example of capitalist waste that would rival any horror story from the Stalinist planned economies.

The stock market boom in Britain was almost as dramatic as in the US. Taking out the effects of inflation, share values have grown by about 3% a year evened out over the century. From 1980 to 2000, the average growth was 13% a year. Increasingly buying shares was seen as a one way bet, the chance to cash in on free money. From a standing start four years ago, the number of investment clubs in the UK, made up of people coming together to enjoy gambling on the stock market, swelled to 6,000.

For those that wanted to hold on to their money, a sense of history was required. What has occurred over the recent past if you invested money for a twenty-year period? From 1950 to 1970 you would have made, after inflation, gains of 3.5% a year. Invested for twenty years from 1960 you would have **lost** 3.9% a year. From 1970 to 1990 the increase in value would have been just 1% a year (18). Advocates of the 'new economy' analysis claimed that such history was irrelevant. We had entered an era in which new technology dramatically lifted productivity and future profits, so justifying soaring share prices.

The theory is rather thin and in any case can only be applied to the USA where there was a large shift in capital investment towards high tech industries. It is easy to accept that information technology has improved productivity, though much of the productivity growth was due to people working harder in strong demand conditions. In the downturn, the voice of the new economist has become more muted.

Another justification of high share prices was the increased value of knowledge. Changes in the way companies are valued have taken place. Knowledge and management skills are now rated more important than assets (property and equipment) (19) but there is little evidence of how the value of knowledge translates to a rapid increase in profits across the economy. Is the historic rate of profit growth really going to rise from mid single figures to 15% a year or more? (20) Even the long time free market guru Samuel Brittan had to point out that to justify global stock market prices at the peak, profits would have to rise to 19% of global GDP. They were then 9% of GDP in America (21).

The Wall Street bubble has burst. Just how far the deflation will go depends on the complex interplay between economics, politics and psychology. By historic standards the market was overvalued by 50% at its highest. As of July '01, that would indicate the mainstream Wall St. Dow Jones Index has some falling yet to do; but all may change by the time this book is published.

So what are the results of a stock market fall? Capitalism is an unplanned chaotic system that relies heavily on the psychology of confidence, so predicting outcomes is tricky. However lessons have been learnt from the 1930s. The 1929 stock market crash did not directly cause the depression of the next decade. Production actually started to pick up in 1930, lending resumed and the stock market levelled off. The secondary crisis that caused political retreat and economic collapse was the failure of the Austrian Kreditanstalt bank at the beginning of 1931, with no bank or government willing to take on its loans. Lending was pulled in sharply internationally and in a desperate attempt to guard their own economies, governments put up import controls and devalued their currencies. With everyone doing it the result was naturally a fall in world trade, collapse in confidence and the world recession. Tariffs and quotas were a response to and not the cause of the problem. The initial cause of the crisis was already there in the form of low demand (22).

In order to avoid this, the American government's response to the stock market crash of 1987 and the dip in 1998 was to do everything to keep demand up and credit lines open. There is only so much they can do though. The stock market bubble is much bigger than it was in 1987. True, confidence kept up in 1998, but a drop in the Dow Jones stock market index of over 20% in little more than a month showed how jittery markets were becoming (23). For those who wanted to see, the figures given above showed that the level of share prices was untenable. What is never known during speculative excesses, is what particular shock will bring investors to their senses. It could have been a drop in the dollar or a rise in inflation. As it turned out, it was a combination of the dot.com emperor appearing completely naked and some disturbing profit warnings from the telecommunications industry.

Once the stock market fall looks permanent, as we have already noted in the section on the business cycle, demand in the economy will drop. People moving towards retirement save more to compensate for their devalued stocks, industrial investment falls and the financial services sector shrinks (24). Recent experience in Japan has shown that once demand has fallen away and confidence been lost, it is very difficult to rekindle, however many times you lower interest rates.

USA listed companies account for half the value of the world's stock exchanges, up from one third in 1990(25). The stock market fall will almost certainly reverberate around the world as fund managers move into the safe havens of cash and bonds, and countries like Britain will experience similar recessionary drag.

Credit, Foreign Exchange and Derivative Markets

If instability is the most recognisable feature of world stock markets, it is even more so for the foreign exchange markets. There was a time when stock markets existed to raise money for trade and production and foreign exchange markets existed to obtain the currency to pay for trade. The principle purpose of both is now to provide on-line gambling facilities.

In 1986 $188bn. was traded every day in the main currency markets of New York, London and Tokyo, that was 7.4 times the amount of goods and services that moved between countries. By 1995 the figure had reached $1.2 trillion, 19 times the value of goods traded and eighty four times the world's non-gold reserves(26).

What we need to understand from these figures is that corporations and financial institutions are trading in currencies to make a profit out of dealing, not because they need the foreign exchange. The state of affairs moved analysts McDonald and Company in America to describe the big three auto companies as "basically banks masquerading as manufacturing companies"(27). Furthermore, the scale of their activity is such that it renders ineffective the efforts of any government to protect its currency and economy. National reserves, even America's, are dwarfed by the huge movement of money.

There has been a relentless push for financial deregulation for twenty years to allow money to go where it produces the highest and quickest profit. Currency speculation and investment in foreign shares are all of a piece. They are a bet on the short-term success or failure of the host. The economist Greider characterises the position thus:

"The case of Mexico (the currency devaluation of 1995 – CH) illustrates in the most horrendous terms, that developing nations make a kind of deal with the devil when they open themselves to the animal spirit of global capital. As liquidity sloshes about in the global financial system, seeking the highest returns, a nation may find itself inundated with 'hot money' from abroad that can ignite a giddy boom, or starved of credit when the foreign money decides, for whatever reason, to leave." (28)

The activities of the speculators follow a depressingly familiar pattern. Money pours in to a country that shows growth potential. This raises consumer demand and encourages borrowing, much of it foreign. Prices, especially property prices, start to rise and the economy looks like over-heating. The government makes some attempt to cool it down, the speculators lose confidence in their ability to gain quick profits, take their money out and in the process try and make profits out of gambling on a falling currency. The companies and banks that took out the foreign loans then find them difficult to repay and the value of their property assets drop in the ensuing recession. They go broke and workers are put on the dole.

Earlier we tracked this process for Indonesia but similar cases abound. In Mexico $90bn. of foreign capital flowed in between '90 and '93. The rise in consumption caused a large balance of payments deficit, so President Zedillo devalued the currency by 13%. This was not enough for the speculators who took the peso down to 50% of its value. The ensuing economic downturn meant a 30% drop in wages and a doubling of unemployment.

South Korea had borrowed heavily abroad in the mid '90s and when in January '97 Hanbo Steel collapsed with massive debts the speculators attacked the won, again reducing it by 50% of its value and making the situation for all the companies with foreign debts twice as bad. For the following months an average of 4,000 workers a day were made redundant and 90% of construction firms went broke. (29)

An interesting thing happens after speculators have caused havoc in these countries. It has come to be known as 'socialism for bankers'. Governments are expected to prevent their banks going bust at the ultimate cost to the tax payer, but the financial rescue packages that are organised by the likes of the IMF do not go near the beleaguered country in question.

Instead they guarantee that the American banks that gave out the high-risk loans in the first place, receive their money back!

To add insult to injury, these same banks advise on rescue packages, earn fees from implementing compulsory privatisations that are part of that package, and pick up assets in the target countries at knock down prices. So it was that America's Federal Reserve Bank consulted with the big six Wall St. commercial banks (including Chase, Bank America, Citicorp and J.P.Morgan) and the big four merchant banks (Goldman Sachs, Lehman Bros., Morgan Stanley and Salomon Smith Barney) about what should be included in the S. Korean rescue package. The meeting took place on Christmas Eve '97. Not many months later several of these banks were in Indonesia entrusted with the privatisation of key sectors of the economy. The world's largest money managers set countries on fire and then are called in to put out the blaze. They ultimately decide which enterprises are to be closed down and which are to be auctioned off to foreign investors.(30)

We cannot leave the crazed and destructive world of high finance without a mention of derivatives. There is no need to fully understand them. Their very existence is dependent on them being complicated. They came into being as relatively straightforward insurance policies, which is why many of them are called hedge funds. They were intended to guard against a falling currency and the like but, unlike the futures market, the deal is not linked to the currency itself but to something linked to it (derivative).

The derivatives market has grown by about 40% a year since the mid '80s and is now valued at twice total world output. In other words, a lot of money (31). Interestingly the market was dominated by 'standard' deals prior to the '90s. These were regulated and transparent. You knew

142

what the package was, who the dealers were and what sort of profits they were taking. From a standing start, 'over the counter' deals now account for almost half of derivatives. These are unregulated specially packaged deals for the client, often used as a way of respectable financial institutions circumventing their own rules in order to obtain a higher income.

Frank Portnoy was a derivatives dealer in Morgan Stanley's New York office in the mid '90s. He was one of seventy Morgan Stanley dealers spread across New York, London and Tokyo. In the two years to 1995 these dealers brought in approximately $15m. dollars each in fees. Enough income to pay for the entire 10,000 staff. The book he wrote about his experiences gives an insight to the bizarre and ruthless world of high finance (32) .

His job was to put together appealing, over the counter derivative deals and go out and find buyers for them. His target clients were often companies banned from dealing in foreign currencies, such as pension funds. Instead he would sell them bonds whose price was related to the level of a currency. One such bond paid the principal back (the amount the company invested) multiplied by the change in the value of the dollar plus twice the change in the British pound, minus twice the change in the Swiss franc! All tremendous confusing fun until we remember that this game is being played with stakes equivalent to $10,000 for every working American (the value of the derivatives market). At least with normal bonds you can expect some interest payment but with derivatives, if the movements in the currencies have been in the wrong direction, you lose your initial stake as well as the return. (33)

The gamblers sometimes have their fingers badly burned. On April 4th '94 the manufacturing giant Proctor and Gamble lost $108m. on two interest rate swop deals. Their accounts for that year revealed that they had $2.41bn. tied up in derivative contracts that did not appear on the balance sheet. (34)

Derivative and exchange dealings add another layer of instability to the financial world. To them could be added the effects of the estimated £400bn. a year laundered money from drugs, arms and illegal immigration (35). Much of this washes up in the tax havens of the world like little Jersey that has £230bn. in its electronic coffers.

The growing instability of financial markets can be distinguished in the changing role of the International Monetary Fund (IMF). In the boom years through to 1974, in the era of fixed exchange rates, the IMF used to lend to central banks who were trying to avoid devaluation in the face of balance of payments crises and a run on the currency. British Chancellor Denis Healey famously turned back from Heathrow airport to negotiate such a deal and save the pound in 1976 (compared to the upheavals of today such a crisis looks fairly small beer). With the debt crisis of less developed countries in the '80s however, the IMF moved to lending to countries to keep them solvent. In the closing years of the century it became the lender of last resort to governments that were in danger of crashing the international financial system.

So what can be done to stabilise the financial system? According to the Bank of International Settlements, probably very little.

"Given how jealously nations guard their sovereignty, proposals for the establishment of a global central bank, an international lender of last resort, a global super-regulator or an international bankruptcy court are unlikely to be acted on in the foreseeable future" (36).

Once gambling has become endemic to the system it is very difficult to remove it. There are welcome proposals like the Tobin tax that would levy, say, 1% on short-term currency deals. This would reduce speculation and raise considerable revenue, but would not alter the logic of currency exchange. Where 'hot money' exists it will still seek out short-term profits. The only sure way of reorienting the system is a mixture of public control of institutional and company funds, combined with capital controls that prevent money being shifted in and out of countries.

It is sometimes claimed that computer technology has ended the ability of governments to control financial dealings, but this is only the case if governments choose to play politics by free market rules. Without entering the discussion as to the benefits of the move, Malaysia showed in 1998 that the power of the speculator could be broken. A remarkably sympathetic editorial in the Financial Times (2/9/98) laid out the case:

"Malaysia yesterday introduced wide-ranging capital controls, which in effect withdrew the ringgit from the international financial system. Along with the Hong Kong government's recent intervention in the stock market this could be the beginning of the backlash against the mantra of free markets. A major rethink of attitudes towards capital flows is therefore urgently needed.

Capital controls have become dirty words in today's economic orthodoxy. But as the crisis in south-east Asia showed, unfettered movement of capital can have devastating effects.

....Controls on short term capital would give these countries greater monetary flexibility, making the banking sector reform easier. Lower interest rates would also give a short term boost to growth."

How the financial system can be made our servant rather than master will be examined further on.

Economics is about the allocation of resources. So far I have argued that capitalism makes a bad job of distributing these resources between people (the growing gap between rich and poor), between countries (north / south divide globally and in Britain) and between productive and unproductive uses (speculating with profits and savings rather than investing them). However it does not follow automatically that what we might call socialism can do the job any better. What can we learn from the experiences of running economies outside the rule of profit?

CHAPTER 3.

THE FAILURE OF CENTRAL PLANNING

Everybody knows that the plans are not going to be fulfilled. It is not the intention that they should be fulfilled. They never will be. The system is as it is. It is a system. Indeed if plans were carried out as intended it would be an absolute disaster! Many people would be out of a job the next day. Enormous numbers of people would have nothing to do. The result would be mass unemployment because there wouldn't be the vast overstaffing which exists at all levels in the Soviet Union

Hillel Titckin in debate with Professor Brus. Critique No.14 1981.

Faced with the economic holocaust in the west that followed the Wall Street stock market crash in 1929, it is not surprising that many political activists and intellectuals became entranced by the successes of the Soviet economy. While unemployment in America and Germany in the early 1930s rose to over 20% and industrial production collapsed, the first Soviet five-year plan of 1928-1932 appeared to show the explosive potential of a planned economy.

Increases over the plan period (1)

	1927	1932
Industrial production (milliard roubles)	18	43
Electricity (mill. KWH)	5	13
Iron (million tons)	5	12
Machinery (million roubles)	1.8	7.3
Labour force (millions)	11	22

Even allowing for statistical distortions, inflationary pressures and the coercion deployed in reaching the targets, the industrial transformation of the Soviet Union could not fail to impress the western observer - a doubling of the economy in five years. Inevitably thereafter "the planned economy" became synonymous with the Soviet model, promoted to the world by the international communist movement. The more obvious the failures of the Soviet economy became, the easier it was for the opponents of socialism to punch holes in the socialist case. Right up to the '80s you could pick up a free copy of Soviet Weekly to see pictures of smiling farm workers bringing in yet another record harvest, when it was clear the whole system was grinding to a halt. The alternative voice, of revolutionaries who did not believe in the centralised plan, was always very small.

In reality the Soviet planned economy had little to do with Marxism, socialism or the interests of workers. It was not born out of an open debate on how the blind forces of the market could be controlled and living standards raised. It had more to do with the internal political struggle of the regime, the centralisation of power around Stalin and the decision to build socialism in one country. The wildly optimistic plan was imposed from above and involved forced collectivisation and the crippling requisition of the produce of 25 million peasant households.

A reported exchange from a Russian biography (2) illustrates the point. The author, a specialist manager in the oil industry, wrote a resignation letter to the Central Committee at the time of the first five-year plan in the following terms "I cease to be responsible for the planning department. The plan figure of 40 million tons I consider to be completely arbitrary. Over a third of the oil must come from unexplored areas, which is like cutting up a bear before it is caught or even located. Furthermore, the three cracking plants that now exist are to be turned into 120 plants by the end of the five year plan. This despite the acute shortage of metal and the fact that the highly complex cracking technique has not been mastered by us".

He reports his central committee respondent as replying "We do not doubt the knowledge and goodwill of the professor....but we reject the fetishism of figures which holds him in thrall....We reject the multiplication table as a basis for policy".

This was planning by political will power in action.

For all the dictatorial distortions of the plan, the economy still surged forward. The system was well suited to the attainment of its chief aim, to mobilise resources and concentrate them on the most urgent needs of the state. It was aimed at increasing the **quantity** of goods produced without worrying too much about quality and efficiency. In a state rich in raw materials and with agricultural workers leaving the land for the towns and cities, such an approach was possible. By the 1960s, when the western world was in the middle of the post war boom, the failure of the soviet planning system to implement new technologies and exploit investments efficiently led to a slowing of economic growth.

Take the production of consumer goods and the percentage increase over the five-year plans (remembering again that these figures are inflated due to hidden inflation etc) (3):

'65-'70	'70-'75	'75-'80	'80-'85
49%	37%	21%	21%

Of course there were specific reasons for the slow down, as well as it flowing generally from the contradictions of the system. Some of the policies of the Krushchev years in the early '60s seem hardly sane - storming campaigns organised from the centre which caused havoc, particularly to agriculture which was planned to expand by 70% between 1958 and 1965 and only managed 14%. Bizarre accounts abound. One such is that in 1963 Krushchev was determined to treble the size of the chemical industry in seven years and to do this he cut plan targets in a series of sectors so resources could be moved across. Particularly hard hit was brickmaking where he closed 8,000 out of 12,000 brickworks! (4) Not surprisingly there were serious shortages.

The explanation for the slowdown however can not be sought in the psyche of Krushchev or his geriatric successors. The increasingly mad-cap schemes of decentralisation and recentralisation, reorganisation and variation in incentives were all attempts to breathe life into an economic system that was tending towards inertia. The only 'allowance' that can be made is the enormous drag on the economy that military and space expenditure represented, absorbing scarce skills and specialist equipment. Although the proportion of the economy devoted to the military had always been high, relations with the United States in this period were such that in '61 alone military expenditure rose by 30%.

When the bureaucratic crown passed to Brezhnev and Kosygin, attempts to kick start the Soviet economy were abandoned and it was allowed to slip into the same comatose state as its leaders, in what were characterised as the years of stagnation. It remained only for Gorbachev from '85 to '91 to conduct the Soviet Union through its final movement of glasnost (openness) and perestroika (restructuring). Sadly the only restructuring that took place was the conversion of the ruling elite into a capitalist elite, taking over great swathes of privatised industries and amassing fortunes on the way. The gangster capitalism that emerged in the former Soviet Union over the course of the '90s has impoverished the majority of its citizens.

What concerns us here is what led to the Soviet economic decline. What was it in the internal workings of the system that failed? Is it true that if the Soviet Union had been a democratic country with workers allowed to criticise the plan and put forward alternatives, the planning and allocation system would have worked? To ask the question is to realise how meaningless it is. If thorough going multi party democracy had existed, the central planning system would probably never have come into being and would certainly not have lasted 60 years. Democracy cannot be pumped in to a crazy system in the hope that it will fine-tune it. Workers' democracy would have ripped down the edifice and started again.

Contradictions of Central Planning

There is a need for clarity when discussing Soviet planning, and planning in general. So often what purports to be an alternative way of organising the economy is just a collection of words that has little light to shed on real life. Take the following contribution to a 'Market vs. Plan' discussion from Katarina Katz :

"You don't have to sit in the World Planning Office of the World Socialist Republic and decide what kinds of shoes should be produced in every village and community of the world! Consumers and producers together can do this. It would mean diminishing alienation. It would lead to the breaking down of the divisions which exist between producer and consumer" (5)

Just what does this mean? How do producers and consumers get together and decide how many shoes are to be produced? Let us start with an iron law. A shoe factory, or collection of factories, can only function in two ways. Either the factory is told how many shoes and of what type to produce, where inputs will come from and where shoes will be sent, or it will operate in the market – buying and selling from whom the enterprise chooses. The first is a system of allocation (the Soviet Union) where money at an enterprise level is almost irrelevant, the second is the market system. Some confusion remains on the Marxist left in this regard. An economy can be socially owned and directed and no longer operate to the rules of the profit system, but still be a market system. Large parts of it may be internally planned and networked, but in the end, if money exists, goods are priced and there is the freedom to establish a business, a market economy exists. Allocation is something completely different. By studying the experiences of the bureaucratically planned economies, I hope to show that the task of modern day socialists is to socialise the market, not create a democratic system of allocation.

Many contradictions flow from the Soviet Union having adopted a system of allocation in industry. It was estimated that 3,000 million planning indicators existed at any one time. A planning hierarchy made these planning decisions independent of the enterprise. Information flowed up the hierarchy, provisional plans came back down, corrections went back up again and then well into the planning period the final targets and distribution information would be passed to the individual enterprise. I once read that a final agricultural planning indicator was the product of 60 in-trays! Even if a gross exaggeration, it indicates a certain inefficiency. It was also a problem crossing the ministerial planning barrier. The ministry responsible for the production of fertiliser was not the one that produced the bags or the ministry that organised the distribution. Lack of co-ordination was inevitable.

But the unwieldy planning hierarchy is only the beginning of the problem. The market at least ensures that if you are turning out rubbish, people will buy off a competitor and the business will go bust. This is a strong incentive to maintain standards. In the absence of a market the Soviet Union used other methods of ensuring quality. The problem was that none of them worked. Under the Soviet system if anything was left to the initiative of local managers it tended to produce distortions. So if a nail factory was told to produce a certain number of nails, the easiest way to achieve the target was to produce small ones. To prevent that happening the planners might specify a certain minimum weight of nail. The distortion is merely diversified, as managers concentrate on weight and numbers of nails, rather than quality and usefulness.

A case from Pravda (2/3/86) illustrates the point:

"We have discovered that, without any changes or renewal of equipment, the factory at Sverdlovsk can produce pipe line which is equal to the best in the world. But if we actually manufactured them, the volume index (which determines the size of the bonus), as well as the incentive fund, would diminish".

To appreciate why local managers were so perverse as to not want to produce a useful product, it is necessary to ponder their life in a centrally planned economy where they occupied the lower rungs of an enormous one-party bureaucracy. Criticism was impossible and problems had to be circumvented by unofficial means. One of life's driving forces for local managers was naturally the want of an untroubled existence for themselves and, by association, their workers. They would be on a fixed salary, with a top up for plan fulfilment. Their vested interest was to be given low targets and to have plenty of resources to achieve them. So the information given to the planners was badly distorted from the start. Materials and labour required would be exaggerated, capacity underestimated and hoarded resources undeclared. That way if inputs from other factories did not arrive or the local party boss started to put on pressure, the unit would still have the wherewithal to meet targets.

It also meant that there was colossal underemployment and waste, recognised by the regime itself. It was estimated in 1965 that 25% of the industrial workforce could be removed without affecting production (6). "We pretend to work and they pretend to pay us" went the Russian quip. Waste was endemic because there was no incentive to reduce costs. The local manager would argue for the maximum amount of materials and once delivered they might as well use them.

Occasionally there were moves to introduce profits as an incentive. But with prices bearing no relation to value (prices were only reviewed three times between 1945 and 1983), and managers having no control over labour costs because of guaranteed job security, the exercise was always abandoned.

In truth, the economy was not planned, but administered. Once the 'heroic' period of building the Soviet industrial state was over, things muddled along in a greater or lesser state of chaos. At all levels workers were profoundly alienated from a system they did not control and that imposed arbitrary penalties on them. These included penalties such as demanding unpaid overtime to reach the plan target, or wage deductions for not achieving the target. Private work was often undertaken in the factories, materials were taken away and an estimated 20 million workers had a second job to try and supplement their income (7).

This communist worker from Minsk quoted in the Moscow News (22/11/87), sums up well the cynicism:

"The negative attitude to work.......is a sort of 'strike', a perfectly natural response to the bureaucracy, to the severity and even rudeness shown towards those who produce all the material wealth of society. The worker repays indifference with indifference. This indifference is profoundly anchored in our lives. It is not something which affects only individuals, it affects the whole of the working class"

In this working culture and with the consumer having to accept what they were given, it is no surprise that poor quality was always a problem and is one of the reasons that statistics have to be treated with so much caution. A great deal of production was useless. For example, it was estimated that two and a half times the cost of a tractor was spent on repairing it over its eight-year life (8)

Perhaps a final dysfunctional aspect to central planning that should be noted is its effects on the implementation of new technology and investment in general. The driving force of capitalism is accumulation. Capitalists invest in new technology to reduce unit costs of production. They do it to make bigger profits by either selling more than their competitors at a lower price or increasing their profit margins. No such motor existed in the Soviet Union. On the contrary, investment in an existing factory caused disruption, threatened the fulfilment of the plan and was to be avoided. There were plenty of inventions coming out of the academic and military research institutions but their take up by industry was poor.

The pattern of progress is that an industrial sector would tend to stagnate until the bureaucracy noticed it. Investment then tended to go into new factories rather than modernising existing ones. The investment itself was often wasteful and poorly exploited. Bureaucrats would typically avoid responsibility and no one had to pick up the tab if the project was a failure. These characterisations of the Soviet economy are not controversial - all were recognised in papers published by the Central Committee of the Communist Party from '85 onwards.

So back to the central question. Were the problems of the Soviet type economies a result of central planning itself or the lack of democracy within it? Workers' control and the freedom to criticise would undoubtedly have removed the worst excesses, but the central failure would remain that central planning removes the whip of the market and takes decision making powers away from those directly involved in production. It removes the incentive to serve the customer, to invest, to do a good job and so forth.

These characteristics can be found closer to home. It is surely not free market mythology to suggest that hierarchically organised public and private monopolies have produced management empire building, bureaucratic arrogance and inefficient systems for the same reasons. To accept the truths within the philosophy of Thatcher and her ilk, is not to agree with their political conclusions.

From the days when the future of the Soviet State was still being fought over in the early 1920s and Central Committee members actually spoke their minds, it is worth plucking out of context Preobrazhensky's waspish comment "Undoubtedly, historically considered, the socialist form is higher than the capitalist. This is very comforting, especially when the higher form works worse than the lower form" (9).

This little advert for the free market is merely to insist that productivity and consumer satisfaction are not the exclusive concerns of the right wing, but should be at the heart of any socialist model. Capitalism in its non-monopolised form is generally a very efficient system of organisation at the micro level – the whip of the market makes sure the slothful die. Its failings are how it impacts at the social level causing unemployment, poverty, environmental destruction and so on. To support public ownership is not necessarily to support central planning; market mechanisms can be incorporated into an economy that is socially controlled.

Some might argue that the same results could be achieved by incorporating greater consumer control into a primarily non-market economy. External inspection and control would certainly help, but it does not avoid the central dilemma. Either a product or service is sold to those who want to buy in competition with others, thereby ensuring sensitivity to customers' demands, or there is no market and sales are guaranteed with all the arrogance of monopoly which that entails.

Trotsky, writing in the 1930s, may not have agreed with everything written here, but was certainly aware of the problems with central planning (10):

"even the most correct combination of all these elements (good information etc. CH) will allow only of constructing a most imperfect wire skeleton of a plan, and not more.

The inumerable living participants in the economy, State as well as private, collective as well as individual, must give notice of their needs and their relative strength, not only through the statistical determinations of plan commissions, but by the direct pressures of supply and demand. The plan is checked and to a considerable measure realised through the market."

If the problems of central planning in developing a modern economy can only be solved, at least in part, by using market mechanisms, we need to examine the results of introducing the market into these systems.

Market Socialism - Communist Style

Hungary

Soviet tanks ultimately crushed the Hungarian revolution of 1956, but the rising had a profound influence on the Stalinist state machine thereafter. The bureaucracy never dared to implement quite the level of social and economic control as their Soviet counterparts for fear of its repetition.

The New Economic Mechanism introduced in 1968 was a delayed response to the rising, as well as an attempt to kick-start the economy. At face value the measures were radical. Central planning was to be largely dismantled and market mechanisms introduced. The proposals were as follows (11):

1) Production patterns to be determined by contracts with customers, rather than being in response to a planning instruction from a ministry.

2) Allocation of inputs to cease. The enterprise would purchase its requirements on the free market.

3) One year plans to be abandoned. The five year plan to act as an indicative guide.

4) More self-financing of investment. The money should come from the enterprise's own funds and not the state.

5) Wages to be fixed by the enterprise and not the state, but a wage increase tax to be introduced.

6) Prices to be controlled more by enterprises than the state and reflect real values.

7) Enterprises to be encouraged to trade more abroad and be able to keep most of the foreign currency they earned.

Such a raft of measures could be expected to have a major impact. Confusingly for those trying to learn from history, not much seemed to change over the following years. This needs some careful explaining.

Economics can never be separated from politics and social organisation in general. In Hungary the existing bureaucratic elite were charged with implementing this policy. The planning ministries did not relish the loss of power involved in the reforms and in any case exercised enormous power over the enterprise managers. This was not the Soviet Union with its 44,000 enterprises; only 800 of them existed in Hungary and they were highly monopolised (12). The managers were appointed by the ministries and were schooled in the practices of central planning. There was no social change involved, no democratic control of enterprises by representatives that might have different ideas as to how things should run, merely a shift in power relations between the centre and the enterprise. Inevitably the heady brew of reforms became diluted.

The dilution took various forms. Firstly despite declared intentions, the state was still controlling 60-70% of investment funds ten years on and the same central planners made key decisions over the social wage that made up 25-30% of total wages (13). If managers wanted to invest in new machinery they would first try to put their hands on 'free' money from the state rather than using their own which built in a tendency to overinvest and complicated any idea of measuring profit. Further the price adjustments (read price increases, as it involved the removal of subsidies), were unpopular with workers and the state continued to subsidise loss making industries to court popularity. This increased the budget deficit.

More significant than any of the above however, was that Hungary became ever more locked into the capitalist system. By 1975, 50% of its national production was traded abroad with the particular problem that its exports tended to be to the Soviet block and its imports from the west (14). To keep living standards rising the state borrowed heavily from western banks in the early 1970s but then interest rates rose and energy prices sky rocketed with the OPEC oil crisis (Hungary imported all its oil). The recession then cut off demand for Hungarian exports. By the end of the decade Hungary was firmly in the debt trap, a debt that doubled again by the end of the 1980s. By then $3400m. a year went out of the country in debt repayment - $650 for every working person. This when the average wage was less than $2500 (15).

Such was the control of western creditors over economic decisions that the International Monetary Fund (IMF) representative was given a place in the cabinet and on the Central Committee of the ruling Socialist Workers Party! Representatives of western creditors however were not so concerned about raising living standards and increasing productivity as making Hungary a country fit for capital. In the final few years of the communist block, most of the pillars of capitalism were put in place - independent commercial banks, a stock exchange, the legal framework for converting state enterprises to companies, the accession to international trade agreements etc. By 1989 there was not much communism left to be liberated from.

If there is little to be learnt from the Hungarian reform experience it is because the economy retained many of the features of the Soviet Union. The reforms were not the result of a democratic resurgence and attempts to exercise new forms of social control over economic life, they were seen by the central planners as a technical mechanism to introduce the self regulating ability of the market. As we saw with the Soviet Union, coating the perversities of central planning with layers of market mechanisms solves nothing.

That said, goulash socialism offered a better quality of life to the majority by removing rigidities in the system. The toleration of small scale private enterprise did not result in big increases in the gross domestic product figures but delivered food to the shops and plumbers to your house. A contrast to Albania where even the soft drink salesman on the roadside was part of the national plan!

Hungarian reforms can be seen as a slow restoration of capitalism. The same cannot be said of Yugoslavia that broke from the Soviet block early on and introduced radically different forms of workers' control.

Yugoslavia

Whatever it was, Yugoslavia was something different. Although traditional central planning was implemented after the war by Tito's liberation forces, by 1949 he had been expelled from Stalin's Cominform and had adopted a more independent stance to socialist construction. The new society was to be built on the basis of 'debureaucratisation and mass participation' (16).

Wariness of words is always necessary, but the social realities of Yugoslavia **were** different to its communist neighbours. It remained a one party state complete with its pampered bureaucracy, security police and political prisoners, but while the state remained strong, real powers were delegated to workers in the enterprises. Typically, a director would be a political appointment from the local commune, but the works council and management boards were elected by the workers (75% had to be production workers and they could not serve more than two years). These bodies had extensive powers. In 1978, out of a population of 21 million, 3 million workers were elected members of works councils.

Much more than in Hungary, the term market socialism properly described Yugoslavia, carrying both negative and positive features. From 1952 to 1972 the economy averaged 8% annual growth, provided a comprehensive welfare system and was much more sensitive to consumer needs than the rest of the eastern bloc. Unemployment was also minimal, but it should be remembered that much like Ireland in the past, the country's potential unemployment was exported - in this case as guest workers to Germany.

Nor was this market socialism just a staging post on a return journey to capitalism. There were no shareholders or dividend payments and in 1970, outside of the agricultural sector, fewer than 3% of workers were employed by someone else or were self-employed. All the rest were members of collectives. Despite enterprises' power to fix wages, inequalities were less than China in the seventies with the wealthiest 5% earning only twice as much as the poorest 25% (17) .

As always, the detail of historical circumstance makes generalisation a problem. The administration of a state with six republics, five nations, four religions and two alphabets was never going to be easy and unification itself was a tremendous victory. Inevitably over the years the balance of power between the centre, republic and enterprise shifted. In 1952 the centralised Communist Party renounced its rights to appoint to all levels of the apparatus which meant that the geographical unit, the republic, tended to become the political focal point, rather than the party hierarchy at the centre. The 1963 constitutional changes further strengthened the role of the republics and enterprises in relation to the central state. The centrifugal forces within Yugoslavia were always to have negative consequences for its economic development.

Though the trend over the years was to grant greater independence to the enterprise, the state or republic tended to intervene in investment decisions and provide subsidies (in 1965 60% of investment funds came from 'socio-political' sources). This introduced some of the problems of over-investment, inflation and political favour seeking that have been discussed earlier. But, like Hungary, Yugoslavia's crisis developed more from economic integration with the west than from its own internal contradictions.

A policy of industrialisation, with the hope of substituting domestic production for imports was followed from the start. Unfortunately such was the federal nature of power and bank ownership that each republic sought to build up its industrial base independent of the others. The steel industry provided the classic example. Logically, there should have been one large steel mill located on the coast to receive the imported ore to serve the entire country. As it was there were six mills - one in each republic! A second problem with the industrialisation policy was that the machinery and spare parts were imported but poor production techniques meant that the final product could not be exported back to the west to pay for the imports either because the quality was poor or the price was too high. Instead the goods were consumed in the country, protected from foreign competition by import controls. Needless to say in the inflation / recession cycle of the 1970s Yugoslavia faced a balance of payments crisis and then a debt crisis even worse than Hungary as it borrowed to fill the currency gap.

By 1982 some 25% of foreign earnings were taken up paying the interest on the accumulated debt. It is worth comparing some figures for 1972 and 1982 to see the cycle of decline the country had entered. Neither year was exceptional - the worsening trend was unrelenting

Annual percentage changes

	1972	1982
Private consumption	5.5	0.5
Fixed investment	6	-6.2
Inflation	16	40
Unemployment	3.5	8.2
Balance of payments deficit ($m.)	992	3089

Economic decline went on to fuel republic and ultimately ethnic rivalries as each vied to protect their resources. Socialist rhetoric was abandoned for a nationalist variant and a flawed self-management system became increasingly manipulated by local power brokers. From 1980 onwards the number of strikes by workers against their own works councils doubled every year so that by 1987 there were over 900 strikes (18). In that same year the war mongering Slobodan Milosevic launched his leadership bid for the Serbian Communist Party largely by exploiting the Kosovan situation. The Yugoslavian people were to pay a heavy price for his descent into political barbarism.

Other Planning Variants

If the object of this chapter is to draw lessons from past planning experience it is unnecessary to examine all variations in their historical contexts. There are really only three essential forms. 1) Capitalist planning or attempts to control the functioning of the free market 2) Central planning and its system of allocation and 3) Market Socialism, here defined as the major resources of the economy being in state hands but market relations being dominant in the economy.

In extreme circumstances, such as in Britain in the Second World War, a high degree of state planning was undertaken with a remarkable degree of success, but that was in conditions of national emergency when the ruling class was prepared to accept state interference. In general while the state has often nurtured and protected industry, particularly in countries such as Japan and South Korea, planning has had to operate within the confines of the laws of the market and profit maximisation. The history of the Asian (ex) growth economies gives the lie to those who argue that the only successful economies are those that rely on free market economics. In reality they were built with state investment behind walls of import and currency controls. They have little to tell us though about the possible shape of a socialist economy, other than perhaps the relationship of the banking system to industry. This will be considered later.

In the case of Britain, vain, and frankly embarrassing, attempts at deploying the ideas of planning such as George Brown's National Plan in the mid 1960s have had short shelf lives:

"Since nothing was done directly to ensure that the plan really happened, the status of the targets was in doubt from the outset. Moreover, it was never clear how growth projections for particular branches should be translated into the concrete investments required to put the plan in to practice. Individual firms received little or no guidance as to what was expected of them and the plan itself provided neither compulsion nor incentives"(19). Eighteen months after it was launched the National Plan was quietly cremated on the fires of the devaluation crisis. There were no memorials. Indeed it marked the death of even thinking in national planning terms. Later interventions such as the National Enterprise Board were faint hearted and partial efforts, seen largely as a sop to the left of the Labour Party.

In fact as the world boom drew to an end and competition intensified, state interference came to be rejected more and more and individual freedom (read business freedom) became the central plank of the Thatcher / Reagan revolution. Today the idea of planning has all but been expunged from the political vocabulary though it still exists of course **within** corporations.

Do the experiences of China or Cuba hold any special lessons? As a regime that seemed to enjoy overwhelming internal popular support in its first twenty years of existence (1959 - 1979) and probably still has majority support today, Cuba looks to offer something different from the Soviet Union. In reality though the economy used to be run in a fairly traditional centralised manner. The leadership banked an enormous amount of political good will at the time of the revolution and as a result has been able to operate a more relaxed political culture. In addition the subsidies provided from the Soviet Union in providing cheap oil and importing sugar above world prices, gave Castro the economic room to make a real difference to the lives of workers and peasants. Despite the deficiencies of the one party state, Cuba came to enjoy one of the highest living standards in central and southern America and an education and health service that rivalled those of the advanced capitalist countries.

Since the collapse of the Soviet Union, despite the rhetoric of Castro, the country has had to make ever-greater concessions to capitalism to maintain itself, particularly in tourism and foreign ownership. There now exists the dollar economy alongside the official one. As stagnant or falling living standards make the political regime more unpopular few are prepared to project the continuation of state ownership and planning much beyond the death of Fidel Castro.

But what of China and its economic miracle - surely it represents a successful resolution of the market or plan dilemma? The country has enjoyed growth rates in the region of 10% per annum for almost 20 years now in a massive leap towards becoming a modern economy. This growth does not represent any economic third way, but rather a successful transition to capitalism compared with an unsuccessful one in Russia.

Both economies suffered the one party, centralist malaise discussed previously, but for political reasons Russia chose to take the shock therapy forced on it by its western creditors and advisers. The shock constituted opening up the entire economy to market forces and selling off state assets at give away prices. The entirely predictable result was a collapse in investment, demand, production and employment with the difference from capitalism being that the workers tended not to be sacked, just not paid anymore. At the same time capital was shifted abroad to tax havens and the new elite, many of them converts from the communist party, set about enriching themselves.

It is worth remembering the human cost of this catastrophe. Take these figures from a recent United Nations report that considered the position of Russia and the former Eastern Bloc (20):

In 1989 about 14 million people in the former communist bloc lived on less than £2-50 a day. By the mid 1990s that figure had risen to 147 million (from 4% to 32% of the population).

9.7 million more people would be alive today if life expectancy hadn't fallen the way it has.

30,000 nurseries were shut in the former Soviet Union between 1991 and 1995.

The Chinese chose a different road. As the events of Tiananmen Square showed in 1989, the Communist Party was determined to control the transition from a centrally planned system to a market economy. State industry was in as parlous a state as in the Soviet Union (half were making losses). However, instead of selling them off, floating the yuan on the international exchange markets and dropping all capital controls, the regime concentrated on releasing free market forces beneath the edifice of the central planning mechanism. Gradualism was the watchword here expressed by Premier Li Peng in 1996 (21):

"We think the market plays a fundamental role in the allocation of resources; but in China, a socialist country, its role can only be brought in to full play under the government's macro - regulation and control". State industry was to be kept going, but the engine of growth would be private and foreign investment. In the medium term the communist party intends to confine state ownership to some thousand core companies but, unlike in Russia, privatisation is subject to political expediency and might be reined in for a period.

The gradual transition of China to capitalism, not just in terms of the use of the market mechanism, but the steady expansion of private ownership, introduces all aspects of capitalism to society. Certainly there has been a marked increase in living standards for the majority but with the drive for profit though increased productivity has come unemployment and increasing inequality. In 1997 between 14 (official figures) and 20 million workers, were made redundant from state owned enterprises. Real levels of unemployment are estimated to be as high as 20% if state employees not receiving wages are included, and there are some 100 million rural migrant workers (22).

During this growth period China has had the advantages of surplus peasant labour moving into industry and working for low wages, a massive home market of over 1 billion people, and foreign investment of over £20,000m. a year. That money flows into the country because corporations can exploit a fairly sophisticated economic infrastructure of communication systems and business practice (at least in the coastal regions), while employing labour at a fraction of the cost. Interviewed on the radio a Dutch investor said that in China his labour costs represented 5% of total production costs compared to 50% in Europe. He also ominously said that Chinese workers had to be 'watched' because in the state enterprises they were not used to working hard (23).

As private enterprise continues to grow, so the state loses its ability to control the economy. The business cycle is asserting itself in a clearer form and there is the classic problem of capitalism that workers' are not being paid enough to purchase the goods they are producing. China will not become a mirror image of America, but unless a workers' movement based on social ownership can cut across events, it will end up a wholly capitalist economy with the thin crust of communist party power being broken in the process. Overall production may rise but so too will inequality, regional differences and exploitation.

Planning - Some Conclusions

Firstly, the world does not stop turning with the end of private ownership of the means of production. Central planning changed the Soviet Union into an industrialised state and world power, albeit at great human cost. Few would argue however that central planning is suitable for an advanced economy for reasons we have discussed.

Capitalist planning outside of its war context has amounted to pushing and shoving between state and industry in the post war era. The state has normally been responding to pressure from the workers' movement (eg. Britain and France) or representing a one nation, social democratic political culture (Germany). Planning has never threatened the power of capital, with the partial exception of the early '80s Mitterrand government in France, and evaporated as a strategy after the end of the world boom.

Hungary and China may illustrate successful features but both were / are on the march from an economy dominated by state ownership to one of private ownership. Only Yugoslavia, however briefly, represented a third alternative of social ownership bound by market mechanisms. Some sort of verdict on its success is necessary.

The Yugoslav system's central contradiction was that enterprise ownership was only social in the sense that it was not private. The works council was often the battleground for state versus enterprise interests. Workers quite naturally tended to favour development plans that would maximise profits and incomes for their enterprise (statistics contradict the notion that workers preferred to take profit as wages and failed to invest). Such enterprise based thinking was often met by the external power of the communist party / commune / republic / state trying to impose their own agenda

171

through their power over investment funds. Strong syndicalist tendencies were at work, and just how the general social interest was meant to be met within the enterprise, was never clear. Three things resulted from this. Enterprises exploited monopoly positions to force up prices. The economy was dogged by manoeuvrings between enterprise and state and local state representatives duplicated investments around the country.

There is no room for naivety here. If there is to be a synthesis between the disciplines of the market and the social interests of a planning mechanism there will be tensions. The tension would be lessened however if the interests of the state were moved **inside** the enterprise. Not in the Stalinist sense of having managers and trade unions alike at the beck and call of the Party, but of placing the state interest (representing the electorate) as a stakeholder on the Enterprise Board.

Talk of stakeholding – the need to represent the interests of workers, the consumer and society at large, as well as the shareholder – is now commonplace in western discussion of corporate governance. Companies like Johnson and Johnson, the babycare group, even have value statements saying that they put mothers first, employees second, community third and shareholders a poor fourth. Sadly this stakeholder-wash has to be treated with the same suspicion as the green wash of the environmentally conscious corporation. External interests are only taken into account to protect the image of the company, as an additional arm to their marketing strategy. No one is talking about stakeholders actually controlling the company and setting its priorities

If the core idea of stakeholder control was to form the basis of a socialist economy, then the Yugoslav model would be adapted so that the Enterprise Boards consisted of representatives of the workforce, state and consumers overseeing the work of the full time management. The state representatives would not necessarily have the final word. They would have to convince the other parties that meeting social need also meant quality production and good working conditions. We will explore this model further in a following chapter but its essence is clear: the state could not impose grand unproductive investment plans and management could not exploit anti - social self-interest.

Clearly another concern about Yugoslavia is that while it seemed to meet the general social interest over the 20 years it was successful, it clearly did not match the productivity levels of its western counterparts. The problem is central to this work and, at the risk of running ahead of ourselves, an initial comment is required

The cornerstone of Marxism is that capitalism at some point becomes unable to develop the productive forces in a way that takes full advantage of the technical abilities society has achieved. Capitalism fails to organise production to meet human need and in its crisis opens the way for a new form of productive relations that will remove those barriers - socialism.

At the society level all is clear. A socially guided economy, with a planning framework should be able to create work for those who want it and bring wasted human and physical capacity into use. Even the malfunctions of the bureaucratic one party states suggest that would be possible. But at a product level, will a computer be produced cheaper under a socialist system than a capitalist one?

It is important to differentiate between the productivity of society as a whole and workplace productivity. As well as full employment, socialism should mean a shorter and more flexible working week, environmental sensitivity, greater social support, childcare and so on. These measures would not be introduced to improve productivity but to improve lives. With full employment, increased investment, elimination of commercial secrecy and increased networking, it may well be that socialist productivity will be higher than under capitalism. Such things are impossible to predict in advance. However there is no reason to expect that the productivity of a particular computer production plant will be higher.

The deregulated and intensively competitive technology industries are geared up to bring new techniques to market in the shortest possible time at the lowest cost (of course inflated profits will be made as long as the competition allows). To achieve this, corporations throw huge incentives at management and development staff and pay third-world assembly workers a pittance, while squeezing as many hours as possible out of everyone. These are not methods of increasing productivity that socialists would wish to copy.

This is not to argue that a socialist economy has to become a caricature of poor productivity like the Soviet Union became. The future of socialism will depend on the overall standard of life it can offer and its ability to show that those standards will continue to improve year on year. Its future will also be dependent on it becoming a global system, not exposed to capitalism competing on the basis of human and environmental exploitation. The collapse of the Yugoslavian system was inevitable once it became integrated with a capitalist world with much higher productivity levels.

Other structural deficiencies existed in Yugoslavia but of a more technical nature. Perhaps the most important was that workers tended not to have any long term stake in the business. They did not own it, they just took their wages. A fairly simple solution that the Mondragon co-operative implemented (see later) is that when the enterprise invests money out of profits it 'borrows' the money from its workforce. They are given an equivalent amount in non-transferrable shares which can be redeemed at some point in the future.

The self-management economy of Yugoslavia was far from ideal but it did give us some clues as to how a socialist economy might be fashioned. In chapter five that structure will be fleshed out, but first we have to accommodate a spectrum of thought that barely existed at the time of debates about Yugoslavia – green economics.

CHAPTER 4.

THE GREENING OF SOCIALISM

The last two chapters have attempted to show that social control and planning of big business is needed and why central administrative planning will not work. Before looking at how an economy might be socially run we first need to ask, what do we want to achieve? If gross domestic product is no longer to be the guide, where are we to take the economy? The green movement has focussed on issues of the alternative economy and it is worth examining their ideas.

Through much of the last century the existence of the Soviet Union framed the planning debate. Both activists and mainstream economists argued on the same ground. What form of economic organisation maximised growth, employment and living standards and minimised poverty? Ideas of democracy, control over your life, domestic relationships, the environment or indeed happiness rarely entered the equation. Full employment, rising wages, greater equality and a strong welfare state more or less covered the demands (not to be mocked!). For the majority of the left, socialism was to be delivered by the state in a mixed economy.

As the domination of the communist party over the intellectual left began to weaken, especially after the crushing of the Hungarian uprising in 1956, concerns began to broaden. The New Left was interested in the more complex ways economic organisation impinged on people's lives, not just the growth in purchasing power. From the sixties on, a plethora of organisations and movements developed that put people and their environment at the centre of the economic debate. The green movement was one such strand and its influence on economic thinking has been profound, rippling far beyond a core of green activists.

To retain some focus, this book can only note the essential environmental struggles taking place against soil erosion, deforestation, global warming, bio depletion, genetic manipulation etc. Our attention must remain with economic systems and the political economy proposed by greens. Suffice to say that the environmental concerns of these campaigns should be common cause to all radical alternatives.

If socialism is a broad church, the green movement is something of a cathedral. It spreads from aristocrats who prefer their venison organic to anarchist revolutionaries. The ideas considered here are those of the UK Green Party, probably near the centre of the spectrum and, as yet, uncorrupted by the spoils of office!

Unlike its European counterparts, the Green Party in Britain had its roots in the right, not the left of politics. Two former Conservative Party activists launched what was to become the Green Party in 1973, concerned that too many people and too much economic growth would lead to catastrophic disruption of the planet's eco-system (1). The party was strongly influenced by Teddy Goldsmith, brother of corporate raider James, and his magazine the Ecologist. The party evolved from being called 'People' through the Ecologist Party to end up as the Green Party in 1986. Like all green parties it spans the spectrum between 'realists' who want to be environmentally minded within the free market system and 'fundamentalists' who want to challenge the capitalist system as a whole. Three themes run through green economic policies – care for the environment, elimination of poverty (justice) and local democracy and control. Each bears examination.

Environment

The emphasis has shifted since the early years. At first the impending environmental disaster was to be that raw materials, particularly gas and oil, were likely to run out with serious results. We had to use less and conserve more. The need is still to use less and conserve more but the emphasis has shifted to the effects of waste rather than a shortage of inputs. The dangers come from many directions - global warming from excess carbon dioxide emissions, increased asthma from car fumes, pollution of water sources from effluent etc. In addition, the call to protect species and habitat has grown louder in the intervening years (2).

It is not just the environment of the earth that needs protecting but the environment of our lives. The sixties and seventies may have brought a booming consumer culture to the cities but they also brought environmental disaster. Motorway feeder roads cut across communities, people were gathered up in anti-social flats, streets became unsafe to play in and growing car ownership heralded the death of local shops. With government policies consistently favouring car use as against public transport, the car now shapes our towns and cities. About half of any urban land area is given over to cars (more in America). Workplaces are located out of town and close to motorways, increasing our journey times, and suburbs are more likely to boast retail parks than green ones. None of these developments are welcome for the 30% of adults who still do not have access to a car.

The tide is now turning, at least in theory, as green thinking becomes the common sense of the age. No government document dares utter the phrase 'economic development' without the word 'sustainable' appearing first. In a modest way city centres are being reclaimed for pedestrians, town centre flats built or converted and high-density residential areas made safe for children. The pace of change is slow though, especially in improving public transport, and without influence on the decisions of major companies the reintegration of work and shopping into the fabric of urban life is particularly difficult. Single-minded commercial thinking still favours the green field site.

So, for a mixture of environmental and welfare reasons the principal target areas for the Green Party are as follows. Improve public transport and tighten planning regulations. Increase the quantity of reusable and recycled goods to avoid dumping and incineration. Promote organic farming to avoid the damage of intensive farming methods, while improving the quality of food and increasing employment. Introduce funding for community businesses to implement schemes such as the insulation of housing (3).

They would use taxation as a means to an end. Taxes would be shifted from employment (income tax and National Insurance) to resource use (e.g. fuel and land) thereby discouraging wasteful consumption and encouraging economic activity.

These measures would be set in the context of redefining what constitutes a good life and what constitutes economic success. General welfare indices would replace gross domestic product as an indicator of progress. This would end the absurdity that if a country cut down all its trees, sold them as wood chips and then gambled the money away, it would appear from its national accounts to have become richer!

The general thrust of these reforms must surely be supported, though the proposals are modest and would leave the basic mechanisms of the capitalist system intact. The controversial area is whether economic growth of any kind is environmentally permissible. Opinion appears divided. Some greens differentiate between good growth (building more trains) and bad growth (building more cars). Others take a more fundamentalist position:

"the consumption we enjoy now is bought at the expense of the consumption of our children or grandchildren...We might view the resources of the planet as being like a bowl of peaches"(4)

This appears a strangely unscientific view, harking back to the 'we're running out of oil' sort of pronouncement. Use of resources is not the same as damaging the planet. We are increasingly able to create goods from renewable resources but may not exploit the technologies because it is not profitable to do so. More important within this debate, is how you could achieve a no growth economy without removing the profit motive as its driving force. Capitalism is based on accumulation. The Green Party appears to have little to say on the subject.

In dealing with issues of economic justice their ideas are potentially more radical.

Justice

The main vehicle for delivering economic justice is the Citizen's Income (C.I.). The idea is powerfully simple. Everyone would be paid an equivalent to income support levels (higher for pensioners, lower for children) and with it all the non-housing benefits would be scrapped. Income tax would be on all earned income. In that way the poverty trap would be abolished as there would be no benefit losses on earned income. The unpaid work of mothers and carers would be rewarded, tremendous savings would be made in the administration of benefits and people would feel more able to work part time if it suited them.

The only problem is, and the advocates are very aware of the criticism, it costs. To implement a Citizen's Income of £50 for adults of working age (£62 for pensioners) in 1996, combined with the abolition of the Job Seekers Allowance, Income Support, Family Credit and Pensions, would have meant spending an additional £70bn.(5). Even with fairly optimistic costings the reform would mean raising income tax to 35% on all earned income to cover expenditure. The redistributive effects would not be large. The purpose of the reform would be to reward the unrewarded and end the injustices of the benefits system.

As a mechanism for delivering social security Citizen's Income has much to recommend it. However it does little to increase the income of some of the poorest sections of society. The level of current pensions and benefits is very low. Any increase would have to be added to the cost of CI. There is also a worrying trend amongst its advocates to combine the measure with the abolition of a minimum wage so people would be 'allowed' to work in less profitable sectors like organic farming and recycling.

The central objection to CI however is political. It swims entirely in the opposite direction to free market politics and yet is seen to fit in to a free market system. The corporate and financial sectors are forever pushing for a reduction in the cost of the welfare state and governments of all types have set about their bidding. Introducing a bill of £70bn. into this climate and taking on the arguments of why we should pay people who do not need the money, and pay people to be idle, is surely a political non-starter. The implementation of CI could only be considered as part of a much deeper economic transformation.

It is a recurring contradiction of green politics that, by side stepping the free market dilemmas, their alternatives become either utopian or life stylist. Nowhere is this clearer than in their thinking on local control.

Local control and democracy

At the centre of the green thesis is the loss of individual and community control to corporations and central government. Where once people produced their own food, energy and many household goods locally, they now import them from other areas. The self sufficiency and dependency networks that were established between people have been lost, as have the jobs in many cases. The case is well made, though it can lead to a certain feudal sentimentality. Instead of producing a vision of a political economy that reintegrates our productive capacity with our social needs, there is often the tendency to want to build an economy within an economy. The conclusion flows from pessimism about large-scale political change.

Two leading green spokespeople give voice to this:

"In the world economy only a very limited range of activities is commercially feasible in most communities because of the intensity of competition from outside. We must therefore build independent, parallel economies if we are to fill more of our needs for ourselves"….. "But these top down tactics (breaking up big business into small co-operatives – CH) are pipe dreams in the present climate and we have no alternative but to work from the bottom up. In other words, rather than changing the law we will have to change attitudes – and consequently ideas – if we are to build peasant system economies strong enough to survive the pressures and instabilities of an industrial system world" (6)

"In many areas of economic life Greens face entrenched power structures that appear so monolithic that any attempt to change them seems pointless. The phrase 'the juggernaut of international trade' is no hyperbole and other issues ranging from world poverty and the international financial system to globalisation and the role of transnational corporations seem overwhelming. But in the field of resource allocation there is some good news. There is actually a great deal we can do as individual citizens and consumers. The most obvious action we can take is to consume less" (7).

To see our own lack of organisation lined up against the multinationals **is** daunting, but unless our politics tackles that level of the system we are building on sand. Of course something can be done this side of the revolution. Green activists have come forward with many ways of organising that make a difference, but as their own literature testifies, the tide of the free market can often sweep these initiatives away leaving only the ideologically committed to soldier on.

Green strategies for local control are:

1) lock in purchasing power locally by use of local currencies and local exchange trading schemes (8)
2) make sure local savings are used for local development and that cheap credit is available (credit unions and development funds) (9)
3) support co-operatives and community businesses. Develop small business support networks.(10)
4) as far as possible provide your own food and power (11)
5) be self reliant and self limiting.

To the uninitiated, local currencies and local trade exchange schemes (LETS) can seem a little eccentric but their economic logic is impeccable.

As long as you can find enough people to accept a local currency they can appear to work like magic. What is happening is that additional purchasing power is created and then is made to circulate quickly in a small area. Before being banned as a threat to the national currency, experiments were conducted in Germany and Austria in the '20s and '30s. In these trials the local authority issued notes as local currency, backed up on a one to one exchange offer with the national currency.

The currency note only had a time life of one month but could be renewed by purchasing a stamp to fix to the back of the note at one per cent of face value. To avoid incurring the monthly charge receivers of notes spent the money quickly. Accordingly in the towns where the system was introduced, taxes were paid in advance with notes, food was paid for via bulk orders, local builders were given credit in the currency by homeowners and the local authority took on the unemployed to do public work.

In Wogl, an Austrian town of 10,000 people, the circulation of Gesellian stamp money reduced unemployment from 35% to negligible levels between 1932 and 1933. Moreover all housing in the town was repainted, streets extensively repaved, local forests planted and a bridge built in homage to the 'new economics' of Silvio Gesell.

However, it is one thing to promote a local currency in times of deep depression, another to do it in modern America. Clearly there are disadvantages to holding the local currency to the national one – there are fewer places to spend it. So when people's need for money, in whatever form, grows less urgent, their preference for the national currency can increase. If the number of participating businesses drops, so inflation can take hold as the local currency is dumped on those businesses still participating.

LETS (Local Exchange Trading Schemes) are when groups of people join a trading club. You register with the scheme and log what skills or products you can offer in exchange for the unit of trade. Your skills can range from baby sitting to car repair. The 'buttons', or whatever name is chosen for the currency, may be equivalent to an hour's labour or be tied to the pound. LETS avoid the danger of inflation by the level of currency being equal to the amount of trade being done. Everyone has an individual account and all transactions are undertaken by cheque, so your account is either in credit or debit depending on whether you are selling more of your time and produce or buying other people's. What it gains in security it can lose in bureaucracy. It is not ideal having to use a cheque to buy a bag of potatoes and someone has to take the time to run the accounts and circulate an up to date newsletter of who can offer what.

Every new idea has to start small, but after ten years of promotion in Britain there is little sign of LETS schemes taking hold. There are over 300 in existence but it is estimated that they account for less than one per cent of one per cent of national income (12). It is easy to be sneering. Greens could well point out that socialism has been around for 150 years or more and does not seem to have had much impact (although movements claiming to be Marxist changed the face of the planet in the 20th century). Mechanisms such as the use of local currencies may be useful in a situation where social control could ensure that major businesses accepted the currency. However it would be perversely optimistic to believe that local currencies or LETS could counteract the powerful forces driving increased competition and inequality. In the conditions of a depression where such alternatives might be sought, we would want them to be part of much more radical measures.

The other elements of local control listed above are gaining acceptance and can have an effect at the margins. The number of credit unions (member controlled local saving banks) and the funds at their disposal have grown enormously. In the United States one in four of the population belongs to a credit union and in Ireland it is one in two. In these countries they are able to offer a service as efficient as a high street bank while charging low interest on loans, lending to people who are turned away by banks and using savings for the benefit of the local community. It is a financial mechanism that should be given full support. Unfortunately credit unions are at an early stage of development in Britain.

Though between 1992 and 1997 the number of credit unions grew from 383 to 584 and their membership from 88,000 to 214,000, many of them remain publicly sponsored goodwill gestures.(13) Some 62% of credit unions are run entirely by volunteers and open only up to six hours a week. Only 10% are economically self sufficient and sustainable. That is nothing against the principle however. The larger ones that tend to be employer based **are** self sufficient and growing quickly. (14)

Community banking does not have an established track record in Britain, but there are examples in the United States. The idea is that loan funds are used as a way to regenerate areas and tackle poverty. Unlike normal banks that tend to lend to the well off and withhold loans from the poor, community banks focus their efforts on a particular area and encourage people to borrow for economic activity. The South Shore Bank in Chicago is perhaps the most well known example (15).

At the end of the 1960s the South Shore area, covering about 78,000 people, began to suffer large-scale outward migration and went into decline. The South Shore bank at that time behaved in a standard commercial manner and effectively 'red-lined' the district. While it held $33m. in deposits from South Shore residents, only $120,000 was out on loan to customers living in the area. At about this time the bank was taken over by a group of enlightened bankers who sought to reverse the situation. Loan managers had to report to the directors if they **refused** a loan to a local resident. This was combined with actively promoting business loans to the community and linking it to financial advice. The bank particularly targeted owners willing to refurbish their flats. After twenty years of this sort of work the South Shore bank had in total financed the refurbishment of 9,000 flats and in 1992 alone pumped $41m worth of loans into the area. The redirection of such a sum of money is significant.

Co-ops will be discussed fully in the next chapter. The point to be made here is that only as part of a transforming strategy can they have an impact. Being controlled by workers or users, they are likely to be better employers and more sensitive to community needs, but in the final analysis they are businesses that cannot make a loss. It is very difficult sustaining a business in an area that is in decline and where purchasing power is ebbing away. Like so much of green economics they would form part of the solution once the 'big economics' is sorted out. Wealth is very difficult to create from nothing. Bring income to an area through a large employer, and the opportunities for wealth to spread and multiply begin to appear.

This is not to decry the efforts of thousands of volunteers active in creating social enterprises and Development Trusts. Through their democratically elected Boards, these organisations are attempting to put communities in control of economic development. But they have little economic clout and generally have to get by on small resources and delivering public sector contracts. To turn an area around requires major and sustained business investment, linked to the needs of local people.

The centrality of 'big economics' is recognised by many activists. Milton Davis, one of the directors of South Shore bank, after recounting the successes of South Shore, told the BBC "Crime has gotten worse recently, largely because we have too few entry level jobs for single young men....Crack cocaine and the ridiculous attitude we have to guns in this country do not help. The missing building block is jobs. We need help on this one."(16)

Richard Douthwaite in his book Short Circuit (sub title 'strengthening local economies for security in an unstable world'), ends with a chapter 'The Future, And It Works'. It describes the regeneration of a small town called Manley, 50 miles north of Brisbane, Australia between 1970 and 1995. At the start of the period Manley was a declining farming community that because of falling prices was forced to switch from labour intensive dairy farming to cattle ranching. Around 1970 a trickle of what the book describes as 'young well educated people from the city looking for a simpler, less materialistic sort of life' began to arrive. Over the next twenty years these incomers formed the vanguard of an alternative enterprise culture.

A credit union was established that by 1993 had 2,500 members and had provided start up finances for thirty new businesses. Partly state financed, an old creamery was converted to a small business incubator. Eighteen co-ops exist consisting of a radio station, clubs, food producers, trainers, retailers etc. and 800 people are involved in a LETS scheme.

Manley must surely be a more interesting and economically successful place to live as a result of these initiatives, but with refreshing honesty Douthwaite also identifies the necessary accompanying flow of wealth:

"It would be wrong to suggest that these co-ops transformed the declining town of the early 1970s into today's vital, vibrant community by themselves, although they undoubtedly helped. Derek Sheppard, a former economic development officer with the Queensland government who resigned and moved to Manley to escape sixteen hour working days, suggests that an influx of retired people from the mid 1970s onwards played a much larger role in halting the town's decline" (17)

Greens stand for a decentralised economy, not a socialist one. They stand for building up from the bottom, of taking economic control back into individual hands. Yet they do that for the most part without challenging the functional requirements of the free market and the power of corporations. To that degree the project remains utopian. Any form of self help and activism should be supported but that does not mean turning self help into a strategy for political transformation. Unless the major levers of the economy are brought into play, high levels of inequality and poverty are likely to remain a permanent feature of the social landscape.

Is it fair to classify green thinking in this way? After all green activists are core organisers of anti-capitalist events around the world. It is an accurate portrayal of the Green Parties, though not of the green movement as a whole. Selected quotes from the Green Party's Manifesto for a Sustainable Society give a flavour of where they stand on economic relations and a selection appears in the reference section.(18)

The document puts forward a series of far reaching reforms. None would alter the fundamental workings of capitalism, but many would be seen by the ruling elite as an intolerable interference with their ability to maximise profits. There is an ambiguous exception. One paragraph is devoted to corporate control:

"The right of the shareholders to dividends must not be the single most important criterion for company policy making. Those with a stake in the company's decisions must have the right to make informed input into those decisions. These 'stakeholders' include the shareholders, the workers, consumers, the local community and advocates for the local environment. New legal and institutional structures will be created to enable these stakeholders to have a voice in the running of companies and other relevant organisations" (page 5).

It would appear that the policy is not one of social control, but rather of interested groups having a voice and input, perhaps in the form of two or three people on the Board. Again, such a reform would irritate but could be accommodated. Maximising shareholder value would remain the criterion for success.

The economics of the majority of the Green Party and its political affiliates consists of mechanisms that develop local and individual control over economic circumstance. If major industry and finance were socialised, the policies would be entirely valid. However a refusal to embrace the politics of power and resolve who runs the economy and in whose interest, turns such a strategy in to a deception. Alternative forms of activist led economic organisation will come and go and, in many cases, we will be inspired to glimpse what might be possible in a sanely organised society.

But to put such a strategy forward as a political escape route from global competition is seriously misleading.

The green movement of course is not the Green Party. Thousands of activists have a more fundamental view of capitalism than the spokespeople of the Green Party and understand that the primacy of the profit motive is incompatible with the protection of the planet and its people. In the coming years there is likely to be a continuous process of realignment at the radical end of politics. Anti-capitalist environmentalists have much more in common with socialists than they do with liberal greens. This dividing line that runs through the green movement has and will lead to new red/green political formations. It also leads to Green Parties adopting a pro coalition stance where, for the price of a few environmental policies, they become enmeshed in free market governments. This is already the case in Germany and France.

Every movement carries its history with it. Twentieth century socialism was dominated by the issues of increasing production and control of the central state. Green thinking encourages us rather to move away from maximising production, to put environmental and personal living issues at the centre of politics, to pass down as much power as possible to local level and to actively encourage small and co-operative businesses. Such a shift should be fully embraced. In return socialists will have to convince greens that sustainable and meaningful change can only be implemented, if combined with the political struggle for social ownership of the pillars of the economy.

Combining these political traditions and learning from the experience of central planning, we can begin to draw the outlines of how a socialist economy might operate.

CHAPTER 5.

OUTLINES OF A SOCIALIST ECONOMY

It is relatively easy to sign up to socialist aspirations, but how are they to be achieved? Too often there is an avoidance of detail beyond the need for a 'democratically planned economy' or 'production for need not profit'. The reason is a worthy one; that you cannot and should not be prescriptive about the nature of a society that will be forged in the course of the struggle for power. But this is surely like suggesting that learning to drive is the same as being told where to go. Over the last century we have accumulated a wealth of knowledge about how economies work. General conclusions must be drawn if socialists are to be treated seriously. "What would you do if you were in power?" is a legitimate question that demands an answer.

The outline developed here is not a blueprint. It will not become reality. Real life is much more surprising and interesting. A socialist economy will be formed by the endeavour of millions acting through new and reshaped organisations. Intricate academic jigsaws of how society could operate if we did not start from here are completely worthless. I would only hope to set a direction, to develop an economic framework that can be argued for now and implemented or altered in the future. Such a framework has to rise from people's experience and be leavened with common sense.

There **will** be a 'day one' of the revolution. If anything worthy of the name socialism is to come into being there has to be a point at which the bulk of the economy comes under social control rather than operating on the basis of profit maximisation. It is hard to see how that can be a gradual process.

In the early '70s a sub committee of the Labour Party's National Executive put forward a policy, later adopted by both the National Executive and Party conference, that a major private company in each sector of the economy should be nationalised – approximately 25 in all. While the policy was understandable in the context of the battle between right and left in the Labour Party, in many ways it represented the worst of all worlds. The struggle for its implementation (there was none) would have invoked enormous resistance from the ruling class. They would rightly have seen it as the beginning of the end. Yet once implemented, even if the public companies did improve investment, training etc, they would have been forced to dance to the tune of the dominant private sector. A failure to seek the lowest cost options would have meant a loss of markets to competitors and gradual decline.

What is needed is the bringing in to social ownership of the major oligarchs of the economy, normally between three and six companies in each sector, along with nearly all the finance industry. The remaining private companies would then fit in with social priorities not the other way around. The transition to socialism is about power, about breaking the grip of the free market on the economy. Slow advance to this end increases the level of aggravation in the system without changing the way it operates. Capitalism does indeed operate best when it is 'free'. To feel that we can relaunch a social democratic mixed economy is surely to fail to learn the lessons as to why Thatcherism arose in the first place and the meaning of globalisation.

Tony Blair understands this. New Labour accepts the primacy of the free market and then looks at what can be done within it.

Raise such ideas of fundamental change in your workplace twenty years ago and the chances are you would end up in a vigorous discussion of the virtues or otherwise of private enterprise. Today you are more likely to be met with a glazed look tinged with sympathy. Is it crazy to talk about large-scale socialisation of industry? We will return to the issue of political isolation in the last chapter, but two points need to be made here:

1) This book has been written at the end of an unprecedented nine year growth cycle for the Anglo Saxon economies. Clearly in such an environment ideas of fundamental change will have limited appeal. However, previous chapters have explained why capitalism remains an unstable system, prone to crisis. What would the general reaction to the socialisation of finance be if millions experienced the wiping out of much of their savings and pensions in a stock market fall? Overnight, in July 2001, Equitable Life reduced the value of 400,000 pensions by 16% for reasons related to falling returns, while the high flying Independent Insurance, valued at £1bn only a year before, went bust at the same time. In future, public ownership could be seen as a way of offering people financial security.

This is not to reason that the worse the conditions, the better the chance for socialism. Politics is more complex than that. But the arguments in this book are predicated on the instability of the growth / recession cycle returning, and probably with a vengeance.

2) Those that feel policies for large-scale socialisation are criminally naïve are perhaps too pessimistic and short term. Granted we may be starting a

political long haul (though events can put political attitudes into fast forward), can anyone really believe that 'this is it'? That two hundred years from now (the lifetimes of just two people), we will inhabit a planet dominated by a few enormous unaccountable companies forming and meeting the needs of unequal and powerless populations?

It may come to that but surely only after the defeat of a historic struggle to create a democratic economy.

Since the fifties the Labour Left has generally kept an embarrassed silence about public ownership. It became more a matter of private belief than political policy. Nationalisation was unpopular, so you could not propose it. End of argument. The blame was apparently with the political consumer, not the product that was being sold. We should not be surprised if people rejected the idea of extending the old corporatist nationalised industry.

Carefully fostered by those with a vested interest, the perceived failings of the nationalised industries, the commanding depths of the economy, became interchangeable with the failings of socialism as a political creed. So the broad band of society that wants greater equality, welfare and control over the economy were persuaded that socialism represented inefficiency, lack of incentive, state interference, curtailment of freedom and bureaucratic arrogance. While nationalised industries probably never had a fair press, like many prejudices, negative attitudes were sustained by an element of truth.

The public corporation was run like a private company except with state targets. There was no attempt to co-ordinate or plan between industries or to involve the consumer and workforce. In a monopoly position, management were often able to ignore consumer needs and to build bureaucratic empires with little attention paid to how productive the work was. It was not all bad as we will discuss below, but there **were** reasons why the Gas Board became the butt of stand-up comedians.

The inadequacies of the old nationalised industries did not lead to the current right wing views of the leaders of the labour movement. There were greater forces at work. Thatcherism and the collapse of the Soviet Union to mention only two. However they do in part explain the reluctance of even the left to raise socialisation as a solution to our problems, which has compounded the marginalisation of socialist ideas in general.

A word more on the insanity of proposing large scale social ownership, remembering we are dealing with psychological not technical arguments here. The Labour leadership claim that public ownership is unpopular (though it did not seem to be that unpopular when the Tories came to privatise electricity, water, the railways and mines) and therefore a political albatross. This one-dimensional analysis fails to notice that corporate culture and the world of big money are falling ever further into disrepute and that people are demanding change.

MORI has conducted a survey of attitudes to business over the last 30 years. In 1999 the approval rating dropped to the lowest point ever.

Asked "Do you agree that the profits of large British companies help make things better for the consumer" 25% said yes and 52% no.

The rating has fallen consistently since 1980 when Mrs Thatcher first came to power and 56% answered yes to that question. The report goes on to say that in spite of business efforts to project a socially responsible attitude, more than two thirds felt that industry and commerce do not pay enough attention to their social responsibilities and that they failed to pay enough attention to their treatment of the environment. What is also interesting is that while the rating of business at least stabilised in the boom of the '80s, the fall was continuous throughout the growth years of the '90s. (1).

It is no surprise that the survey also found that the vast majority disagreed with the nationalisation of these major firms. With only perceptions of the Soviet Union and previous nationalised industries to react to and with no significant political current arguing for a new form of ownership, could it be any other way?

Socialisation in practice

Socialisation as used here is not a politically cowardly way of saying nationalisation. It represents a different way of running enterprises. Its meaning is that those with the interest of society as a whole should be in the majority on the ruling bodies of companies. At the same time representatives of the state should only form a minority.

The anchor of the policy is that power over enterprises should be divided between the representatives of workers within the industry, consumers and the state, with management there to advise and implement decisions. While such a division could be enshrined in company law, to have any meaning, the power of shareholders would have to be removed and taking the company into public ownership is the only way to do that.

Inevitably, as corporate power has been called into question, half-way house solutions have come to the fore. One such idea is the creation of Stakeholder Councils to supervise Boards of Directors (see for instance Roger Crowe, Stakes not Shares, New Economics Foundation, 2001). The Stakeholder Council would be the governing body of the company. Under this proposal it would have the power to elect and remove directors, approve or veto their pay and vote on key policy issues at the annual general meeting, just as shareholders do now. Radical though the proposal is, it is an attempt to reconcile the irreconcilable. The company would be expected to run in the interests of stakeholders - the workers, community, suppliers etc. - and yet would still be owned by shareholders who expect the company to be run on the basis of profit maximisation. The move would not resolve this tension, nor would it integrate the company into a system of economic planning. Yet, as Will Hutton points out in the Introduction to Crowe's pamphlet, the move would be fiercely opposed by big business. If we are going to enter the political fray, we need to be armed with a policy that will be certain to work.

Why do I suggest a three-way division of control between consumers (and suppliers), employees and the state? If only employees controlled a large enterprise or industry it would inevitably tend to be run in their interest. Employment, working conditions and wages are likely to be prioritised over productivity, quality and social benefit. This would only be a tendency. Many examples could be given of both altruistic and socially conscious planning emerging from a situation of workers' management. Within a socially directed economy there would remain ample scope for workers' management and co-operatives, but it is easy to envisage cases where employee management of industry would conflict with social benefit.

Workers generally want to maintain their particular factory or field of employment, but technology and consumer needs change and the structure of the economy needs to change with them. For instance the number of workers in the finance industry should probably be reduced, the issue is how it is done. In the mining industry tens of thousands were thrown out of work with scant opportunity of finding alternative employment. Social control of an industry ensures that dynamism is maintained, needs met and productivity taken advantage of. Planning mechanisms would ensure that in areas where employment is reduced, other needed jobs were created. At the same time workers' representatives within the power structures would ensure that the transition was phased, retraining took place and incomes maintained.

Conversely, if the state took sole control of industry many features of the Soviet Union would become apparent. Planners have a safe job to retreat to. They would have a tendency to look for the easy life, until the boss started to ask difficult questions or the Central Planning commission started to storm a particular sector. Also the planner's penchant for headline-grabbing large and dubious investments predates capitalism. They should not be in a position to impose their political will. State representatives could come from a variety of sources. A state planning agency is likely to be built out of the existing planning sections of corporations linked to a delivery backbone of a publicly owned banking system. So a banker on the enterprise board pushing government priorities is one option. At a district level it may be appropriate to have a local government representative to promote links between the town and enterprise, or at a lower level still, someone from the local tenants and residents' association.

The essence of the new structure is that the vested interests of the representatives would be clear, and that they would not be able to impose their will without winning over others who approached enterprise planning from a different perspective. A state planner sitting on a national industrial board may want to locate a new research centre or office in an area of high unemployment. Workers' representatives would want to know how that impacted on current staff, and the consumer representatives to be

199

convinced that it improved services. Decision-making would be challenging, transparent and like the minutes of the Monetary Policy Committee, out in the open.

Who are these consumer representatives? At one level it would build on the experience of what already exists with the Consumer's Association and the regulation bodies (2), but taken to a much higher level. To call it consumer representation is really a misnomer, as it conjures up an image of people who cannot see beyond the price and suction power of their vacuum cleaner. These should be people trained in the complex business of seeing that manufacturing and service industry are meeting our needs.

As we saw in the first chapter an increasing number of people over 50 are ceasing to work. The majority of this is involuntary. However it is unlikely that the numbers of people interested in part time work before or after sixty five will diminish. There is an enormous pool of accumulated experience to be tapped into. Departments in Universities could specialise in training people to be consumer representatives in particular industries. The Departments could become information points for everything related to that industry with consumer representatives accessing information on the web. Elected consumer associations for each sector would assign trained representatives, paid the same sort of expenses as local councillors (around £7,000 a year), to the national and local management boards of that industry. They would develop consultation systems with the consumer, come together to thrash out priorities, share ideas and develop interactive information points accessible in everyone's home. A sort of extended on-line 'Which' magazine that would give unbiased information.

Their job would be to make sure that new products and inventions were being taken up, that they were designed to meet the needs of all sections of society, that enterprises were not dropping behind what was on offer elsewhere or abusing their monopoly position and so on. This is surely not fanciful. The volunteers almost certainly exist, the information technology definitely does and they would cost little more than the salaries paid to existing directors.

Worker representatives play a vital role. They not only bring the interests of the workforce into decision making but also convey a fund of knowledge about how the enterprise works. The idea of putting workers in controlling positions is far from revolutionary. The government appointed Bullock commission in the '60s recommended that company boards be made up of one-third shareholder representatives and one-third worker representatives with the remainder to be agreed between both sides. Welcome though this reform might have been (the Wilson government ran a mile from it!), it would not have altered the capitalist mission of profit maximisation. In fact it highlighted the dual role of a worker representative. Would they be on the board to represent workers or to run the company? The conflict is softened under socialism but is not removed. Worker representatives could be elected through the trade union mechanism but they are on the board as management. There will still be a need for trade unions to protect their members from the company they in part control. Emerging from the hard school of Stalinism, when workers in Czechoslovakia began to democratise their enterprises in the Prague Spring of 1968, they made a point of separating the functions of trade union and works council representatives. Worker representatives of the future will do well to study their experience (3).

It is difficult to avoid presenting the three thirds formula as something that seemed to solve the world's problems just before the pub closed. Precisely

201

one of those 'clever ideas' that are so unhelpful in convincing people of the practicality of socialism. It seems such a common sense way to run things though – and not just businesses. Why should not council departments be overseen by boards of users (consumers) councillors (the state) and workers? It would increase understanding and awareness of needs. In some cases it is already happening. It is not a rigid prescription but shows a way in which the economy could be organised.

How could this system of management be implemented? On coming to power a socialist government would have to take into public ownership the major corporations and financial institutions – perhaps 150 companies in all, the number is not important, their economic weight is. When taking over the financial institutions all deposits, pensions, insurance policies etc. would be honoured and their return put on to a fixed rate rather than being dependent on the stock market. In the case of Britain this would, by proxy, bring the bulk of the major companies into majority public ownership (4). There **would** be cases where low-income individuals had savings in directly owned shares and guidelines could be established for fully compensating shareholders with interest bearing bonds up to a certain financial limit. However in general I see no moral imperative for compensating major individual shareholders.

The issue is in any case hardly a real one. If there were even a threat of a socialist government, most of these individuals would have sent their money abroad. The flight of capital abroad is of course a major concern, but then it is because this is likely to be happening in an economic crisis that we are advocating a socialist solution! Ultimately unless individuals follow their money abroad, and some will, there should be every chance of pulling it back.

Much of British manufacturing industry is now foreign owned and in sectors we would want under social control. If they are viable as independent enterprises they should be taken over. If not, they could be exchanged for British assets overseas or agreements could be reached on the way they should operate under foreign ownership. There should certainly be no political concession that foreign owned assets will not be touched.

Ownership is about politics, and the strength of the political movement, not technical difficulty. The ease of nationalisation has been shown on many occasions. On the weekend of the 30th September 1984 the Bank of England summoned nearly 200 bankers to the City. They announced the nationalisation of the failing secondary bank Johnson Matthey. They charged the bank £50m. for their trouble and organised £250m. support loans from the other banks. The nationalisation was completed ready for the bank to open its doors at 8-30am on the Monday morning. (5)

At a more fundamental level, at the beginning of the eighties the French Mitterrand government vastly extended state control of the banking sector with little opposition from a demoralised capitalist class. Thirty-nine banks were taken over, all with deposits of more than £1 billion francs. In the end the state controlled 75% of all issued credit and most of the rest was with mutual organisations that do not have shareholders. (6)

Having workers, consumers and state representatives on the boards of companies and ending the power of shareholders, does not equal socialism. It is a breaking point. The start of being able to do things in a different way, to look at what is socially required and not just what will maximise shareholder value. It must be stressed that the scale of the political movement needed to effect a change at the top, is also the guarantee that the entire system will be overhauled. You cannot make a revolution behind people's backs. Socialism is not about new faces around a boardroom table, or a legislative seizure of power. It is about breaking the inhuman power of capital and replacing it with an economy where people can treat each other as human beings and not as units of consumption. Only when the majority are motivated by such ideas, can something called socialism be brought into existence.

Democratisation of the economy is an end in itself, but it is also a means of achieving other goals – a decent minimum wage, universal child care, full employment, well funded welfare and pension systems, environmental protection, educational and cultural enjoyment, personal security, integrated communities and so on. Before addressing the critics of socialism we will first look at what making the break with capitalism might produce.

What can socialisation achieve?

One of the worst dictums rolling out of the Labour Party in the eighties was that management was everything and ownership nothing. As a rationalisation for the retreat from nationalisation it looked convincing. What a company did was important, not who owned it. Changing company behaviour was best achieved through watchdogs, regulation and consumer campaigns not through old style nationalisation.

The argument for socialisation is that it changes the **objectives** of the company. Inevitably a profit maximising company views regulation as interference and something to be avoided. Currently, if environmental legislation exists the question is not 'how do we best protect the environment?', but 'what is the least we can spend to conform to the legislation?'. However if people with a social interest (consumers and the state) dominate the power structures, they are there precisely to represent the general good and promote the welfare of the environment.

In these circumstances regulation and guidelines become a powerful tool rather than an irritant. When the government distributes funds for urban regeneration projects they define a maximum that can be used for administration (5%). Perhaps a similar system could be used for reducing bloated advertising budgets. A certain percentage of turnover would be the maximum allowed. If the blunt tool of government regulation was backed up or replaced by the voluntary maximisation of social benefit by enterprises themselves, all sorts of possibilities arise. Some regeneration projects in recent years have run a '1% for art' programme, whereby all grant aided construction work has to devote 1% of the budget towards the integration of art into the building. In Batley, West Yorkshire, for instance, this led to a boring crinkley-roofed business centre having a magnificent modern stain-glass window and an old mill boasting a 60 foot gable end mural.

At the moment company social contributions rely either on the quirks of senior management or the calculations of the public relations and marketing departments. Any stronger steers from government produce cries of 'uncompetitive restrictions' and 'state interference'. By moving social control from an external force to an internal one, you move from a system that achieves its objectives by bureaucratic stranglehold, to achieving them because that is what the company wants to do (and the system would work at a more fundamental level than wall murals). The change is of great significance. Far from increasing red tape, introducing legislation and policing it, the implementation system could afford to be much more open and fluid. The priorities and guidelines set nationally would have a good chance of being implemented at enterprise level because there would no longer be the conflict between the social interest and a board of directors charged with maximising profits. (7)

The economy envisaged here would operate within a form of slack planning (not to be misinterpreted!). Each sector of the economy would have its planning council, an expanded version of what appeared under the National Economic Development Council established by the '60s Labour government. As well as planners these would be staffed by representatives of enterprises from the sector. Within that structure, short and long term plans would be developed as to where the sector should be in the future, where it was now and what needed to be done to move from one to the other. Alternatives would be submitted to the government so democratic priorities could be set and the plan would want to be at least loosely co-ordinated at a European level. A central planning agency would be responsible for drawing sector plans together to make sure they were balanced over the economy as a whole. Most would agree that the establishment of a coherent national plan was possible. What you do with it is the difficult part.

In the past Labour largely crossed its fingers and hoped that everything would fall into place. Within a socialist economy the planners / state representatives would be expected to take targets that had been broken down to major enterprise level, back to their boards to seek implementation. It would not always happen. The consumer and worker board members may reject proposals. The removal of planning arrogance has to be a central plank in the democratic economy, but equally any rejection of planning targets should come from a general and not sectional concern. The closure of a factory for instance should not be blocked for the very legitimate reason that the workers want to hold on to their current jobs. Hence the insistence that large enterprises are socially and not worker managed.

So what would be the gains of such a planning system? An immediate start could be made on tackling almost all the dehumanising aspects of capitalism discussed in the first section of this book. Unemployment would probably not be a problem anymore (though the possibility of inflation would be). The reason is fairly straightforward. Economic growth under capitalism tends to be consumer led, with investment in new capacity following on after. This leads to the familiar feature of demand moving ahead too quickly for supply, with prices rising as a result. The government increases interest rates to slow the economy down, demand and investment fall and the economy moves into recession. A planned system opens up the possibility of reversing the relationship, investing in new capacity as a way of increasing demand. The plan can look at the likely demand pattern that would result from a 5% increase in living standards. Investment could then be made to meet that demand and by creating incomes in the process of that investment make sure the demand actually appears. This does not have to be a completely accurate process as long as general economic balance is maintained.

Productivity is poor in Britain. Output per worker is currently 36% less than in the US, 25% less than in France and 15% less than in Germany (8). The figures are worth a second look. Take the case of the US. Their productivity advantage drops to 26% when it is taken into account that they work longer hours and have fewer holidays. It drops again to 15% when you take into account the efficiency of machines (total factor productivity). In other words a large slice of poor British productivity is that workers have to use outdated inefficient machinery (9). A massive investment drive is required that governments are currently impotent to produce.

Such investment would be produced through the plan. The finance sector would be geared up to lend the money that could not be found within the enterprise. Business investment is about £100bn. a year. Ignoring the ability of the present banking system to find additional funds, even devoting 10% of pension and insurance funds to such purposes could comfortably increase that amount by 50%.

Of course, an economy cannot be thrown into fast forward without bottlenecks appearing. Shortage of labour and skills are the most obvious examples. Again a planned system would show tremendous advantages over the free market. There is no shortage of graduates in Britain, in fact in economic terms there is a problem of over education with a large percentage of graduates doing non-graduate level jobs (10). However there are shortages of specific skills (particularly in computing and technology) and in what might be termed personal and problem solving skills across the population as a whole. The latter needs to be tackled as part of general social and educational revolution, but for the specific skills there needs to be a sharp rise in in-house company training.

The capitalist firm is always likely to be niggardly about spending money on training because they do not want to lose workers to other firms after spending thousands of pounds on their training. In a socialised economy this is not an issue, as it is the general increase in the skill pool that is important. The only restriction is how much can be afforded (more of this later). The same line of argument applies to research and development. Outside of the industries that live or die by research (pharmaceuticals, computers etc.) the British record is poor, as noted previously, in part because research has no direct relation to increased profits.

With both skills training and research, academic institutions would move closer to enterprises and there would be a partial shift of costs from the state to the enterprise. It is a process already underway but whose growth is stunted by the profits system. Companies are only prepared to devote small resources to activities that are not directly profitable and educationalists are suspicious of their students being exploited for profit. Divisions between education and industry in terms of staff secondments and student placements could be blurred as large areas of technically based academia became devoted to addressing the satisfaction of need, working closely with the consumer organisations.

Labour shortages would be addressed by concentrating expansion in regions with job shortages. The carrots of government assistance that exist at the moment could be removed. The siting of new facilities is bound to be controversial, but the dispersal of many government offices from London to the regions showed it is possible to aim for geographical balance. Diffusion of growth would have the added advantage of relieving congestion and the need for green field development in the South East.

Surrounded by policies of capital, trade, price and wage organisation (below), a socialised economy stands much more chance of taking Britain towards the high skill, high investment, high wage full employment economy so longed for by Chancellors of the Exchequer. Such a change need not be environmentally damaging. Enterprises would be moved towards a circular rather than linear approach to production. In other words, instead of just considering the cheapest way of producing something and then not caring what happened once the product was sold, enterprises would be encouraged to operate to environmentally sensitive standards. They would use the minimum amount of materials and energy, make sure the product lasted as long as possible and was repairable, and look to recycling possibilities at the end of the product's life. Efforts would be made to make sure that any waste could be used as raw materials for other businesses. As a small example, the technology now exists to create high quality plastic mouldings from nearly all types of waste plastic. There is no need for it to go to landfill.

A traditionally successful economy is by no means the end of the possibilities of the socialised economy, but it is perhaps best to deploy further arguments to meet opposition from the critics.

The Case Against

Arguments against the socialised economy tend to be of four types. They claim that such a system would be:

➢ Against human nature
➢ Anti democratic and freedom threatening
➢ Inefficient
➢ Unaffordable and impossible to achieve.

The first two tend to be either mischievous objections or come from a one sided but understandable reading of history. The other two cannot be dismissed lightly and require detailed and practical refutation that will be discussed in the 'Networked Economy' below.

The transitional socialist society envisaged here is not an egalitarian one, it is just more egalitarian. The revolution will be in power relations, the scars of inequality that mark society will take years to eradicate. Money will still be one of the main incentives to get us out of bed and differentials may still be as large as between £12,000 and £100,000 a year. No one will be expected to function on altruism alone. Pay levels at the top end will be an entirely practical matter. You would not want to pull wages down to a level where highly skilled people decided to exit en masse and there will still be an element of paying the 'going rate'. The difference is that instead of the going rate being decided by the richest in society (fellow Board Directors), it will be decided by representatives of the enterprise and society as a whole

One thing is sure though, that as well as ridding us of obscenely large pay packages and establishing a decent minimum wage, the labour market would be shaken up to reflect the demand for the jobs. It has always been a feature of capitalism that executives will moan about how highly paid certain semi skilled jobs are, despite the fact that they would never dream of doing those jobs even if they could stay on their executive wage. If under full employment no one wanted to be night cleaners on the London underground but plenty of capable people wanted to be senior executives, then the wages of cleaners would rise relative to executives. It may well be that unskilled and unpleasant jobs come to be paid more than those requiring years of training. Graduates would always be welcome to apply!

Fear of loss of freedom, individualism and democratic rights comes from crucifying socialism on the cross of Soviet communism. The effects of the First World War, civil war and isolation quickly distorted the Russian revolution. Without defending every action of the revolutionary government, anti democratic measures and use of terror were deployed to ensure survival of the state, not create a socialist society. The choice was not between the Soviet state and a liberal democracy but the Soviet state and

White terror (the right wing opposition in the civil war). It does us well to remember the desperate circumstances of the time. Between 1917 and 1920 manufacturing fell to 13% of its 1913 level. The population of the cities collapsed; Petrograd lost 57% of its population and Moscow 44%, either through deaths from malnutrition related illnesses, or from people fleeing to the countryside in search of food. The 1921 drought brought 22 million southern Russians to a state of starvation (11).

This may be a contentious interpretation, requiring a detailed discussion beyond the scope of this book. However what can be generally agreed is that from the time Stalin came to power in 1924 and consolidated the power of the bureaucracy and the one party state, the spectre of totalitarianism has haunted the socialist movement. Regrettably the bulk of the left, communist influenced as it was, presented the failures of the revolution either as virtues or unfortunate incidentals in what was otherwise a successful march towards socialism. Stirred up by conservatives, there is still a residual suspicion that socialists have a hidden undemocratic agenda.

In reality, far from reducing democracy, socialism would extend democratic control over the majority of the economy. This contrasts with our ability every four years to vote for people who have very little control over what happens. There is no question of socialists defending a one party state, and a directly elected national assembly must continue to be part of any democratic system.

The Networked Economy

We must recognise two things. Firstly, productivity is important. It is how much each worker is able to produce that gives us our material standard of living (though not necessarily our level of happiness). If half of us still had to work on the land to produce the population's food, a great deal of other goods and services would not exist. Increasing productivity comes from human skill, investment in modern techniques, and the efficient use of resources (good management). Effective management is crucial to any form of economy.

Secondly, in situations where the whip of the market does not operate (and sometimes even when it does) it is easy for management to build empires and hierarchies, concentrate on internal systems rather than satisfying the customer and generally conspire to lower productivity by having people do useless things. Competition between enterprises, **or some equivalent external discipline**, is needed to keep this tendency in check.

Capitalist competition is cut-throat. If your rate of productivity is not rising faster than that of your rivals then over time you are likely to go under. The pressure to increase productivity eases under socialism. To be sure, it should carry on increasing, but output per worker and profitability are no longer the only measurements of success. Take agriculture again. The cash crop farms run by corporations in the developing world achieve impressive outputs per acre, but have they benefited the societies in which they exist? Large numbers of self sufficient, bio-diverse farmers have been driven from the land into poverty. Should a shop or factory that is wanted by a local community and is making a small profit be closed because it is not making as big a profit as elsewhere? Profit maximising logic would say yes. A preferable logic would be to consider local and social needs and work on meeting them in the most efficient way.

A free market critic would suggest that this is the sort of liberal-minded woolly thinking that leads to low productivity and state subsidies that have to be paid by the taxpayer. Not so. There is every hope that the components of productivity - investment in modern techniques, investment in skills training and in improving management - will improve at a faster rate under socialism. However, within the constraints of the market i.e. the demand from customers, local needs will be met. Clearly if a shop is making a loss because demand has fallen, decisions will have to be made about whether its importance is such that it should be subsidised. As a real example, this might be the case with village post offices.

The nature of competition will become blurred. Competition between small privately owned businesses and co-operatives will continue much as before but what of the socialised corporations? Planning structures would exist to cover each industry, but that would not necessarily mean that all companies would be grouped together in one large concern like the old nationalised industries. Competition can be useful. Different groups of people may start to do thing in different ways and avoid the abuse of monopoly. What will make a crucial difference is that commercial secrecy will be abolished. What use does a co-operative economy have for it? Management accounts, business plans, new designs would be placed on the internet. Enterprise board members, managers and workers alike would be able to compare or benchmark all areas of their performance against other enterprises in the sector. (12)

In a socialised economy this would serve the dual purpose of keeping managers on their toes as well as encouraging collaboration. The planning system would be entrusted with avoiding wasteful duplication. Under a shareholder economy, with company pitched against company, sharing and openness is difficult to achieve. Despite the growth in strategic alliances between companies in recent years, studies have suggested that the parties have concentrated or protecting their own returns from the joint activity rather than utilising it for continuous innovation and mutual benefit (13)

There should be little scepticism that such openness can be achieved in a socialised economy. Independent enterprises would be controlled by Boards where the majority were interested in collaboration (consumer and state representatives). The state of affairs that exists within the best of the multinationals would start to spread across the entire economy.

GKN, for instance, produces drive line units for cars in forty-seven factories around the world. All information used to be kept on a national basis but during the nineties they introduced systems of information sharing. The production process was broken down into six parts, each with an international committee responsible for introducing innovation. Staff secondments were introduced to transfer best practice and every year a thousand workers gather at a host plant to join workshops on production improvement techniques. These provide the personal contact that cements the continuous co-working over the internet. At the same time common information systems have been introduced to measure plant performance (overhead costs, machine utilisation, value added per worker etc.). Unsurprisingly, the company reports that at first the better plants wanted to hold on to their information and didn't want to share it, but that after several years a culture of reciprocity was established. (14)

A more unusual example of networking can be drawn from the Britain's car industry. Unusual because it involves collaboration across company boundaries. The reason it worked in the motor trade is that the major car manufacturers had a vested interest in improving the productivity of their suppliers and were prepared to collaborate to that end.

In 1998 with funding from the Department of Trade and Industry, the Society of Motor Manufacturers and Traders launched an Industry Forum. Eight master engineers led the programme from Honda, Nissan, Toyota, General Motors and Volkswagen. The team had a dual role. To go into companies to address productivity problems and to train 32 elite Industry Forum engineers to continue their work. Even allowing for exaggeration the results are impressive. Of the 190 projects tackled in the first two years, the average increase in output per worker was 30%. (15)

The dawning of the internet age and access to unlimited information has transformed our ability to create a planned **and** high productivity economy. Consider the new generation of online market places. The principle of their operation is simple. In the past large purchasing companies would have mixed reasons for ending up with certain suppliers – price, service, quality, location, friend of the manager, historical accident etc. Now all details of trade, price and specification will appear in one visible electronic marketplace. All the suppliers in the world will have to compete with each other.

Most estimates of business to business e-commerce suggest that the value of transactions will reach $1,000bn to $2,500bn globally by 2003. Analysts at Merrill Lynch estimate that about $400 - $500bn of this business will be conducted on exchanges. (16) Here an insider from Chematch, an electronic exchange for the chemical industry, describes how it works.

"The beauty of the new market places consists of the bounty of information they make available. Traditionally, data about transactions in the commodity chemicals industry was exchanged by telephone and fax. Industry telephone surveys were conducted sporadically and the findings published. Price discovery was very opaque.

Compare that with how Chematch operates, publishing details of trades on its market – their price, size and location – as soon as they are agreed. That transparency may be particularly useful for smaller companies that have traditionally not had access to the same pricing information as their larger brethren."

Recent developments in the car industry illustrate, in a small way, that the global scope and co-ordination requirements of large-scale industry are outgrowing the constraints of private ownership. In early 2000, Ford, General Motors and DaimlerChrysler came together to form their own electronic trade exchange that will handle their combined $200bn direct purchases a year. All suppliers will have to use the exchange and the effects of increased competition are likely to be dramatic. Goldman Sachs estimate that these on-line initiatives, partly by reducing staff numbers in purchasing departments, but mostly by putting the competitive squeeze on suppliers, will reduce the cost of a car on average by $1,065. In their most basic form these internet auction houses put tremendous pressure on suppliers and push the buyer towards countries with the lowest wages and few employment rights. However, in order to capture the goodwill of suppliers, exchanges are already moving towards a not-for-profit model run by the industry as a whole. As well as offering the buyer competitive prices, they offer the suppliers the ability to share resources and spare capacity. So it is that Transportal Network allows truckers to trade spare capacity that ensures they are not making return journeys empty. It also gives them the chance to pool their purchase of benefits, insurance and equipment, so gaining from bulk buying. (17)

The information contained in these exchanges, added to and open to everyone, would be a tremendous tool of industrial management in a socialist economy. Current suppliers need not be abandoned but would be expected to aim for the productivity levels achieved elsewhere. The buyer would work with the supplier to make the improvement. It could be argued that as capitalism is throwing up a growing number of examples of collaboration, socialisation was no longer necessary. The reverse is in fact the case. If the economy was not revealing the **need** for collaboration, the ideas in this book would remain an irrelevant abstraction. As it is, we can observe the new mode of production trying to burst out of the shell of the old, restrained by the need of capitalism to privatise knowledge and information in order to gain a profit advantage.

Some commentators feel that the private corporation is particularly unsuited to take advantage of the networked economy. A discussion paper produced for the Department of Trade and Industry in August 1999 considered various scenarios for the 'knowledge economy' through to 2015. While they foresaw a growth in the number of skilled, self employed contract workers, it was within an economy still dominated by corporations. As possession of knowledge increasingly equates to profits, corporations have to keep knowledge to themselves, not share it. The document saw as the main features of this future:

a) An economy built on the basis of stable, large corporations that have developed to protect and exploit the knowledge of their employees.
b) Concept, design and manufacture undertaken in a single organisation or within a group of companies, in an attempt to capture the full value of the production process
c) Large companies retaining dominance by protecting their brands, trade marks and intellectual property.

It is likely that only a socialised economy, with no interest in privatising knowledge, could fully take advantage of the state of comprehensive and universally accessible information that the internet offers. Knowledge and information products, unlike physical ones, do not deteriorate if they are used and passed on. The more they are shared the better the economy will function.

What is envisaged with socialisation is not so far from some capitalist realities. For twenty years the Japanese keiretsu system was praised for delivering the fastest growing economy in the world. The system brings companies and their suppliers together through interlocking directorships and a permanent relationship between them. The problem of the supplier is seen as the problem of the buyer and both are involved in its solution. Within a socialised economy all the enterprises within a certain sector could operate as a 'virtual keiretsu'. They would all be on the same information intranet, able to move in and out of project solving alliances and be able to learn from each other.

It is worth exploring a little further what competition comes to mean in these circumstances. For sake of argument take the brick manufacturing industry (a near monopoly anyway). It would be quite straight forward to organise the industry into one enterprise – the British Brick Company – with various production sites producing different types of brick, one head office, one research department and so on. It would probably work well. Overheads would be kept to a minimum, production and investment would be well co-ordinated and social ownership would ensure that standards were kept high and customer needs met. The tripartite board system in the brick industry would in all likelihood include representatives of building companies as board members to present the interests of users. There is always the problem though that monopoly can lead to a certain inertia – you are not going to lose any sales if you do not improve the quality of the bricks, so that complex improvement plan you were told to work up can wait until tomorrow. Capitalist corporations may have finely tuned, efficient internal processes that do not depend on market mechanisms, but part of the reason they remain efficient is there is usually another multinational waiting to put them out of business if they come off the boil.

Say then that the industry was split into three enterprises. Information is still shared and all send representatives to the industry planning board. The only difference from the above model is that they have independent management structures. Each of the enterprises wants to increase their income. However the consumer and state representatives that dominate their boards will not allow them to compete in the farcical way that the privatised electricity suppliers do, vying with each other to supply exactly the same product to the customer by dint of duplicated sales efforts and heavyweight marketing. The market for existing bricks will be carved up, probably on geographical lines. Where they will compete is in developing improvements that increase productivity or improve quality e.g. a brick with better insulation qualities or one that allows spray paint to be removed easily. If one of the enterprises started to produce basic bricks at a lower cost, or had a better delivery system, then all customers should be free to buy from them. It would be up to the directors and management of the other two enterprises to adopt the better systems.

But if all information is shared immediately with competitors what is the point in creating improved products? Presumably no sooner is the proto-type out than the other two companies will be producing it as well. First of all in an economy that is improvement driven and not profit driven this should not matter, but say it did appear to be a disincentive to creativity, an adaptation of the patent system could deal with the problem.

As the economy becomes more knowledge-based the functioning of the patent system under capitalism is called increasingly into question. At the moment you can patent anything that is 'useful, novel and non obvious', which means you can even patent ways of doing things, not just products. The attempt to patent information relating to the human genome brought the problem to the public's attention, when an American company tried to claim ownership to the knowledge of human DNA make-up. A patent should never prevent an idea being used by anyone. It should only guarantee an income to the creator (royalties), and knowledge itself should be unpatentable. So in the case above it may be that the creative brick company earns an income from the other two paying for the right to produce an improved brick.

Is it utopian to imagine that enterprises could compete and collaborate at the same time, share information and yet be part of different organisations? It certainly flies in the face of traditional economics. The argument is crucial to the superiority of socialisation over corporate competition. To give a clear answer we again have to look at the meaning of competition in a socialist economy.

The small business sector would compete much in the same way as it does now, particularly in the service sector. The size of the Yellow Pages is unlikely to shrink. At the other end, some industries should become natural monopolies (transport, water, energy supply, drug manufacture and so on) this time with democratic control and data banks open to everyone on the internet. In the middle you would have most of today's large corporations. In particular product areas, many of these are near monopolies in Britain already (think of the white goods industry – washing machines, fridges etc. How many British manufacturers are left?). Most of the competition is from abroad.

The challenge would be to improve the product and introduce new ones in response to the needs of the consumer (this applies to service as well as manufacturing industry). Creating separate competing enterprises may best do this, but information sharing would be a precondition. All society should be able to benefit from the raising of the level of technique and commercial secrecy limits that development. The output of research and development departments could be posted on the internet and be added to and adapted by academics, consumer groups, suppliers and other interested parties. Good ideas would be taken up by other enterprises and incorporated into different products. This is all gain.

Product monopolies would not be able to exploit their position by charging too high a price or offering an inefficient service because of foreign competition, open accounts and having enterprise directors charged with preventing the abuse of monopoly. There would also be the non-socialised small business sector ready to punish any failure to meet needs.

The advantages of open information systems do not end with product manufacture. If major retailers knew what each other were doing in advance (and they make great efforts to find out in any case) consumers might gain from greater variety as they sought to service different markets. Consumer groups could examine the internal accounts of financial service companies and give reasons as to why one was better than the other, and so on.

Of course ideas will be 'pinched' by foreign or even domestic enterprises, but in an economy where profit maximisation is no longer the objective, it really does not matter that much and could be handled by a revised patent system offering a right to royalties. As an indication of the latent pattern of development, Yale University in the US has established an electronic exchange for inventions (TechEx) and in the first three months of year 2000 logged four hundred inventions in search of licensees.

To grasp the nature of competition in a socialised economy is not easy. Management of a given enterprise may take the traditional view of capitalist competition, that they should be out there selling as much as they can at the biggest profit. Yet the majority of the Enterprise Boards (state and consumer representatives) are there to guarantee maximum social benefit from the industry. In essence they are from a single national organisation and have a vested interest in wanting universal access to new products and techniques, expanding provision and minimising the duplication of competition. The tension is a healthy one and there is no single way that it will be resolved. It is precisely putting up the 'efficiency' benefits of hard-nosed capitalism against the general social interest and arguing it out. An instructive example is currently being played out in the German power industry.

Unusually, German power stations are local municipal utilities (Stadtwerk). Many of the nine hundred plants are candidates for privatisation. The Stadtwerk tend to put an emphasis on providing benefits to the local economy and employing local people. Any surplus they make goes to subsidise loss-making public services like local transport. There is little doubt that the power stations could employ fewer workers and provide cheaper electricity if they were privatised, but the threat has unleashed numerous campaigns and a public debate around facts that are available to all (18). In a different form the debate anticipates the discussions that will be continuous within socialised industry – immediate product cost and price vs. broader social benefits. No one is promising that socialism will be straightforward!

Forms of organisation need to be dealt with pragmatically. Sometimes a democratically run monopoly will be appropriate, sometimes the form of competition described above. My intention has only been to show that a socialised economy would not face any crisis of inefficiency. Openness may not come naturally at first in a culture steeped in the traditions of commercial secrecy for two hundred years. However defenders of the status quo have an uphill struggle. They have to argue that knowledge that is instantly accessible and useable by all, should remain the private property of corporations for the sake of the dubious benefits of free market competition.

Effective Management

A final argument for the vigour of a socialist economy lies in improving management. By 'management' is meant the ability to organise resources effectively, not the individuals in the hierarchy. Almost everyone should be a manager of some sort. Throughout the nineties this has been the common sense of management theory. Books like Tom Peters 'Liberation Management' (1992) or Koch and Godden's 'Managing Without Management' (1996) considered traditional corporate management to be defunct. Instead of the self-serving hierarchies, companies should consist of small customer driven teams serviced by sophisticated IT systems providing them with information.

Koch and Godden, both business consultants, were fairly damning. Their book starts from the premise that managers generally, not just those at mid levels, subtract rather than add to the value of their organisations. Management, they argue, not only takes an increasing share of corporate wealth but add complexity to decision making and internal processes and have precious little to do with the customer.

For all their downsizing, delayering, re-engineering and empowering, big firms are little different from what they were 10, 20 or 30 years ago – just smaller in headcount. Nor have managers become any more productive than when Henry Mintzberg discovered in 1973 how they really spent their time (mostly in firefighting and being interrupted). A survey by Booz-Allen and Hamilton found that only 20% of senior executives' time was spent on external, non-organisational matters and of that only 5% went on direct customer contact. (19)

Koch and Godden may represent the para-military wing of management theorists, but it does not sound as though a socialised economy has much to beat. In Britain what has gone right has largely been imported from Japan in the form of the team ('kaizen') system. Ambi-Rad, the Birmingham heater manufacture employing 150 people, introduced a team system, making each of eight groups responsible for an aspect of production and producing suggestions for quality and efficiency improvements. Time and again this form of devolved management or workers' control has been seen to increase productivity, even though under present arrangements the fruits of your good idea might end up in senior executive bonuses or shareholder dividends. Despite this, the ideas of the Ambi-Rad workforce produced a £300,000 reduction in costs in the first year. (20)

Socialist management techniques are nothing to do with deciding everything by committee. The key principles are control at the most local level appropriate to the task, external collaboration and sharing the fruits of success. All forms of workers control could be used, without denying the need for management co-ordination and specialisation. Only on rare occasions does management suggest the thinning of management. It would be another advantage of active external and worker control that outsiders would regularly be brought in to see if enterprise management could be improved or was indeed necessary.

It is easy to envisage a representative of the Institute of Directors being called on to demolish the above arguments. They would suggest that the boards of socialised enterprises would be made up of interfering amateurs with confused objectives. The system of control would make it impossible for managers to manage. It has to be admitted that life for senior managers might become more complex. Instead of just maximising profits, targets might be set for environmental performance, local purchasing, community benefit etc. Some corporations have elements of these already. But boards, and their reflections at lower levels of the enterprise, are not there to manage. They exist to set objectives for the enterprise and it these that will be revolutionised in a transfer of power. This is not to deny the problems. There will be times when workers and management collude to protect the enterprise interest against the social interest. This is no different from senior executives leading Corporate Boards by the nose and withholding damaging information. Such possibilities highlight the need to take the socialisation process deeper into the enterprise than just Board level.

Tight financial control

A preoccupation of the critics of socialism is the 'soft budgeting' that would exist under such a regime. What they mean is that enterprises would always be able to borrow money from the banks at low interest, so would not bother sorting out their problems. They would merely borrow their way out of trouble. Bad debts would accumulate and one day someone would have to pay for them.

Since the Japanese economy moved into recession, it is an accusation levied at the keiretsu, and the South Korean equivalent, the chaebol. These conglomerates, with interlocking directorships between companies and banks, are reckoned to have been the cause of the build up of bad debt. When the companies were unable to afford to pay the interest on their loans, they borrowed more to cover the payments and then their borrowings were justified by hugely inflating the book value of their assets.

While this is all true, it has little bearing on the economy envisaged here. The Japanese and South Korean corporations were able to indulge in these corrupt practices because they were accountable to no one (the failure of corporate governance is universally recognised). The deals were done between a few people in secret. In a socialist economy, not only would the company be publicly owned but also the books would be open to inspection on the web. Banks would lend expecting a modest real rate of return and if an enterprise was unable to meet its payments an open intervention and discussion about what needed to be done would take place. Corruption and mismanagement are possible under any system, but the transparency of the commercial world with decisions out in the open, will offer tremendous protection against it.

Individual incentive

Economists, even left wing ones, raise a strange concern over socialist economics that they call the principal / agent problem. This is that if the boss of the company is not the same as the owner of the company, will they work as effectively? The argument is a valid one if we were suggesting that every enterprise should be socially owned. There are clearly budding entrepreneurs who will work all hours for their own small company who would not be prepared to do the same if they were answerable to a board. However wholesale social ownership is not suggested here. In our target for socialisation, the corporation, the chief executive is already answerable to a board and the shareholders (the owners). It only becomes a question of whether they work more effectively for £80,000 or ten times that amount. It is surely the case that once a person is on a very good salary, incentives to perform well are more the human ones of responding to respect and expectation than monetary reward. There may be many hopeless chief executives, but they are unlikely to be playing with paper clips all day. The reason for them being rewarded so handsomely has nothing to do with increasing efficiency and everything to do with corporate power brokers internationally seeing what they can get away with!

Related to this is the argument that management is likely to be weak because of political interference and investment decisions being taken at state level. Without wanting to dismiss inevitable tensions in the system, the position of the enterprise manager is unlikely to be any worse than if s/he was part of a corporate holding company. Political pressures will be evident, and rightly so, from the central planning agency, but those planners will sit as equal partners with consumer and worker representatives on enterprise boards when it comes to pursuing the implementation of investment plans.

Managers will not be at the beck and call of the state, nor will they have an amorphous bureaucracy to hide behind.

One last point on the efficiency or otherwise of socialism. A final comment is due on old time nationalisation. I did not seek to defend it earlier because it is not the ground on which supporters of a socialist economy should fight. However we need to be disavowed of the mythology that the private sector always does it better. Detailed comparative studies of nationalised industries and similar private ones, and of companies before and after privatisation, indicate, through a collection of mixed results, that overall the form of ownership had little impact on efficiency (a condemnation of how governments failed to exploit public ownership). In addition, over a 35 year period public ownership improved the performance of the UK mining, gas, electricity, water and transport industries relative to their private US counterparts. (21)

Socialism – affordable and practical

So to the last variant of criticism, that socialism is an unaffordable wish list that is practically unachievable. It is true, the list is long. Conditions need improving for millions of workers and non-workers alike, so how can it all be afforded?

The Thatcherites were always keen to remind us that you had to produce wealth before you could distribute it. While this ignores the possibility of reorganising **how** we produce wealth, the point can still be taken. The total amount of goods and services in the economy needs to be increased, especially the services that relate to our needs for care, health, fulfilment, interaction etc. At the same time we need to make sure that access to these goods and services is more evenly distributed than now, so it is not all about increasing government spending.

However taxes should remain the main source of funding for health, education and welfare, so government income needs to be increased. Estimates vary, but it is likely that some £40bn. additional spend could be made available through a combination of increased tax on those earning over £50,000, an effective inheritance tax, higher profits tax and cuts in defence spending. There is no shame in such 'tax and spend' policies that New Labour have conspired to turn into an insult. Increasing taxes on the well off is supported by a majority of the population and the country would no longer be seeking to attract multinationals in search of cheap landing points, so additional taxes could be taken out of profits rather than people's wages.

More significant than tax rises though is the effect of growth on government finances. Both the US and UK economies have shown the benefit of this during the '90s. An expanding economy means more people move into work and pay taxes, while the number claiming social security falls. While implementing modest increases in both taxation and spending throughout the period, the UK government's budget has swung from a £30bn deficit in 1993 to a £16bn surplus in 2001, based on an increase in gross domestic product of just under 3% a year.

It is very likely, with its ability to increase demand through useful investment, a socialist economy could grow at 4% a year or more until those who wanted to work had a job. If public expenditure rose by the same amount this would put about £16bn a year extra in government coffers on top of the £40bn identified above, which itself would swell with an expanding economy. (22)

In real life figures, this means that we could start with about £1,000 a year extra spending for every member of the population and build from there.

The fiscal virtues of the expanding economy are really only half the story though. There is a need for redistribution within corporations. Sums are impossible to do in advance since no one is likely to be keeping a tally of unnecessary expenditure. The aim would be to transfer resources from excess profits, large salaries, corporate expense accounts, advertising, unnecessary sales support and so on, to a decent minimum wage, additional company training, environmental protection and involvement with the community. Company accounts are not helpful on this score. Research work needs to be done by insiders to give an indication of what level of resources might be released for other uses.

Radical economic restructuring will produce income from interesting sources. Ninety five per cent of the new money produced in the advanced capitalist countries is created and put into circulation by the banks. They simply create the money and put it into customer's accounts as interest bearing, profit-making loans. This licence to print money gives UK banks additional profits of £21bn. a year. If the right to produce money reverted to the state, credited to the public expenditure account, it has been estimated that it would add £45bn. to revenues, the equivalent to 12p on income tax. (23)

There is no need to go into detail about economic instruments that might be deployed by a future socialist government. However it is important to recognise that careful economic management will be required to avoid inflation. With the political will to expand investment and the power to do it, the economy is likely to tend towards over demand. In such circumstances enterprises will have to be restrained from exploiting a situation of high demand by raising prices or agreeing to excessive wage demands.

Price and wage control policies have a predictable history under capitalism. The price controls hardly exist and the wage controls are put in to make sure that wages rise less fast than prices when inflation has taken off. For these reasons both under Labour at the end of the '70s (5% wage limit) and again a few years later under the Tories, the labour movement ended up in conflict with the government to maintain earnings. To be in favour of an incomes policy under socialism is somewhat different to being in favour of it under capitalism. One is designed to limit the level of increase in earnings to maintain economic balance, the other to cut real wages.

Guidelines would be set by the National Economic Assembly, or whatever the central representative body for economic planning was called, and would be policed by the state and consumer representatives who dominate the Boards. Implementation could remain flexible, the sole purpose of the directive would be to keep wages broadly in line with increases in productivity over the economy as a whole.

The same goes for prices. As we have witnessed in the privatised industries, the consumer watchdog bodies control prices quite effectively. BT for instance, had to operate on an inflation – x arrangement meaning that their prices rose by less than inflation each year. The consumer bodies could continue to undertake this function for key prices in the economy, backed up by a Prices Commission capable of undertaking detailed audits of prices suspected of being too high.

The economic mechanisms of socialism – a summary

To be worthy of support, the ideas of socialism must be firmly tied to present day realities. Socialists should be clear in their own minds on what criteria socialised corporations would function. Do they maximise sales?

Do they maximise profits under certain constraints? What are the incentives to innovate and how is poor performance disciplined? How do you balance the interests of consumers and producers?

To briefly rehearse how a socialised corporation might function. They will be reorganised around the products and services they provide – some will be structured to face competition from other enterprises, some will not. Most are likely to face competition from small companies. All will be compared to what exists internationally. Operating within the guidelines of the socialised board and what they have confirmed of the national plan, enterprises will seek to maximise sales and profits.

Innovation will tend to accelerate, not the opposite. True, we may lose the hysterical 'innovate or die' of capitalism with its obsession with the new and faddish, but socially productive innovation will improve because it is dependent on effective management (self management), collaboration, comparison and the fostering of new ventures. Behind these positive features, the long-term threat of competitive failure will remain if enterprises fail to update.

The same line of argument applies to the punishment of poor performance. Let us accept the future of an enterprise should not be guaranteed if it performs its job badly and its products are not wanted. But why should we suspect that a social enterprise would be incapable of responding to evidence of poor productivity? Operational details will be open to all and will be compared to similar enterprises at home and abroad. Far from having a vested interest in covering up the position, controlling bodies will want to expose and improve the performance. Managers will be put under pressure to sort things out. A system wide problem can only be anticipated if we adhere to the mistaken belief that a secure job inevitably produces a slack workforce. This was the position of the majority of workers in the most productive period in the history of capitalism, during the 1950s and 1960s!

If products and services are to be paid for, they should be provided on a market basis i.e. they should be freely purchased with the knowledge of alternatives, even if those alternatives are not available within national boundaries. The socialised economy will have private and co-operative enterprises as an insurance policy against management failure in large enterprises. In fast moving areas of the economy, lack of innovation will be punished in just the same way that Microsoft exploited the failings of the giant DEC and IBM corporations. However, the removal of profit maximisation as the sole enterprise objective, and the democratisation of industry in general, will allow progress towards a whole range of socially determined objectives. There will be many areas of tension. For instance, achieving a balance between consumer and producer interests is difficult. The balance has swung too far towards the dictatorship of the consumer over our conditions as workers, but how far should it swing back? This will be one among many critical discussions.

Socialism may be a practical proposition once you reach it, but is the journey navigable? There are of course problems. As already touched on, closing down the City of London as a financial centre has repercussions for jobs and export earnings in the short term. However, the glib assertion that globalisation has made the ideas of socialism untenable has to be treated with a degree of contempt. International companies are not buildings, machinery or human skills but systems of organisation that can be tackled if governments have the political will to do so. More at issue is how a country like Britain, locked into international trade, would survive if it went socialist?

CURRENCY AND TRADE CONTROL

The achievement of free movement of goods, services and capital around the globe is a defining goal of globalisation. In a world of free movement, the first country to break from capitalism can expect runs on its currency, balance of payments crises and attempts to block strategic imports. Speculators would move their money abroad and, without counter measures, planned increases in demand would suck in imports. Steps will have to be taken to control both trade and currency movements.

Importing more than you export is of concern even when there are no currency speculators. It means that wealth is leaking away from an area and is as true for a town or region as it is for a country. For economic health, a good deal of purchasing power needs to circulate in one place, creating jobs as the money moves from person to person (the multiplier effect). Purchasing power is lost if it goes on imports from somewhere else. The balance of payments for Liverpool would almost certainly show that it imported more than it exported. Too little money spent by Liverpudlians is going to sustaining jobs in the city, while not enough goods and services produced in Liverpool are being purchased by outsiders.

Before outlining what might be done, it is worth examining the case for free trade. The supporting theory is appealingly simple. The law of 'comparative advantage' tells us that if two countries are good at producing different things then it is to the advantage of both them to trade. Concentrating resources where production is most efficient will increase the total sum of wealth. Further, the increased competition that results from free trade will make sure that all producers are under pressure to be efficient. Differences between rich and poor are not a problem because every country will be good at producing something, even if it is only cheap labour - in this case, making the country an attractive destination for foreign capital.

As with all economic theories, those supporting free trade are only concerned with world growth rates and completely ignore other human needs. People are merely transferable resources. As he so often did, Keynes provided a clear rebuttal:

"If it were true that we should be a little richer, provided that the whole country and all the workers in it were to specialise in half a dozen mass produced products, each individual doing nothing and having no hopes of doing anything except one minute, unskilled, repetitive act all his life long, should we all cry out for the immediate destruction of the endless variety of trades, crafts and employments which stand in the way of the glorious attainment of this maximum degree of specialised cheapness? Of course we should not." (1)

To this could be added that free trade theories take no account of the environment, preservation of local culture, maintaining local communities or local sovereignty. For little overall economic gain, free trade unleashes a system of winners and losers, and is likely to result in the destruction of communities and loss of local control to corporate decision makers. Participating governments are not allowed to protect or assist local industries and communities are victim to closure and relocation. This can be observed from recent trade agreements.

The North American Free Trade Agreement was implemented in 1994. It created the largest single free trade area in the world between Mexico, Canada and the US (360m. people). In a phased approach over 10-15 years, the intention is to remove all tariffs and subsidies, plus restrictions on capital movement and investment. The effects on Canada do not look promising (though hidden by the extraordinary growth of the US economy during the 1990s). A large survey of Canadian firms at the outset found that 60-70% had intentions of shifting to the US or Mexico because of cost advantage. Canada's labour costs are 40% higher than the US, 154% higher when welfare costs are included. US social spending relative to GDP is now about the same as South Korea and Brazil (2).

Nor are the gains accruing to Mexico as large as might be expected. Certainly there has been considerable investment in the country from US corporations relocating their manufacturing facilities, but the movement does not appear to be closing the wealth gap as the free trade theorists tell us it should. With the latest machinery and management techniques, Mexican manufacturing productivity is often 80-100% of its US equivalent and yet wages remain at one tenth of the US level, and have not risen since the 1960s (3).

So what of the benefits of the movement towards free trade? The dramatic rise in world trade since the Second World War clearly had wealth creating benefits. It would be absurdly inefficient to encourage every country to be self-sufficient in all its needs (remember Enver Hoxha's Albania). However the growth in trade was only partly related to the removal of tariff barriers (a charge on imports) and elimination of capital controls. It was as much a matter of large corporations becoming world players.

The reduction of barriers has been achieved through a series of 'Rounds'. The last successfully completed one was the Uruguay Round. One hundred and thirty four countries signed up to it in 1993 after 7 years of negotiation. It contains an appendix of 26,000 pages listing what the countries had agreed to. It was heralded as a breakthrough in eliminating restrictions on imports. Countries would have to reduce both import duties and requirements that imports reach a certain quality standard (non-trade barriers).

Even the authors of the agreement recognised that there would be losers and that they would be concentrated amongst the poorest countries (4), but the anticipated gains were also exceptionally modest. One study estimated that over the first ten years, the direct benefits of the Uruguay Round would add between 0.2% and 1.3% to world growth, "within a rounding error" as the authors commented (5).

Trade may be a good thing, even if freighting things around the world is always going to be environmentally questionable, but we should not be intimidated by free trade theorists who claim a barrier-free world is essential for our economic well being. Interestingly, the loose-cannon Keynesian economist Paul Krugman once calculated that if overall demand was maintained but world trade fell by 50% it would only cause a 2.5% drop in living standards. This is because living standards are determined primarily by domestic productivity, not trade. Most trade consists of only slightly different items going between countries. Major efficiency loss would only be in industries like aircraft manufacture that need a global market. (6)

Free trade means greater incomes for the better-off who can buy the imports, and no income for those made redundant in the restructuring. Far from leading to benign growth in all countries, free capital movements ensure that multinational investment is directed to a few favoured locations. In exchange for a marginal increase in world growth, free trade again reinforces the tendency to increase inequalities within and between countries.

To reject free trade is not to advocate a siege economy. Socialism in one country never was, and is ever less, a viable strategy. The future of the first socialist country will be determined by how quickly the revolution can be exported, in Britain's case, at least to a European level. Survival is possible, but no such economic system can thrive, surrounded by antagonistic free market countries (witness Cuba). The double-headed difficulty of how you break free of globalisation and, at the same time, internationalise the social economy, probably gives rise to more scepticism about the prospects for socialism than anything else. It is a fear fed by political isolation. With so few adherents internationally, a call for world socialism inevitably has the ring of hopeless fanaticism. Objectively though, the increasing economic integration of the world makes the appeal less utopian than in the past. The chances of political isolation of a single country, as occurred with the Russian revolution, is far less in our economically linked and communication rich world. It does, of course, require a leap of faith and imagination to foresee millions of activists worldwide pushing for the transfer of power. Perhaps we should take comfort from Trotsky's reminiscences of the Zimmerwald conference of the socialist international in 1915:

"The delegates, filling four stage coaches, set off for the Swiss mountains. The passers-by looked on curiously at the strange procession. The delegates themselves joked about the fact that half a century after the founding of the first International, it was still possible to seat all the internationalists in four coaches. But they were not sceptical. The thread of history often breaks – then a new knot must be tied." (7)

Three years later, the internationalists were not treated as such a joke as revolution blew across Europe. Such an historical comparison may be glib. It would be wrong to belittle the political mountain that has to be climbed, but at the same time economic realities must always be differentiated from the mass psychology of the moment. In certain conditions, popular moods can change rapidly and in such an interconnected world, politics easily crosses national boundaries. In a climate of political ferment, European governments would be extremely unlikely to refuse to sell goods to a neighbouring state that underwent a revolution, for fear of invoking sympathetic action in their own country. Military intervention by the US would be even more unlikely. After all, forty years on, Cuba still exists! The possibilities of socialist advance will be revisited in the last chapter. In the meantime, let us return to how international trade relations **should** be organised.

Britain has everything to gain from economic co-operation and integration with Europe, but European Union rules could not be allowed to halt the socialist transformation of the economy. The political battle would be to create a socialist federation of Europe and beyond.

In a socialist Britain, the intention would not be to reduce imports but control their rate of growth to avoid a balance of payments problem. The method of achieving this would be to make sure that socialised companies purchased locally whenever possible to create wealth in the regions and minimise environmental costs.

Studies of multinational companies in Britain during the nineties have shown that, on average, less than 20% of their three main categories of input purchases were bought within the region they were based and less than 45% within the UK (8). Given that the purchasing power represented in these figures would create thirty additional jobs for every hundred directly employed by the company, this would be a very effective way of redirecting wealth and avoiding pulling in imports.

The problem is that these international purchases, while in part due to company policies and purchasing arrangements, are increasingly a result of the product not being available in the UK as de-industrialisation continues apace. Socialised companies would have to be encouraged to form links with suppliers and, once again, help them to rebuild their productive capacity. In all likelihood there would be a small cost disadvantage to purchasing locally at first, but, as already discussed, suppliers would be benchmarked against the best and be expected to improve performance over time.

Trade problems could probably be kept in check by the activities of socialised enterprises without imposing restrictions on consumer imports, though the right to impose duty on luxury imports would have to remain part of the reserve economic armoury. The same could not be said of capital movements and currency speculation. Speculation could be stopped internally through public ownership of the finance industry and major corporations, but further measures would be needed to insulate the economy from international attack.

The technical feasibility of such measures is not in doubt. As already noted, Malaysia effectively detached itself from the international finance system in '98 with no calamitous economic results. Foreign currency needed for trade had to be obtained through the government. Similarly, the giant Chinese economy, though now on the road to liberalisation, operates behind capital and currency controls.

There is nothing like exchange controls to give free market commentators apoplexy. This was the reaction of Forbes Global to the imposition of controls in Malaysia:

"In the real world, exchange controls restrict both capital movements and the currency trading necessary for trade flows. Once exchange controls are in place, governments can dictate to citizens that they must spend and invest their wealth at home. Capital controls also gives politicians a free licence to destroy their citizens' wealth by debasing their currency and procrastinating on tough but necessary reforms. Malaysian Prime Minister Mohammed Mahathir has just imposed exchange controls. Foreign investors in Malaysia have been expropriated and the Malaysians will bear the cost of their distrust for years."

For this commentator, the prospect of politicians destroying citizens' wealth was clearly worse than the reality of speculators already having done it! What is being defended here does not concern us. Of course, currency should be made available for trade and personal use. Countries with excess savings should also lend them to countries who are short of savings to use for investment purposes, but a socialist government would not recognise the 'right' of rich individuals, corporations or financial institutions to speculate with short-term investments. The taxing of short term 'hot money' would alleviate the problem but would be difficult to administer. Speculators are best removed at source.

Exchange controls are not desirable. They are bureaucratic and inflexible. Controls might have to be used in a transitional period, but the end point should be a common currency for a socialist federation, with exchange controls only existing against those beyond the federation. A common currency is both predictable and convenient.

The downside to a common currency is that it hides problems. The poor south of Italy cannot devalue its currency to make it more competitive with the north of the country. However the importance of being able to devalue the currency is often overrated. It does little more than gain a breathing space. Unless the productivity of the currency area improves the problems will just re-emerge in another form – probably inflation. The problems of southern Italy, or Cornwall for that matter, are better tackled through investment and training being channelled into the area, as would be possible under a planned economic system.

Various workable currency options exist. There could be a common trading currency while retaining local currencies, or alternatively there could be something like the Euro, with a layer of local currencies underneath it, as was discussed in the chapter on green economics. There is no contradiction between aspiring to some sort of common currency as a vehicle for international co-operation, and opposition to the establishment of the Euro. The Euro, as envisaged, is part of the free market European project, tying all countries down to the rules of unrestricted competition. Political resistance to that project is widespread and opposition to the Euro has to be evaluated in that context.

The intention here is not to draft the details of new currency arrangements. The point to be made is that a nation state need not lie victim to trade and currency movements as it moves to reorganise the economy. There are measures it can take to protect itself and systems it can advocate as ways of co-operating and combining with like-minded countries. Globalisation is no excuse for abandoning a programme of economic change.

If the socialisation of major industry and finance is carried through and steps taken to both protect and export the revolution, what would the economy look like below the commanding heights? One feature is likely to be the growth of co-operatives.

CO-OPERATIVES

Worker-controlled and user-controlled co-operatives will form an essential part of a democratic economy. A large enterprise or industrial sector should not be run as a co-operative because co-ops represent their members' interests not those of society as a whole (though arguably, a social enterprise could be called a stakeholder co-op). Below the socialised sector though, the presence of co-operatives should be as pervasive as possible.

Co-operatives have something of an image problem in Britain. In the popular mind they can often be associated with either a great movement of the past that has quietly faded away ("I can still remember my mother's divi number"), or, alternatively, are seen as the chosen form of organisation for politically conscious life-stylers. At least that was the case until the nineties when Britain's only large co-op, the Co-operative Wholesale Society (now the Co-operative Group), began to turn itself around. Beyond the Co-operative Group and the smaller consumer societies that chiefly run shops, co-operative enterprise does not form a significant sector in Britain. There are about 1,500 worker co-ops accounting for an estimated 15,000 jobs (1). Globally though, the movement is still vigorous, with some 700 million co-operators in 100 countries.

Co-operatives can contribute to social and economic progress in three ways. By being owned by their members, normally on a one-member one-vote basis, they can:

a) increase the control of workers and consumers over their workplace, suppliers and facilities.

b) use capital more efficiently, not having to pay shareholders a dividend

a) by the nature of their organisation and value system, operate in a different way to a privately owned firm.

It is of course true, that co-operatives cannot be an island of socialism in a sea of capitalism, but even in head-to-head competition with corporations, we can see the social benefits of co-operative business practice. The history of the Co-operative Group is instructive on this score. First though some co-operative theory.

Little work has been done in Britain on comparing the performance of employee owned firms relative to their private competitors. However "one of the few pieces of research, into the profitability of John Lewis in the 1980s (not a co-op but an employee owned trust – CH), suggested the department store group was at least as competitive as its competitors, if not more so" (2)

Lack of research is not the problem in the USA, where "studies consistently show that when broad employee ownership is combined with a highly participative management style, companies perform much better than they would otherwise be expected to. Neither ownership or participation accomplishes these significant gains on their own." (3) This is an important point. A co-operative of five people operating a one-member-one-vote system is easy to understand. They work collectively, each member has a high degree of influence over the company and no one exploits anyone else. The structure is not so clear if there are 500 staff.

Employees can own 51% of a company and everything remain the same. Their ownership becomes merely a way of distributing benefits via shares.

In the US, active workers' control can be written out of employee ownership agreements, maintaining the right of managers to managers. Even when worker control is written into the constitution, it can remain a dead letter unless there is a co-operative culture.

Employee share ownership plans (ESOPs) are big business in the US. An ESOP is essentially a trust that is allowed to borrow money to purchase shares, repaying the loan from company profits in following years. About half the ESOPs in private companies are used to buy out the owner. There are over 10,000 of them involving 9 million workers, and 2,500 of these companies are now fully employee owned. Yet because the culture often does not change, neither does the practice of the company.

There is tremendous scope for increasing the number of co-ops in the small business sector in Britain, but this would have to be combined with support to develop new management techniques in any enterprise too large to operate 'total democracy'. Perhaps the major source of future co-operatives would be from family businesses. At present, only 24% of family businesses survive to the second generation. An amazing 30,000 private companies across Europe fold each year because they fail to successfully transfer ownership (4). In a socialist economy, ESOP-type trust funds would be promoted to enable businesses to be passed on to their workers. Employees would also be given the right to exercise that option if the business was faced with closure. In addition, the tax regime could be altered to favour co-operatives (at the moment it does the opposite), and national advice and training systems provided.

The US has shown the growth potential for transforming private firms into employee owned ones, but the situation of just giving workers shares that can later be sold would have to be avoided. In many cases, it has led to reversion to private ownership. One of the key co-operative principles coming down from the Rochdale Pioneers, who started it all back in 1844, is that a co-op should be no one's to sell. Its assets should only be passed on to another co-op. Any tax breaks etc. given to private owners for selling to the workforce would have to be on condition that a co-operative structure was adopted.

So what advantage does a co-operative bring over and above the benefits of workers' control? Well, co-ops are not just about people as workers, they cover every facet of social life; how we organise ourselves as consumers (group purchasing), as residents (housing co-ops), as savers and borrowers (credit unions), as sellers (agricultural co-ops). In every case, their content is socialist. They put the membership in control, cutting out the profiteer and representative of authority. By means of involving members in the running of the organisations, they are also more likely to spread much needed self-confidence and skills throughout the population than their private counterparts. As the product of collective effort not primarily motivated by profit, co-ops invariably have a more concerned and caring approach to people and the environment. An example of what a co-operative can achieve is best drawn from another country, where they exist on a larger scale.

The Seikatsu Consumers Club Co-op in Japan is an organisation of housewives formed in 1965 and now serving over 230,000 households. It began when a single Tokyo housewife organised 200 women to buy 300 bottles of milk in order to reduce the price. The Co-op operates on two basic principles: one is democratic autonomous management encouraging all members to participate, and the other is to maintain a close relationship between members and producers.

With an advance ordering and joint buying system, Seikatsu members are able to plan their consuming life and provide sustainability to producers. The co-op is dedicated to the environment, empowerment of women and improvement of workers' conditions. They refuse to handle products detrimental to the environment or human health and they oppose wasteful lifestyles. They procure quality produce by signing contracts with local farmers to ensure produce is safe to eat. The co-op buys the produce in exchange for a guarantee that only organic fertilisers and the fewest possible chemicals will be used. When they cannot find products of adequate quality, they will consider producing it themselves, as they have done with milk and natural soaps.

With the growth in female participation in Japan's workforce, Seikatsu has set up women's workers' collectives to undertake both distribution and other service enterprises, including recycling, health, education, food preparation, child care and a not-for-profit insurance company. Presently, there are more than 200 organisations and 8,000 workers.

The co-op is organised in 'hans' (a local unit averaging about 8 people). Each hans elects a representative to its Branch (consisting of between 50 and 100 hans), which in turn develops its own agenda and sends representatives to a General Assembly to set policy and elect Seikatsu's Board of Directors. 95% of the co-op members are women.

The fundamental principles of Seikatsu are:

1) Create a new lifestyle in order to protect the environment and health. Stop passive and resource wasteful lifestyles based on commercialisation.

2) Abolish differentials and discrimination, realising that prosperity based on the sacrifice of others should not be forgiven.
3) Establish the autonomy of people through the daily activities of collective purchase.
4) Enable women, who are the majority of members, to be independent. (5)

But isn't this precisely the sort of lifestylist endeavour that confines co-ops to the margins, even if the margins are sometimes big ones? Will not the majority want to carry on consuming as much as possible, including cheap well-marketed food? Much of the cynic's case has to be conceded. In a capitalist society, it is very difficult for co-ops to service a mass market in competition with major corporations. These corporations are good at ignoring ethics and driving down costs. In the short term, pouring chemicals on the land, despite the long-term damage it may do, increases yields per acre. We can enjoy buying our pack of 99p Kenyan green beans because the farmer has only been paid 4p for them and so on. Some costs would increase in a socialist society to pay for better wages, adopt environmentally sustainable techniques and the like, but it should be possible to maintain and improve the standard of living for the vast majority despite this reallocation.

Another reason co-ops struggle to flourish in a free market economy is that workers with skills will tend to leave for the better wages in the private sector. While co-ops are able to adopt familiar management hierarchies, underneath a democratically elected board of directors, they are more egalitarian than their private counterparts. As we have already witnessed, the free market tends to reward those who have, while further squeezing those with nothing.

The Co-operative Group does serve a mass market. It has more than 1,200 stores and supermarkets, the Co-op Bank, CIS insurance, farms (80,000 acres), dairies, funeral parlours, motor traders, travel agents, opticians and most recently a wind farm! In many ways the Co-operative Group shows just how little room for social manoeuvre there is under capitalism - when you live amongst wolves, you cry like a wolf. Wages for the staff are similar to other large retailers and what they sell appears much the same. At the same time, we can see how the business **would** operate differently in an economy that was, in the majority, socialised. Scott Bader for instance, is a British manufacturing co-op (resins and polymers, not wholemeal pasties) with a Quaker history and a turnover of £100m. Its statutes dictate that at least sixty per cent of profits must be reinvested in the business and five per cent should be donated to charity or a community use of the employees' choosing. In fact in the last financial year it gave over eight per cent to charity (6). Such internally determined business principles could become the norm within a social economy.

The 1950s through to the mid 1990s were a disaster for the UK consumer co-ops. The number of shops fell from 30,000 to 4,600 and their share of retail trade from 11 to 4% (7). Co-operative societies collapsed into each other and management seemed to have no clear answer as to where the co-op was heading. Then in the early nineties, the democratically constituted board of CWS, now easily the dominant force in the sector, appointed a Chief Executive prepared to launch a co-operative assault on corporate competitors. The results have not been revolutionary, but are worthy of note (8):

➢ The Co-op bank adopted an ethical investment policy and marketed itself as the socially conscious bank. The trebling of profits that resulted from tapping this niche market led to a renewed investment drive by the Co-operative Group as a whole, increasing capital expenditure from £66m. in 1994 to £157m. in 1997 (recent figures are not comparable due to the merger with the Co-operative Retail Society). In 2000 4% of the bank's profits went to community causes.

➢ Stores are being acquired and refurbished. Unlike most chains, the Co-op will open stores in poor areas.

➢ They have led the way on matters of clear labelling of food contents, 'freedom food' that avoids animal cruelty, the banning of GM foods, and the introduction of fair traded goods that give improved guaranteed payments to the grower.

In May 2000, the Co-operative Group published a document called 'Food Crimes', produced after an extensive consumer survey of concerns about food. It illustrates the contradictory position of a co-op in the free market, both being against and yet a part of the system. It is worth a closer look. (9)

The seven food crimes are identified as (and note the language. This is a business and not a campaigning organisation):

1) The insidious targeting of the public by global big business putting huge marketing muscle behind products that fail to fit in with healthy eating advice.
2) The unnecessary use of chemicals on land and in livestock – interference with nature's way
3) The disregard of animal rights to keep costs down, or even worse, to pamper our taste buds with so-called luxuries.

4) The destruction of the planet by the intensification of food production systems.

5) The practice of permitting animals to be fed with the remains of their own species or herbivores with animal by-products or giving animals feed made from the blood of other animals

6) The careless exploitation of countries, cultures and creeds by multinational concerns milking the so-called global economy.

7) The deliberate assault on the taste and appearance of food.

The document goes on to say what should be done and then the CWS puts its own position:

"As a consumer owned business run for its members, the Co-op cannot ignore the overwhelming sense of unease among shoppers on these issues. We recognise the implications are potentially enormous for agriculture and the food chain as well as governments and the scientific community. There are powerful vested interests for maintaining the status quo.

The challenge looks awesome, but the Co-op is committed to an inquiry within the industry. Where evidence emerges, it will respond to these concerns with specific initiatives involving its own products and policies. Giving power back to the consumer will not happen overnight. It requires co-operation from all parties".

The Co-op wants to change things, yet is party to many of the problems. It cannot move first because it is part of the competitive system. The 'crimes' have to be dealt with at an economy-wide and global level. I have dwelt on this example because there is a strand of left thinking that thinks that co-operatives are the complete solution and distances itself from any notion of the planned economy, however loose. As self-contained enterprises, co-operatives will always be part of a market system competing to maximise income. The case of food shows the need for social planning and socially controlled big business. The only alternative is to impose endless government investment instructions, regulations and inspectors on individual enterprises.

We cannot leave consideration of the role of co-ops without a look at Mondragon, the much-studied co-op in the Basque country of Spain. It is an interesting question, beyond the scope of this book, why Mondragon appears to be so much out on its own as a symbol of commercial co-operative success, but if proof were needed that co-operative organisation is not inimical to high productivity and economic growth, this is it. The lessons that can be learned are as relevant to how major social enterprises could be run, just as much as small co-ops, because of the size to which Mondragon has grown. (10)

The Mondragon network was founded by a Catholic priest, Don Jose Maria Arizmendi, a man who narrowly missed being put to death by Franco as a result of his participation in the Spanish Civil War on the republican side. With the help of collections from the citizens of Mondragon, he founded an elementary technical school in 1943. The first graduates numbered amongst them five men who, in 1956, founded a small worker-owned and managed factory named ULGOR with 24 members. They manufactured a copied kerosene stove.

At the end of 1999 the co-op employed 46,000 people in 120 companies covering industrial production, finance, retail, training and research. They are the eighth largest company in Spain. The growth has been exponential:

| | in billions of pesetas | | | |
	'74	'84	'94	'99
Industrial Group sales	16	93	227	360
Retail and distribution sales	1	28	268	594
Funds administered by Financial Group	11	119	456	1,059

While these figures have not been adjusted for inflation (a little higher than Britain's over the period) the expansion remains remarkable and in the Industrial Group about 60% of the sales are now international.

The Co-op grows by continually incubating new firms as well as increasing sales. They have made it a rule that no co-op under the Mondragon umbrella can be bigger than 500 employees because of the negative effect that has on workers' democracy. New start businesses can be proposed by existing members or by outsiders. The bank then has a special unit that will not just lend them money on flexible terms but will be involved at all stages of business planning and implementation. A whole infrastructure of support has been built up – a university, technical college, a research and training centre as well as the bank. In Britain some 80% of start up firms fold in the first five years. Mondragon has had just two failures in its entire existence. The funds created by these new co-ops then have to be deposited with the bank to be lent out for further economic development.

To be part of a co-op a member must pay a large membership fee, up to a year's salary into his or her own employee account. If necessary they can borrow the amount from the bank. Each year approximately 70% of profits will be put into workers' accounts and then be borrowed back by the co-op at a rate of interest decided by the workers. The account will be closed when the worker leaves the firm or retires and they will be paid 75% of the amount of profit that has been placed in the account plus the interest. In 1995 across the co-op as a whole, the average account was worth £43,000. For workers with long service, it was much more.

The system has two benefits. The co-op has no shareholders and can use all the profits it makes for reinvestment by borrowing from its own workforce at a reasonable rate of interest (a proportion of profits are always set aside for community use). In addition workers have a good pension and have a vested interest in the long term success of the company.

Each of the 120 co-ops is organised on the same one-member one-vote lines. An annual General Assembly of all workers elects a General Council who appoint management on four year contracts. Once appointed, management are given a fairly free hand, although there are consultative bodies and workers have the right to convene a General Assembly that can exercise its supreme power. Each General Council then sends delegates to the 350-strong Mondragon Co-operative Congress that acts as an advisory, not a ruling body over the group.

It is right to be enthusiastic about the structures of the co-op and the dynamic and supportive economic environment they produce. At the same time, we must not to lose sight of the CWS type problems of existing in a capitalist environment.

➤ Wage differentials that, for years, were kept to a maximum of 1:4.5 have been widened so that managers can be paid more.
➤ There is an increasing tendency to employ contract workers (up to 30% of the total) who do not become co-op members and are given the worst jobs.

> Although the record is a good one, workers' pensions are largely based on profits that can go down as well as up.
> The international divisions of the co-op that are being established do not operate as co-ops
> The company is not particularly environmentally conscious, nor does it make a point of sourcing its inputs locally.

Other problems will potentially exist in a socialist society. Although the formal structures of democracy are very good and workers receive plenty of information, they are not given the time to consider plans and work up alternatives. The battle for real rather than constitutional workers' control continually needs to be fought and some works time needs to be allowed for participation (11). Further, at the central Co-operative Congress level, representatives are overwhelmingly from management, not the shopfloor, creating something of a class divide. Tensions between productivity and human needs are also not abolished. Should expensive machinery be worked twenty-four hours a day, despite the damage to workers' social life?

All this said, Mondragon represents a significant step forward for human economic organisation. It stands as a beacon of denial to the 'no alternative' school of business theorists. In a less competitive and more egalitarian society there will be plenty of room for co-ops. They will be part of the way the new society is created.

PRIVATE ENTERPRISE

It is hard for socialists to fully embrace the world of small businesses. It would be economic nonsense and political death to promise to bring them into public ownership, but they are the collecting point for the worst pay and conditions and naked exploitation that exists under capitalism (1). Even so, I believe we have to offer far more serious support to the private entrepreneur than the Tories ever do, but only on condition that a whole raft of workers rights are adhered to.

Small business is needed not so much for its innovative potential, but for its flexibility - particularly its ability to adapt services to customer need. A supportive approach to private enterprise (as opposed to corporate enterprise) is politically needed because the right to get out there and have a go, however many of us actually do it, is now deeply ingrained in the culture of capitalist societies. Some socialists would argue that there should be no right to employ anyone - that as soon as you move beyond self-employment, all enterprises should be either co-operatives or publicly owned. The objection to this is as much on practical as principled grounds. No government would surely **force** the employees of small businesses to take them over. They may not want to. In any case, unable to employ people, would-be employers would continue to run their business with spuriously self-employed workers, as often happens now.

There is also the more serious point, that as long as the enjoyment of being your own boss and making money by your own efforts exists, people should be helped to do it, as long as it is not at anyone 's expense. This has nothing to do with a **political** reconciliation with small business interests. The history of such broad or popular fronts have been a disaster for the socialist cause. A small businessperson is often caught in a pincer movement between the remorseless downward price pressure of the corporate buyer and the rising costs of running the business. In such circumstances, they cannot be expected to have progressive attitudes to wage levels, workers' rights and social legislation. Only in exceptional political times will the business owner be a friend of the left, but that does not stop us being clear about what support a socialist society might offer.

First, some facts to give the discussion some context. International definitions are that a micro- business is one employing less than ten people, a small one between ten and fifty, medium between fifty and two hundred and fifty, and large above that.

Proportion of businesses, employment and turnover in small, medium and large businesses in Britain, start 1998

	% of total businesses	% of total employment	% of national turnover
Large sized businesses	0.2	43.7	48.2
Medium sized businesses	0.7	11.6	13.8
All small and micro sized businesses	99.1	44.7	38.0
Businesses employing less than five	25.2	10.9	11.1
Self employed (no employees)	64.0	12.7	4.6

From 1980 to 1990, the number of enterprises increased from 2.4m to 3.8m. Three factors were driving the development – redundancies and 'outsourcing' of the early eighties (e.g. making your factory maintenance workers self employed), the availability of equity to home owners as house prices started to rise sharply, and the free enterprise culture of Thatcherism. Since 1990 the number of enterprises has remained static, as has the proportion of people working in the small business sector. Of the 3.8 million enterprises at the start of 1998, 2.3 million were run by self-employed people not employing anyone (2).

What is not immediately obvious from the above figures is the alarming rate of turnover in the small and self-employed business sector. An estimated 400,000 people a year try to start their own business, though for many it is not the first time. One third go bust within one year, another third within two years. By year five around eighty per cent of new start-ups have ceased trading. For the individuals involved, that can mean an enormous amount of stress, and often debt (3). On top of the insecurity attached to the work, self-employment is often poorly paid. Overall self-employed earnings are close to the national average, but conditions are polarised, and studies indicate that the self employed are three times more likely than the average employee to be in the bottom ten per cent of earners (4).

Starting a business is precarious and difficult, which is probably why not many of us do it (3% of British adults have tried, compared to 8% in the US) (5). But how much does it contribute economically? We are constantly told that small and medium sized companies are the engine of job creation and an important source of innovation. There is some doubt that this is the case.

In 1994, the OECD did a special study of the job creating potential of small businesses in Britain and concluded "that the large claims made for the job creation ability of small enterprises are often based on faulty statistics. A more correct statement is that small establishments are disproportionately responsible for both gross job gains and losses. The latter is partly due to the relatively high mortality rate of new small establishments." (6)

The whole contribution of small businesses to economic success has been questioned in a recent book by a business school academic (7). As well as general research, the book is based on interviews with the founders of 100 of the fastest growing start-ups in the USA. The author, Amar Bhinde, first notes that the vast majority of new businesses start small and stay that way. These are the hairdressing salons, corner shops and landscape gardeners. They are mature predictable industries and, for just that reason, they are the least profitable. The success stories come in areas of high uncertainty where the markets are changing fast because of technology, regulation or fashion. Unsurprisingly, a very large proportion is in computing.

Mr. Bhinde goes on to develop two statistically backed lines of argument that run counter to all business school received wisdom:

1) Entrepreneurs are not innovative.
2) Entrepreneurs are not risk-takers.

Big innovations tend to come from big companies. They are equipped to screen ideas and to fund them. The entrepreneur's job is to fill the gaps – to take small, uncertain ideas and run with them. They normally take an idea from someone else, then change it constantly to fit the market. The starting point is much less important than what happens next.

Nor are entrepreneurs risk takers. They are typically young people with no money, expertise or status. They have nothing to lose. Risk arrives later on when they have made their money and have to decide whether to invest in long term growth or sell out.

What they do have is a high tolerance of uncertainty, self-confidence and selling ability. Big companies may be happy with risk but cannot deal with uncertainty. They can invest billions in a microchip plant or oilfield, but only when they can calculate the odds. Few of Mr. Bhinde's interviewees began with any kind of business plan: the future was simply too uncertain. When the odds are unknown the entrepreneurs come into their own. They need to be supported in fulfilling that function.

Ironically, when socialism is being portrayed as the end of all initiative, one of the arguments tossed in, is that there will no longer be any venture capitalists (people with a lot of money wanting to make more) left to back the adventurous entrepreneur. Yet only five of Mr Bhinde's most successful one hundred had received any financial backing, precisely because venture capitalists cannot cope with uncertainty and lack of information.

It would be hard for any economic system to make a worse job of backing the entrepreneur than British capitalism. Not only do venture capitalists generally demand a rate of return of 60% a year on their investment (8), but venture capitalist firms have to find almost 75% of their money abroad, as British financial institutions only invest 0.5% of their funds in small and growing companies, compared to 5% in the US (9).

The needs of small businesses are fairly straightforward. They need access to finance at reasonable rates for start up and expansion, full order books and the ability to operate on reasonable profit margins. They also need a great deal of management skills (not always realised by those involved!).To this list could be added the needs for more hours in the day and the linked hatred of 'red tape' and external interference.

In terms of financial support and healthy demand, there is every reason to suppose that socialism could improve on what exists now. For start ups and early growth finance, special institutions could be established that were charged with being adventurous and prepared to lose some of their money, but the Mondragon model of support would be favoured where possible. Existing business people and bankers would give continual advice and guidance in parallel with the financial support. This contrasts with the very hands-off relationship offered by British banks. Many of the business support schemes that exist on a modest scale at the moment, would be built on. Student placements, research links, specialist advisers, low cost business incubators, skills training of all sorts etc.

A socialist economy, operating on a planned rather than chaotic basis, is also more likely to deliver steadily rising demand. However well run they were, many small businesses were thrown against the wall in the recessions of the early eighties and nineties.

So what of profitability and interference? It is not a matter of 'profit being a dirty word', only that it should not be made at the expense of someone else's pay and conditions. To protect workers in small businesses, there would have to be regulation; the right of all workers to a decent minimum wage, a minimum number of holidays, a reduced working week, access to education and training, sickness benefit and occupational pensions, to be represented by a trade union etc. All would have to be enshrined in legislation. There need not be any additional paper-work attached to these rights, but there would have to be a well-staffed inspectorate to make sure employers did not abuse them and were heavily fined if they did.

We live in an age when it has become intellectually fashionable to dismiss talk of rights as an obsession of the sixties. Instead, we should consider our responsibilities. In the economic sphere our responsibility is to make a success of the free market, and that means being flexible as workers, to price ourselves into jobs at the pay and conditions level the employer thinks fit. The limited rights that European workers have won over the years are under concerted attack from the deregulated free market model of the US. If socialism is to have any content, it must reinstate and extend these rights to everyone.

This will pose difficulties for the small business sector. It is awkward to find a replacement for someone on maternity leave. Sending staff to college for half a day a week involves lost production. Some costs will be borne by the state but others will fall on the business (e.g. the higher minimum wage). Hard choices are involved here. While some increase in costs could be absorbed by reduced profits, there may have to be some rise in prices. However, the income of the low paid would have risen by a greater amount to enable them to absorb the increase. It may indeed be that some marginal businesses that rely on low pay, and the absence of all benefits to make them viable, cease to exist. As the general position would be one of full employment, that is perhaps no bad thing.

There would always be the option to exempt small co-operatives from some aspects of social legislation, on the grounds that people have a right to exploit themselves if they so wish. While this might create flexibility, particularly for a young business, it would create a two-tier small business sector with the more socially progressive tier being associated with low wages.

It might be felt that any private sector at all, still based on the profit motive, would threaten the stability of the entire socialist system. This is unlikely but will be discussed further below. It would seem to be sensible though, at some point, to introduce a maximum size for private companies based on employment or turnover. When that point was reached the owner, with some compensation, would be expected to either join up with a socially-owned enterprise or transform the enterprise into a co-operative.

Is this all too soft? Many small business people work all hours for little reward; others though, encapsulate all the nastiness of the exploitative boss that we want to be rid of. Bearing in mind the rights to decent conditions and the progressive taxation system that will exist, it comes down to what sort of socialism is to be created. Is it a libertarian one that seeks to eliminate poverty and democratise the bulk of the economy, or a prescriptive one that seeks to block any exceptions to a socialised rule? As a first step in the socialist transition, it must surely be the first.

ALL MARKETS AND NO SOCIALISM?

The economy outlined above consists of a dominant socialised sector and, underneath it, a mixture of co-ops and privately owned firms. While the activities of the publicly owned enterprises would be planned and a large degree of co-operation exist between them, transactions would be money based. Below them, co-operative and private businesses should form long term supplier relationships with enterprises in the socialised sector, but essentially they would be operating in a market system familiar in capitalism. Such an economic structure is normally described as market socialism, and as such attracts trenchant critics from some of the Marxist left. The criticisms are important because they question whether market socialism actually changes much at all.

Many Marxist critiques of market socialism exist. The one I have chosen to answer is that written by the late Ernest Mandel, who wrote extensively on economic subjects and can be said to represent the orthodox Marxist school of thought. 'A Critique of Market Socialism' was written in 1986 in response to Alec Nove's work 'The Economics of Feasible Socialism'. There are many variables of market socialism and the version proposed in this book is, perhaps, more planned than Nove's conception. Nonetheless, the criticisms made by Mandel would equally apply.

To classify positions on workable alternatives to capitalism as either Marxist or non-Marxist is somewhat false, since Marx gave little consideration to the subject. However the orthodox position is as follows: the economy can be likened to a giant corporation. The corporation will decide how much it is going to produce in a year and organise its internal systems to achieve that production. Money may be used as an accounting system but production is really organised through target setting and instructions. "So much of x will be delivered to y every month". Everything is planned and geared to meet the needs of the next stage of production. The socialist economy would likewise meet the needs of consumers, finding out what they wanted before production, not after it.

By contrast, the individual producer of pedal bins in the free market turns them out without being clear how many are being produced elsewhere or what the demand for them will be. Sometimes there will be a glut, sometimes a shortage. The threat of redundancy from over-production and lack of

265

demand is always around the corner. What is true for the individual producer is also true for the economy as a whole.

So a system of pre-production planning is superior to the free market, as long as it can be made responsive to people's needs. Mandel outlines how this might be done through different levels of workers' self management. National and international annual congresses of workers' and popular councils would determine the great divisions of the national product (length of the working week, maximum and minimum incomes, resources to be distributed free, resources to be bought for money, investment funds etc.). Self-managing bodies in each sector would then take these aggregates and break them down to enterprise level targets. Above their allocation of goods and services, enterprises would be given a money income to spend as they will, "indexed to quality control and customer satisfaction within a given spread, with a coefficient for work stress". The role of money in the economy would be small, confined to trade in 'non-essential' goods with everyone receiving an allocation of essential goods. "Private and co-operative enterprises would survive in small scale production...and individual entrepreneurship would not be forbidden".

Such an economy would also avoid the dictatorship of the consumer over the producer. "For the system of reward and punishments through the market, ingenuously extolled by so many on the Left nowadays, is nothing but a thinly disguised despotism over the producer's time and efforts, and therewith their lives as a whole.

Such rewards and punishments imply not only higher and lower incomes, 'better' and 'worse' jobs; they also imply periodic lay-offs, the misery of unemployment, speed-up, subjection to the stop-watch and the assembly line, the authoritarian discipline of production squads, nervous and physical health hazards, noise bombardment, alienation from any knowledge of the production process as a whole, and the transformation of human beings into appendices of machines or computers. Why is it obvious that millions of people should submit to such constraints for the sake of assuring 10% more customer satisfaction?"

Market socialism is merely 'mixed misery' and, like Yugoslavia, leads "to a growing combination of the ills of bureaucracy with those of the market, each reinforcing rather than mitigating the other." Mandel's system of self-management would differ from market socialism in the following ways:

➢ There would be no competition
➢ No money would be exchanged between socialised enterprises
➢ Enterprise incomes would not be dependent on the difference between the costs of inputs and outputs
➢ Essential goods would be allocated to consumers

Mandel's proposals are mistaken. Like many others, he has failed to take account of how socialisation can change the nature of the market. His invective against consumer dictatorship over the producer may be warranted against capitalism, but not the market socialism described here. There would be constant discussion between consumer, worker and state representatives about what sort of work pattern could be socially justified. On top of that workers' rights legislation would exist relating to all areas of working life to prevent exploitation.

It should also be recognised as politically difficult to convince people that they should accept less disposable income in favour of more allocated goods. At the moment, Education and the NHS are allocated resources, paid for by taxes. It may be acceptable to extend the principle to public transport and utilities, but how far could you go? Workers councils may chose to allocate fridges i.e. provide them free. They are essential and have a low elasticity of demand, i.e. if they were free people would not rush out to get a second one. If the fridges were free however, the fridge manufacturer would have no income to provide the factory's workers with cash to buy non-essential goods. The only body that could provide the cash is the government, and the government would have to raise the money through taxes.

A transition to a system of consumer allocation necessarily involves more and more goods and services being provided free, while tax increases or lower wages reduce disposable income. If disposable income were not reduced, there would be shortages or inflation in the priced goods sector, as an increased amount of money chased the same amount of goods. It is not at all clear that this is the way people would want to go. In fact, if the Mandel model of consumption represents socialism, it is best kept to ourselves:

"In factories manufacturing consumer goods, the product mix would flow from previous consultation between the workers' councils and consumers' conferences democratically elected by the mass of citizens. Various models – for example, different fashions in shoes – would be submitted to them, which the consumers could test and criticise and replace by others. Showrooms and publicity sheets would be the main instruments of testing. The latter could play the role of a referendum – a consumer having the right to receive six pairs of footwear a year, would cross six samples in a sheet containing a hundred or two hundred options. The model mix would then be determined by the outcome of such a referendum, with postproduction corrective mechanisms reflecting subsequent consumer criticisms. Compared with the market mechanism, the great advantage of such a system would be the far greater consumer influence on product mix and the suppression of over production – the balancing out of consumer preference and actual production essentially occurring *before* production and not *after* sales."

There is nothing wrong with consumer testing – even certain corporations are catching on! Beyond that, the system is bizarre. The consumers of a rich country like Britain would be expected to vote for their best six shoe styles (do I want six pairs of shoes this year?) and hope that their choice reaches the 'most demanded shoe charts' so that it is actually produced. We will leave aside how the consumer will know whether it has been produced, when and where they pick it up from, and what are they supposed to buy if it has not been produced.

Allocation is all done in the name of pre-production planning and balance, but the arguments are highly contradictory. It is suggested that planning without prices and the market is, in part, possible because needs are predictable, and patterns of demand change slowly. If that is the case then planning can also be undertaken using prices, money and the market. Consult widely on what shoes styles are wanted, presume that overall demand will be roughly the same as last year, adjusting for increased incomes, then put them in the shops and see how they go.

The only justification for the allocation of goods, is that, without such a method of industrial organisation, the economy will continue on a path of boom and bust, consumer dictatorship and inequality. This chapter has attempted to show that need not be the case.

The errors of Mandel's line of arguing do not end with consumption. His determination to remove prices and money ("it will be quite possible to reduce the role of money in the economy as a whole, as non-priced goods and services become more numerous than goods and services bought"), shows a failure to learn from the experience of Soviet central planning. Prices that reflect cost and money, a universal equivalent, are essential if workers, users and consumers are to make decisions about resource allocation and efficient methods. The form of competition argued for in this book involves comparing and testing one enterprise against another by using prices and money, income and expenditure. It is less about head-to-head competition in the marketplace. Falling profits would indicate a problem and initiate the need for corrective action.

Finally Mandel fails to recognise the downside of workers' self-management of enterprises and the partisan interest they have in the future of the enterprise. For him, there is only capitalist control or workers' control. The necessity and possibility of **social** control goes unmentioned. Representatives of users and the state have to be involved to make sure the needs of society as a whole are met.

SUMMARY

The socialisation of the major corporations and the bulk of the finance industry under the control of consumers, workers and the state will allow the economy to be planned while using the mechanisms of the market. The nature of the market will itself be transformed by open electronic information systems being an integral part of all enterprise and government. All the major levers of the economy will be under democratic i.e. plannable control. That will include major investment, interest and exchange rates, currency movements, money supply etc.

Development of consumer networks will ensure responsiveness to need, while the tripartite system of control will avoid the dangers of bureaucratic arrogance from the state.

Socialism is not just about changes in the boardrooms of corporations however. The socialised economy is the means towards the 'irreversible shift in the balance of wealth and power' that the Labour Party once talked about. Poverty would be eliminated and inequalities reduced. New forms of co-operation between enterprises, institutions and the community would be encouraged. Democratic experiments in the workplace, such as teams electing their managers, would take place. Making work enjoyable would be a key priority.

This is socialism from day one. As the working class learns to exercise its power and responsibilities, socialism will continue to evolve. It would be no surprise if in 200 years there was no money, that we turned up voluntarily to do what work needed to be done, and consumed only what we needed to. But that is not for now. One of the challenges of socialism will be to reintroduce the notion of not working for your living, at least not all of it (the forty hour fixed working week is a uniquely capitalist notion). We need more time for the human activities of helping and enjoying other people, childcare, organising communities and enterprise, and just relaxing. As it is, free market mechanisms force business to create an ever-expanding range of services in order to generate profits and consequently employment. Somehow, we used to get by without all those marketing and business services.

The shift to being more active in the non-financial economy can be achieved through a progressive reduction in the working week without loss of pay, combined with the introduction of the Basic Income. The movement will have to be accompanied by a change in culture, as, in effect, the benefits of future productivity growth would have to be taken as time off rather than increased purchasing power. Such a culture change might be expected in a less competitive and accumulative society.

CHAPTER 6.

PROSPECTS FOR THE LEFT

You tell us
It looks bad for our cause
The darkness gets deeper. The power gets less.
Now, after we worked for so many years
We are in a more difficult position than in the start.
But the enemy stands there, stronger than ever before.
His powers appear to have grown. He has taken on an aspect of
invincibility.
We however have made mistakes; there is no denying it.
Our numbers are dwindling.
Our slogans are in disarray. The enemy has twisted
Part of our words beyond recognition.

What is now false of what we said:
Some or all?
Whom do we still count on? Are we just left over, thrown out
Of the living stream? Shall we remain behind
Understanding no one and understood by none?

Have we got to be lucky?

This you ask. Expect
No other answer than your own

(To A Waverer. Bertolt Brecht. socialist playwright, 1935)

Gloomy stuff. There were good reasons to be politically downcast in 1935. In Brecht's Germany, Hitler was in his second year in power and the threat of war was mounting. Yet the same words still speak powerfully to socialists who formed their ideas in the mass movements of the 1960s and 1970s. The political isolation is of a different sort, but no less daunting.

In the thirties, the active membership of the European left (communist and left social democratic) could be measured in millions. However mistaken the policies, the socialist movement was a mass human force. It was certainly not the absence of a left wing that allowed Hitler to take power, but rather a history of mistaken strategies and tactics (1). The picture today is reversed. By and large, the democratic structures of advanced capitalist countries are intact. There is no immediate prospect of them being destroyed through naked force. The problems socialists face are of ideological isolation, of, indeed, being "thrown out of the living stream". The numbers of people adhering to the economic programme represented in this book has been reduced to small pockets around the globe. The question is whether this phenomenon is a temporary conjuncture of political psychology and economics, or an echo of something more fundamental. An era of long term stability in the advanced capitalist countries. The end of history decided in capitalism's favour.

I have argued that the unrestrained free market tends to increase inequality and poverty and replace human values with market ones. In addition, the absence of social control makes it enormously difficult to tackle the mounting environmental crisis. I have also argued that globalisation has increased the pressure for the free market to be unrestrained – pedalling backwards to capitalist social democracy is ruled out because of global competitive pressures. Further, the increased mobility of international capital will accentuate the economic damage done in any future economic downturn.

These processes were somewhat masked by the, ultimately unsustainable, long American boom of the nineties. Even before any synchronised recession in the west, great sections of the world are in economic and political turmoil, including large parts of Africa, Central and South America, Indonesia, and the former communist states. The growing international refugee crisis is a reflection of this. Even China and Japan face problems of industrial overcapacity with insufficient demand to absorb potential production.

However, the absence of a strong left in the advanced capitalist countries can only partly be laid at the door of the nineties boom. The collapse of the Soviet Union and the ideological offensive of the Thatcher / Reagan days undoubtedly succeeded in convincing people in general, and political activists in particular that there was no alternative to capitalism. At the same time, and the process was most clear in Britain, the forcible transfer of workers from manufacturing industry to services, combined with a tightening of management control in the industry that remained, had a crippling effect on traditional working class organisations. The emptying out of activists from the trade unions allowed workers leaders to drift to the right virtually unchallenged. In Britain, the defeat of the miners' strike in 1985 gave the ebb-tide tremendous force.

Yet there has been no generalised rightward drift in outlook measured by Social Attitude surveys. Voters, rather, combine a belief that nothing can be changed, with increasing contempt for the political system that makes sure it doesn't. Political non-engagement is the fastest growing movement in most countries. It is significant that probably more people under 25 went on the J18 (June 18th 1999) 'Carnival against Capitalism' in London than voted in that year's European elections, not to mention more voting in 'Big Brother' than voted in the 2001 General Election!

So if the battle is worth engaging, where in Britain should our energies be directed? Into the Labour Party, into a new party, or in to no party at all? The subject is a book in itself, but some political conclusions need to be drawn from the preceding analysis.

In the seventies, anyone with a feel for mass politics would have to have been in the Labour Party. Though the Labour government, as always, had a right wing agenda, the party itself contained thousands of socialist activists. Trade unionists had direct links to the Party at national and local level and community activists would always see the party as the vehicle for their demands. Any political formation to the left of Labour was universally ignored and the Communist Party had abandoned any serious attempt at party building.

Some would still argue that to abandon the Labour Party as the traditional organisation of the working class is a mistake. Whether to do so can only be decided after answering three questions:

> Have Labour's links to its working class constituency effectively broken down?

➢ Have the changes in the Party's organisation and ideology been so fundamental as to exclude the possibility of radical change?

➢ When the number of political activists begins to turn up again, will they turn to organise within or against the Labour Party?

The third question is the most significant.

It may seem strange to argue that Labour's claim to be the natural party of the working class has dramatically weakened. They achieved a landslide victory in 1997 and repeated it in 2001. Yet the days when it was said that a donkey with a Labour rosette on would be elected in many urban areas, are long gone. The mirror to the end of conviction politics of parties, is the end of commitment politics by the electorate. Everyone is convinced that the main parties will say anything to be elected, so why offer more than shallow loyalty? The stable political bedrocks of Tory middle England and Labour urban heartlands have both been shattered.

The loosening of party ties can, to some extent, be measured by the success of the Liberals in cities like Sheffield and Labour in traditional Tory areas, but its most powerful expression is in the growth of the 'not interested' tendency. Voting in the general election fell to its lowest level since the First World War (60%) and in local elections there is a crisis of non-participation with the turnout often below 25%. A post war record was established in my own Labour-held constituency, Leeds Central, when in 1998 a parliamentary by-election inspired only 19% of the electorate to vote (2).

Political cynicism is not to be welcomed. However, the growth in the numbers of non-voters and floating voters does make the political ground more fertile for alternative parties than it was thirty years ago. Potential is not sufficient though. The question remains: will activists and working class voters desert Labour? In a more politically charged atmosphere, will they be willing to support a new left party?

The role of the activist is crucial. They give a flavour to politics that the media reflects back to the population as a whole. At the end of the seventies left activists and trade unionists overwhelmingly turned to the Labour Party and supported Tony Benn MP and the left wing programme he represented. This movement reached its peak in 1981 when Benn lost the election for Deputy Leader of the Party by a whisker. Though inevitably speculative, there is strong evidence to suggest such a process will not be repeated.

At one level, Tony Blair's free market 'third way', and the internal struggle he has conducted to sweep away opponents, has made Labour an unnatural home for people desiring socialist change. Add that to the organisational counter-revolution that makes the new consensus almost irreversible and it becomes hard to see why anyone would become involved in party activity.

No one could accuse the modernisers of not being thorough. Their aim has been to eradicate the elements of representative democracy in the party that allowed activists to be effective. These are some of the changes:

➢ Local general management committees of the party used to keep a check on the MPs and apply pressure on the National Executive. Though not yet abolished, all their power has been removed.

➢ The right to submit motions to Labour's annual conference has been curtailed. Policy is formulated within the safely manage-able National Policy Forum and the conference converted to something like a rally.

➢ Panels supporting the leadership tightly vet nominated local candidates. One such Panel removed Ken Livingstone from the mayoral short list.

➢ Regional conferences have been abolished.

➢ The National Executive has been reformed so that fewer members are directly elected.

➢ Secret ballots have been dropped for elections in the Parliamentary Party.

The whole package makes the Party easier to control from the centre and organising an opposition much more difficult. The only reason the union link has not been ended is that their influence is too weak to impede the modernisers. Denied the chance to influence events, it is likely that future activists will turn to campaigns, alliances and parties outside the Labour Party. Already, on a small scale, trade unionists have threatened to take their political contributions away from Labour and use them for ends that the union supports (e.g. in the firefighters, railway and postal workers' unions).

The lack of any independent left wing breakthrough at this stage is not an argument for staying in the Labour Party. The influence of any section of the left, at the moment, is modest to put it at its most cheerful. The Labour Party left for instance are barely represented on Labour's National Executive, a body they used to control throughout the seventies. If events do not turn to produce heightened political awareness and greater self-confidence, then the socialist project is dead, whatever the strategy. Our economic analysis indicates that such a revival is likely. So political positioning should be based on an assessment of how activists are likely to move in the future. The direction of that movement is likely to be different from the past. Of course, any generalised discontent will be echoed in the Labour Party, if only from its remaining core of left wing MPs (Socialist Campaign Group members). However, a few parliamentary speeches and rallies are unlikely to persuade people to put their efforts into an activist-free Labour Party.

Much of this analysis would be accepted by the left wing MPs themselves. The current Chair of the Campaign Group, John McDonnell, describes Labour left leaders "as the political equivalent of stand-up comedians on tour" producing "the occasional demagogic speech delivered to a declining activist audience and to a media listening with less and less interest" (3). He emphasises that, far from achieving Blair's stated aim of building a party of a million members, membership is at its lowest level since the war - 200,000. However, unable to accept that the cause of socialism could best be forwarded outside the Labour Party, he advocates the forming of a broad-based socialist group within the Party. The outlook for such a group is not promising. They would start by diluting their programme to accommodate non-socialists. The group would find it difficult to organise in communities for fear of being dominated by non-Labour activists. If they ever were effective, they would be closed down and members expelled from the Party in much the same way as the Socialist League was in the thirties and Militant in the eighties. Times when the party had a stronger socialist heart than now.

Anti-capitalism

There is a third choice for the would-be activist though – to avoid both socialist alliances and the Labour Party. Just get out there and do it, unhampered by political hierarchies and bureaucracy. Political parties are not popular amongst the under twenty fives. There is no doubt that radical direct action movements like 'Reclaim the Streets' have had the most success in engaging youth throughout most of the nineties on issues such as road building, animal protection and genetically modified foods. It would be wrong to pin ideologies on the participants but many draw on the spirit, if not the letter, of anarchism.

"They organise in loosely associated groups which are voluntary, functional, temporary and small. They depend not on membership cards, votes, a special leadership and a herd of inactive followers but on small, functional groups which ebb and flow, group and regroup, according to the task in hand. They are networks not pyramids" (4).

This is appealing stuff. Parties, and organisations in general, can be frustrating and dull places. Anarchist inspired movements have much to teach us about flexibility and the imaginative use of peaceful direct action. The anarchist rejection of big government and corporate power is a healthy one. The problem is that at its core, their political strategy makes no sense.

Take this extended passage from the People's Global Action network manifesto, agreed at their founding conference in Geneva in Feb '97. 300 delegates attended the conference from seventy one countries. These were people involved in serious struggles involving great self-sacrifice, not small groups of masked window-smashers, as the television likes to picture anarchists.

"Organisations have to be independent of government structures and economic powers and based on direct democracy. These new forms of autonomous organisation should emerge from and be rooted in local communities, while at the same time practising international solidarity."

They should have the aim of "delinking their communities, neighbourhoods or small collectives from the global market. Direct links between producers and consumers in both rural and urban areas, local currencies, interest-free credit schemes and similar instruments are the building blocks for the creation of local, sustainable and self-reliant economies based on co-operation and solidarity rather than competition and profit. While the global financial casino heads at increasing speed towards social and environmental disintegration and economic breakdown, we, the people, will construct sustainable livelihoods." (5)

Doubtless, there would be objections that this is not pure anarchism, but movements that refuse to look beyond direct action are doomed to offer only the politics of 'delinking' and autonomous zones. The ruling elite would be delighted if all opponents of the regime became autonomous and self-sustaining. For the vast majority left behind, whose lives are bound tightly to the corporate world, it would be business as usual. Anarchism offers an intoxicating brew of individual freedom and collectivism. Its spirit will be strong within any movement to a new society. But in terms of where we want to go now and how to get there, it offers nothing. The idea that episodes of direct action can, at some point, spill over into revolution, without any bridges from one to the other, is surely false.

Since anti-capitalism burst into the news at Seattle, it is anarchists who have grabbed the headlines as supposedly being responsible for the violence. Of course, the western media have a very slanted view of the anti-capitalist movement. They try to characterise the participants as students and middle class disaffected youth, scaring us with stories of 'spikey' anarchists, bent on destruction, gaining the upper hand over 'fluffy' anarchists. By this means they try to discredit activists as being both silly and dangerous at the same time. The reality is much more profound.

The backbone of the anti- capitalist movement lies in the developing world, in the struggles of working people to protect their livelihoods against the institutions of global capital. This is not rhetoric. In the year between Seattle and the IMF meeting in Prague (1999/2000), there were at least fifty outbreaks of civil unrest in thirteen poor countries directed at IMF policies alone. More than one million people, including teachers, farmers, trade unionists and priests, were involved in these protests, half of which ended in violent clashes (6). It is true that in the developed countries, workers and their organisations are only starting to put their mark on the protests, but it would be wrong to overplay the role of anarchism.

More significant is that many of the anti-capitalist movement's leaders share the belief in delinkage from globalisation as a strategy - a strategy that avoids the need for socialist change. To be accurate, we should not talk of leaders or even an organised movement at this stage. At least seven hundred organisations were represented on the demonstration of 300,000 people in Genoa in July '01 (7). Rather than leaders we are talking about opinion formers, people like Naomi Klein, Viviane Forrester, Susan George, Walden Bello etc.(8)

Their opinions differ, but in the solutions they promote, a pattern emerges:

1) Democratise / abolish / change the roles of institutions like the IMF, World Bank, World Trade Organisation.

2) Reinstitute capital controls and particularly support the introduction of the Tobin Tax on currency deals.

3) Support indigenous development that is not dependent on corporate inward investment and export growth.

In philosophical terms, Bello talks of it being "a strategy that consciously subordinates the logic of the market and the pursuit of cost efficiency, to the values of security, equity and social solidarity" (9).

These reforms should be supported, but haven't we been here before? Isn't this the social democratic dream that imploded in the eighties? On the moderate wings of anti-capitalism, the nostalgia is sometimes quite specific. The Third World Network stands for a return to the understandings that backed the post-war Bretton Woods agreement - a) financial markets subservient to industry b) international financial organisations regulating trade and ensuring fair prices for commodities c) returning the IMF back to its original role of controlling the free flow of capital.(10)

May we all be spared from activists who see it as a moral imperative to be more revolutionary than the next person. I want to be as reformist and accommodating, as reason will allow. But in the founding moments of a new movement, it would be fatal to set ourselves the task of rediscovering the economic wisdom of Maynard Keynes. The social democratic consensus broke down for reasons that were discussed earlier. It wasn't just a change in political thinking at the top but related to profound developments in the global capitalist economy. The tiger has broken free. It cannot be forced back in the cage with the whip and stool of taxation and controls. The mass movement required to turn over the existing world financial order would be no smaller than that needed to socialise economies, with far more doubtful results.

Nor does some of the moderate programme even make sense. The developing countries **need** trade and inward investment to develop. The issues are that the money should not enter the country for the benefit of global corporations and speculators, nor be controlled by any ruling elite within the developing country. Similarly, trade needs to be organised in the social interest of the country concerned and not be organised within some foreign-dominated enterprise zone. The politics of class and power cannot be avoided.

A New Left Party

It is necessary for socialists to swim against the stream in the current period. Many argue that a Party is no longer needed to organise action against the system. For the sake of argument let us concede the point. What is more certain is that you need a Party to project your voice within the existing democratic structures of society. The notion that you can move from where we are to the overthrow of capitalism, without the movement ever registering its presence in the electoral process, strikes me as absurd. A new workers party with a left wing programme is needed to engage people - not just those who might be touched by any direct action, but the population at large. A left wing party must be fully involved in direct action in support of people's day to day concerns, but it also needs to generalise an outlook, to challenge free market common sense with a socialist one. This can often be best achieved through electoral challenges that attract media attention and hopefully register growing support.

If a left party is to be built, it cannot resemble the small, centralised and sectarian caricatures of the past. It will take some time to create, and is bound to involve alliances between different groups and campaigns in the early stages. Openness, inclusivity and organisational flexibility will be crucial, as will the presentation of its programme.

This book has tried to give a vision of what socialism might be in economic terms. To their credit, the Greens have also tried to paint a picture of how society could be organised, though without showing how it might be achieved. Too often, the left has confined itself to supporting struggles and demanding more of whatever is on offer. Necessary though that is, we need to inspire with an alternative. There is a need to re-emphasise what Marxists used to call the 'maximum programme' and to explain the need for the socialisation of major industry and finance. There is profound disillusionment with powerful institutions and the time is right to argue that they should be democratised. We need to learn to fight with both hands - for every reform, but also for the complete transformation of the economy.

The programme of a new party will be labelled extreme. Its presentation needs to be exactly the opposite. A socialist party should always base itself on fighting for the poor and not be embarrassed that it still believes there is such a thing as the working class! However, the nature of modern class society, and the complex routes to self-identity, demand that it be made clear that socialism is the property of ninety per cent of the population, not only the downtrodden. It is a feature of modern politics that the less there is to choose between the parties, the more venomously they attack each other; the more extreme the language becomes. The programme of a left party will mark itself out as representing a complete change in direction. There is plenty of room for anger about the injustices of society, but the programme should be presented in the most moderate, reasonable and humorous way possible. In media rich societies, style is not a secondary matter.

'Build the New Left Party!' It's a cry that has been heard many times through the decades. How will a new left party break through the credibility barrier to appear a real opposition party, rather than a marginal tiny group? What social forces will bring it into existence? There are no certainties in all this, but we must dismiss the superficial pessimism that takes the realities of reduced trade union organisation and greater individualism and concludes the death of the socialist project.

It is true that the number of trade unionists has shrunk from twelve to seven million and that their democratic structures have weakened (though their **power** remains in utilities, transport, telecommunications etc). However, the specific weight of trade unions in society has only ever been one factor in developing socialist politics. Consider the mass movements that have taken place in countries like France and Greece, where trade unions have only ever organised a relatively small proportion of the population. It is also likely that the birth of a new political opposition will breathe life into the trade unions and vice versa. Our hope for the future would be that the unions grow to be combative organisations involved in both workplace and community matters.

Bemoaning greater individualism is also a mistake. This is psychology and can / will change. What does it mean anyway? Certainly society is structured to promote personal gain over social solidarity, but it does not follow that the potential for collective action has been destroyed. People may go to less political meetings but, as an example of social awareness and concern, the UK's leading eleven environmental organisations have a membership of 5.4 million between them (11). There are plenty of examples of dramatic political shifts. Who would have thought that Ken Livingstone, living a quiet life on the backbenches of parliament, would have been overwhelmingly elected as an independent mayor of London? Who would have thought a retired doctor would have been elected an independent MP for Kidderminster by a landslide, as part of a campaign against a hospital closure?

The social forces that will bring a new left party into existence are those people whose lives and needs are not reflected in the existing parties. 2002 is not 1972. In that period of heightened struggle, the Labour Party was still a pole of attraction and Labour Party trade union leaders like Jack Jones and Hugh Scanlon cast a long shadow over the movement. If the economy re-enters rough waters, a significant minority this time may choose to vent their frustrations in a new direction.

Fortunately, the political canvass for this speculation is not blank. An outline of the future can already be seen. The Scottish Socialist Party was formed out of an alliance of left groups, though mainly Militant Labour, in 1997. Tommy Sheridan was elected to the Scottish parliament in the '99 election. Just four years after its founding, the SSP had the capacity to stand in all 72 Scottish seats in the 2001 general election. The result was a respectable 3.3% of the vote across Scotland, but significantly around 7% in Glasgow. In a poll a month after the election they were registering 6% support across the country for the Scottish parliament (12). They now have branches across the country and picked up an additional thousand members during the election campaign. The SSP has an open structure and is rapidly becoming the first point of call for any group or campaign moving in opposition to government policy. It is evidence of two of the points above. 1) Since breaking into parliament the Party has vastly increased its media coverage and consequently support. In September 2001, the Party's support in the opinion polls was only one percentage point behind the Tories . 2) The behaviour and presentational style of a nationally recognised activist and parliamentary representative, in this case Tommy Sheridan, can win respect from supporters and opponents alike and has raised the standing of socialism in the country.

Political conditions for the left in Scotland are more favourable than in England and Wales (13), but a parallel development could have taken place south of the border in the mayoral election in London in May 2000. If Ken Livingstone had chosen to use his candidacy as an independent to launch an organisation of those wanting a more radical alternative to New Labour, he almost certainly would still have won, as well as attracting thousands of members. Unfortunately, the idea of being accountable to anyone did not appeal to him. As it was, the combined vote for the Greens and left groups in the top-up list for the Greater London Authority was over 16%. Livingstone's stance will undoubtedly frustrate the birth of a sizeable left organisation, but the experience showed how fluid politics has become.

Exactly how a new left party will emerge in England and Wales is not yet clear. The Socialist Alliance, despite its modest general election haul of 1.7% of the vote in 92 seats, should be supported as a formation bringing together existing left groups and individuals. However, any attempt to create a tightly organised party at this stage will condemn it to a future similar to its past - as just another left group. The organisation should grow, but only if it is active and federal in nature, and supportive in how it approaches other new formations.

Looking a little ahead, it must be recognised that the membership of a broad-based left party is not going to be united behind a single strategy. That much is clear in the new formations that have appeared around Europe since the collapse of the communist parties. Such a party is likely to have its own 'Clause IV' as the Labour Party used to have. It will declare a belief in the socialisation of major industry and finance, but the membership will split between wings that see the transfer of power as an immediate objective and ones that see it as an ever-receding horizon of principle. The struggle for dominance between revolutionary and reformist wings will determine what role the party is to play.

Laying the foundations of a new mass party of the left is an enormous political undertaking. We have to confront almost thirty years of free market mental moulding and residual loyalties to the Labour Party stretching back even further. It will require the abandonment of many old ways of working, organisational concessions and learning to co-operate with people in other groups. Such ambitions have rightly been scoffed at in the past, but there is a danger of seeing future events as photocopies of the past. The world has moved on. As a source of egalitarian reform, the role of the social democratic parties is exhausted. Globalisation is removing their power and their ability to raise taxes to fund the welfare state.

New factors favour the emergence of the left. While the collapse of the Soviet Union disoriented and demoralised much of the international left, in the medium term it allows the next generation of activists to consider the ideas of socialism, free of the millstone of the one party dictatorship. In addition, as discussed earlier, the loosening of party ties and political instability makes it easier for a fourth party to emerge.

The danger is that political instability is a two-way street. The far right also view the future with optimism. Virulent nationalism and intolerance will be waiting in the wings, if the working class fail to resolve any future crisis in its favour.

An argument for the new left party has been presented in the British context. That it could be applied to many countries is no coincidence. The general political crisis of the world is that humanity's technical ability to meet social needs has far outstripped the market's ability to organise it. International socialism is needed more now than it ever has been. If this book has helped in any way to show that the socialist alternative is both practical and achievable, it has served its purpose.

NOTES AND REFERENCES

INTRODUCTION

1) Examples are the reduction of German company profits tax from 40 to 25% in the year 2000. At the same time, the newly adopted European Union take-over directive prohibits companies from taking defensive measures to protect themselves from take-over bids. 'Tax Evasion'. Haig Simonian. Financial Times. 14/7/00.

2) In the four categories of shopping, cleaning, washing and cooking a recent survey showed that only in the case of shopping was the work 'shared equally' in more than 20% of households. On all categories the work was done 'mainly by the man' in less than 10% of households. The figures have not altered much over the years. Richard Scase. Britain Towards 2010. Economic and Social Research Council. Aug. 1999.

3) National Strategy for Neighbourhood Renewal. Report by the Social Exclusion Unit. Cabinet Office. April 2000. p.101.

CHAPTER 1 – WHAT'S THE PROBLEM?

THE GLOBALLY EXCLUDED

1) Adrian Berry. The Next Five Hundred Years. Headline Books. 1995. p.40.

2) Barclays Economic Review Second Quarter 1999. In 1999 commodity prices, excluding oil, hit a 40 year low.

3) Statistics from The Politics of the Real World by the Real World Coalition of 30 voluntary and campaigning organisations. Earthscan Publications. 1996.

4) Forgotten Wars, Financial Times p.22 6/5/99

5) Per capita income in various parts of the world as a percentage of per capita income in the advanced countries, 1938 – 1988

	1938	1948	1960	1970	1980	1988
Latin America	19.5	14.4	16.7	15.5	19.8	10.6
Middle East and North Africa	n.a.	n.a.	11.5	8.1	11.1	7.1
sub-Saharan Africa (west and east)	n.a.	n.a.	3.6	3.4	4.7	1.6
South Asia	8.2	7.5	3.6	2.8	2.0	1.8
South East Asia	n.a.	n.a.	6.6	3.8	5.7	3.7

Advanced countries consist of - United States, Canada, Australia, New Zealand, the Benelux and Scandinavian countries, West Germany, Austria, Switzerland, France and the United Kingdom.

From Giovanni Arrighi, World Income Inequalities and the Future of Socialism. New Left Review No.189 Sept. 1991. Tables II, III and IV.

6) Also see Attacking Poverty. World Development Report. 2000/2001. Oxford University Press. and Capital Flows and growth in Africa. Unctad. July 2000. www.unctad.org and Branko Milanovic, True World Income Distribution 1988 and 1993. World Bank .1999. and Shaohua Chen and Martin Ravallion. How did the World's Poorest Fare in the 1990s. World Bank. 2000. www.worldbank.org.

7) Quoted in Global Turmoil. CWI Publications. 1999. p.39.
8) The Politics of the Real World. ibid. p.64

BRITAIN AFTER THE BOOM

1) Maddison A., Phases of Capitalist Development, Oxford University Press, 1982 p.91.
2) Barclays Economic Review Second Quarter 1999 p.10 and Economic Trends quarterly review Spring 2001.
3) Across Europe taxes were shifted from capital to labour. Between 1980 and 1994 taxes on capital and self employment fell from 50% to 34%, while taxes on labour increased from 35% to 40%. 'Taxing Matters'. The Economist. 5/4/97.
4) Barclays Economic Review November 1987 p.138
5) Will Hutton. The State We're In. Jonathan Cape.1995. p.69
6) Harry Shutt. The Trouble with Capitalism. Zed Books. 1998. p.50

POVERTY AND UNEMPLOYMENT

1) Department of Work and Pensions. Statistical Summary. July 2001. www.dwp.gov.uk
2) The minimum wage will have risen to £4-20 by October 2002. The rate of increase from the time of its introduction will actually be slower than the average increase in earnings. www.lowpay.gov.uk , www.statistics.gov.uk/statbase/tsdataset.asp?vlnk=392
3) Average gain figures from Andrew Glyn and Stewart Wood. New Labour's Economic Policy. Oxford University. 2000.

A comparison of total income (work and benefits) can be made with the following examples (thanks to Mansfield Unemployed Workers Centre). In both cases the claimant is presumed to be paying £60 a week rent and rates in April 2001. The Family Credit figure is for 1998 before it was replaced by the Working Families Tax Credit.

Total Weekly Income

A couple, one working for 37 hours a week for £200. Three children - 8, 10 and 13.

Income Support £237   Family Credit £228   WFTC £273

Single parent working 25 hours for £95. Children of 10 and 8

Income Support £176   Family Credit £165   WFTC £204

In 'Work in progress - CAB clients' experiences of the Working Families Tax Credit', (National Association of Citizens Advice Bureau, Feb 2001), the authors report that some people **are** still better off on income support. They cite a case where a woman with three kids and a disabled husband ends up with a £32 a week cut in income as a result of taking a 16-hour a week job at the minimum wage.

4) Working Brief. Oct.1996. p.17
5) Michael Barratt Brown. May Day Manifesto. Independent Labour Network.1998
6) Barratt Brown (above) p.56.
7) Financial Times 16/1/98 and Department of Work and Pensions July 2001.
8) One in six over 50s claim incapacity benefit. Through tougher medical tests and by making it impossible for the long term unemployed to claim the £58 a week, the government hoped to take 170,000 people off the benefit. Newsnight 17/5/99.

9) Financial Times 6/8/96 p.5

10) Britain's spending on the NHS is 6.7% of GDP, the lowest in Europe. (NHS Support Federation Bulletin August 1999. nhscampaign@hotmail.com).

11) Even without an economic slowdown, the Institute for Fiscal Studies in May 2001 reckoned that the Chancellor would have to raise taxes by £5bn. to achieve his spending targets through to 2004. Public spending statistics taken from 'No new spending spree'. Nicholas Timmins. Financial Times. 1/4/99 and 'Ministers challenge lies in delivery'. Institute for Fiscal Studies. Financial Times 19/7/00. Also 'Extended spending needs extra £5bn. a year'. Chris Adams. Financial Times.10/5/01

12) The link between unemployment and Incapacity Benefit is accepted by most commentators (see for instance Local Work. CLES. Oct. 1999). The number of claimants doubled between 1985 and 1995 in a period when general health levels were not declining. Recipients are concentrated in a small number of areas where manufacturing industry has disappeared and unemployment is high. The increase in inactivity for the over 50s is not in the main due to voluntary retirement. Of those men between 50 and 64 not working in 1998, only 25% had retired compared to 60% who were sick. Also, survey information indicated that 50% of those retiring had done so involuntarily i.e. as part of a redundancy package. Gregg and Wandsworth. The State of Working Britain. Manchester University Press. 1999.p 50. Also S.Tanner. The Dynamics of Male Retirement Behaviour. Fiscal Studies 19:2. 1998. pp. 175-196.

13) Tackling the Regional Jobs Gap. Academic research undertaken for the Alliance for Regional Aid. Employment Policy Institute. Sept. 2000

14) Bentley and Gurumurthy for Demos 1999. Quoted in Local Work. CLES. Oct.1999

15) In Sept 1999 the unemployment rate in the North East was 10% compared to less than 4% in the South East and a national average of 6.7%. 5,000 jobs had been lost in the previous year compared to 65,000 additional jobs in the South East. In a period of GDP growth the manufacturing heart of Britain - the East and West Midlands - also lost jobs. Figures from Labour Force Survey in the Financial Times. 13/9/99

16) Milton Keynes Citizen. 30/11/00

17) Britain is probably worse than most countries. In 1987 British companies spent 0.15% of turnover on training compared to 1-2% in Japan, France and West Germany. David Finegold. The Failure of Training in Britain. Oxford Review of Economic Policy. Vol. 4 No 3. 1988.

INEQUALITY

1) Economists argue about the role of increased global competition from low wage countries in reducing the demand for and consequently the wages of unskilled labour. This supply and demand explanation, which seeks to depoliticise the downward pressure on wages, does not explain why the number of unskilled jobs has risen in the US and yet wages until very recently continued to fall. The real hourly wage rate for Americans without a high school diploma fell from $11.85 in 1973 to $8.64 in 1995 in real terms. See Flanders and Wolf 'Investigating the causes of growing inequality in rich countries'. Financial Times. 24/7/95 and Robert Taylor 'Outlook grows bleak for the unskilled' F.T. 29/5/96

2) A Class Act. Andrew Adonis. Penguin 1998 pp.8-9.

3) Up to Feb 2001, according to the Institute of Fiscal Studies, Labour had through their tax and benefit changes, directed another £3bn to the poorest 30% of the population. A modest amount in the context of an economy worth £950bn. Nicholas Timmins. 'Labour's quiet redistribution policy exposed'. Financial Times. 12/2/01.

4) Even after some redistributive budget measures, in the year 1999/2000 the poorest twenty per cent saw an increase in their income of 1.4% compared to 2.8% for the richest twenty per cent. Institute of Fiscal Studies. May 2001. www.ifs.org.uk.

5) Between 1979 and 1994, the share of wages in the Gross Domestic Product declined by 3.3%, the share of profits rose by 4.8% and the share of dividends rose from 1.5% of GDP to 5.4% - a massive increase. 'Wages, Dividends and Investment - the choices for Labour'. Socialist Economic Bulletin. Published by Ken Livingstone MP. June 1995

6) Jo Rogaly. Financial Times 7/2/95

7) Will Hutton. 'A Million isn't what it used to be'. Observer. 11/4/99. For those who enjoy putting names to money, and would be amazed to know that Englebert Humperdink is worth £98 million, a useful directory is maintained at www.businessage-online.com .

8) As above. Also Inland Revenue statistics for 1997, and an estimate from Datamonitor consultancy for year 2000. See Ed Crooks. 'Who isn't a millionaire?' Financial Times. 22/11/00

9) A Class Act. (above). pp.85 and 88, plus a survey by the consultants Inbucon quoted in the FT article of the 22/11/00 (above)

10) Financial Times 25/2/97, plus Inbucon (above). The talent of the executive directors of the top 100 companies to increase their pay remains undiminished in the slow down. The Aug 2001 Inbucon survey,

reported a twenty eight per cent increase in their pay - six times the increase of their employees.

11) Monks Partnership report on boardroom pay. Aug 1996
12) Observer. As above
13) Au pair and Mintel figures from Class Act (above) p.101.
14) Paul Ryan. Inheritance: Symbols and Illusions in Paying for Inequality. Ed. Andrew Glyn and David Milliband. Rivers Oram Press.1994.
15) Tony Edwards. Education : Opportunity, Equality and Efficiency. p.63. in Paying for Inequality (above).
16) Children of parents in social categories D / E obtained on average 1/ 3 of the A-C GCSE passes as children from higher social groups at state schools in '95. Terence Kealey. High Cost of Free Education. Sunday Times. 10/3/96.
17) Spending on school infrastructure was slashed in the 1980s - '74/5 £1.82bn. '84/5 £604m. (spending in real terms). Observer. 3/3/99.
18) Financial Times 18/8/99.
19) Financial Times 26/10/99
20) We Should Know Better. George Walden. Fourth Estate. '96.
21) Varsity 1/10/93
22) Independent Inquiry into Inequalities in Health. HMSO. Sept. 1998. Part 1. Web site ref. www.official-documents.co.uk/document/doh/ ih/part1b.htm.
23) 'Private care bonanza as sick spurn NHS'. Anthony Browne. Observer. 18/3/00

LEEDS – 'NEW BRITAIN' IN ACTION

1) Financial Times Survey 14/4/89
2) Statistics in this section have been gathered from three sources. A)

Leeds City Council's web site (www.leeds.gov.uk) Economy – facts and figures. Downloaded 17/10/99. B) The Case for Objective 2 Status for Leeds Inner Area. Leeds City Council. May 1999. C) 'Better Neighbourhoods and Confident Communities' Single Regeneration Budget. Round 5 bid. Leeds Initiative Regeneration Partnership Unit. Dec 1998.

3) The Leeds Finanacial Services Initiative (Dec 2000) now calculate that 23% of Leeds employment is in the financial and business services sector. It also claims to be the leading UK city for telephone delivered banking with 30 call centres employing 17,000 people. They include First Direct, Direct Line, Green Flag and Halifax Direct.

4) Dark Heart. Nick Davies. Vintage. 1998. pp. 113, 116 and 123.

ARE THE BETTER OFF HAPPIER?

1) Office for National Statistics. Reproduced in the Observer. 11/4/99.

2) Seamus Milne. Guardian. 4/1/99. The Workplace Employee Survey of 1998 found the average working week in Britain to be 43.6 hours.

3) Ben Taylor. Daily Mail. 25/9/99. The findings were reinforced by a government sponsored survey a year later that covered 7,500 staff. It found that a third of staff put in over 49 hours a week and one in eight more than 60. Rosemary Bennett. 'Minister highlights long hours culture'. Financial Times. 21/11/00

4) Seamus Milne. Guardian 5/1/99.

5) Guardian. As above. 4/1/99

6) Alex Klaushofer. Red Pepper. Sept. 1999.

7) Peter Marsh. Financial Times. 1/2/96.

8) Andrew Bolgar. Financial Times 23/10/96.

9) 'Growth in jobs will be caused by flexible working'. Financial Times.

12/1/99.

10) Helen Wilkinson. Family and Work Institute, New York. In the Guardian 6/1/99.

11) Guy Evans. The Observer. 19/1/97

12) Survey evidence indicates that for all those that use their car to travel to work, the average time spent commuting is 45 minutes a day. The highest in Europe. Financial Times. 2/12/99.

13) Oliver James. Britain on the Couch. Arrow Books. 1998. All statistics in this section are drawn from the book.

14) B. Young. Television, Advertising and Children. Clarendon Press. 1990.

15) Financial Times. 15/3/99

16) 17% of households contained one person in 1971, by 1991 it was 27%. Oliver James (above) p.157.

17) Living Together: community life on mixed tenure estates. Demos. 1999.

THE SPECTRE OF THE BUSINESS CYCLE.

1) Soros on Soros, John Wiley. 1995. p.194

2) Marx saw unpaid labour is the only source of profit. Capitalist can make more profit by investing in new machinery that increases production while employing the same amount of workers. Costs per unit of production fall, so if the price stays the same, profits go up. The problem comes when all capitalists have invested in the same machinery. Competition forces prices down. Total profits may still be greater but the capitalist has the cost of renewing the machine in a few years. The rate of profit - profit as a percentage of the value of equipment in the business - falls. The capitalists then have insufficient

profits to increase investment further.

3) National Statistical Office. Profitability of UK Companies. 10/11/99.

4) Financial Times Survey of Indonesia 24/11/97

5) Two thirds of the sixty recessions that occurred worldwide in the 1990s remained undetected seven months before they occurred. 'The arcane art of predicting recessions'. Prakash Loungani. (IMF Senior Economist). Financial Times.

6) Christopher Swann. 'Fears over funding add currency to doubts over dollar'. Financial Times. 24/10/00

TRENDS IN TECHNOLOGY AND EMPLOYMENT

1) Marvin Minsky. The Massachusetts Institute of Technology. The Society of Mind. Simon and Schuster. 1987.

2) Report from the Bartlett school of architecture at University College London, commissioned by the builders Ballast Wiltshier. Reported in the Guardian 20/11/99.

3) Colin Lomax, Brave New Economy, New Start publication, 8/10/99

4) World Travel and Tourism Council 1995, quoted in Leon Kreitzman. The 24 Hour Society. Profile Books. 1999.

5) Peter Schwartz in the Future of the Global Economy. OECD. 1999.

6) Dan Dimancescu et.al. The Lean Enterprise. Amacom. 1997

7) Datamonitor. Call Centres in the UK. Quoted in Financial Times 13/7/99.

8) Joseph Rowntree Foundation June 1999 press release.

9) Mark Goyder. Living Tomorrow's Company. Gower. 1998. p.49

10) Living Tomorrow's Company (above) p.71.

11) Calderdale and Kirklees Training and Enterprise Council. Economic

and Labour Market Assessment 1997/98. pp 14 & 15.
12) The Basic Skills Agency interviewed 8000 people in 1996/1997.

SOME CONCLUSIONS

1) The Index of Sustainable Economic Welfare takes the Gross Domestic Product , the yardstick of success for all governments, then makes adjustments to account for eighteen aspects of our lives that GDP ignores. The adjustments put a value on environmental damage, travel time, household labour etc. While there is sometimes a problem measuring these things, they do clearly have a value to us, that GDP puts at zero. Interestingly the Economic Welfare index, after showing constant improvement from 1953 to 1975, has been in decline since. A sharp contrast to the inexorable rise in GDP. John Gray. False Dawn. Granta Books. 1999. p116.

2) The Institute of Fiscal Studies calculated that by Oct. 2001, as a result of increases in child benefit and benefits aimed at low income families with children, the bottom twenty per cent of households would be 8% better off than they were when Labour came to power. Ed Crooks. 'Chancellor's strategy stays focused on the poor'. Financial Times. 5/3/01.

3) The prison population of the USA was just under 2m. in 1999, up from 500,000 in 1980. Bureau of Justice Statistics. www.angelfire.com Also Ed. Molly Cato and Miriam Kennett. Green Economics. Green Audit. 1999. p123.

CHAPTER 2 – CORPORATE POWER, BIG MONEY AND THE NEED FOR SOCIAL CONTROL

CORPORATE POWER

1) The maquiladoras on the Mexican side of the US border is a good example. In 1980 there were 620 plants employing 119,000 workers. Twelve years later there were 2,200 plants employing over half a million workers. All the major multinationals are involved – Fords, General Electric, General Motors, Westinghouse etc. Average wages in 1992 were $1-64 an hour compared to $16 in US manufacturing industry. Independent unions were banned, there were few public services and pollution was chronic. In 1987 Fords sacked 3,400 workers and reduced wages by 45%. In 1992 Volkeswagen sacked 14,000 workers for refusing to sign a new contract.
David Korten. When Corporations Rule the World. Earthscan. 1995. p.129.

2) On the continent Boards tend to split between a Supervisory Board dominated by independents, and a Management Board. The structure tends to give more power to managers.

3) A. Demb and F. Neubauer. The Corporate Board. Oxford. 1992. Their information was based on interviews with 71 directors serving on more than 500 boards.

4) The Corporate Board (above) p51.

5) Maria Maher and Thomas Anderson. Corporate Governance: Effects on Firm Performance and Economic Growth. OECD. 1999. p16.

Distribution of outstanding corporate equity amongst different types of shareholders.

Type of shareholder	USA '96	Japan '94	Germany '96	UK '94
Banks	5	28	10	8
Pension funds, insurance, investment co.	40	16	20	58
Non financial enterprises	-	24	42	1
Individuals	48	24	15	21
Foreign	4	6	9	9
Other	3	2	4	3
	100	100	100	100

6) Financial Times. Jane Martinson. Shares in the action. 27/4/98.
7) Corporate Governance (above) p.23 onwards.
8) Corporate Governance (above) pp.38&39
9) "At the aggregate level , a survey on Japanese transnational companies in 1989 (the most recent available year) shows that less than one half (47%) of firms acquired by Japanese transnational companies improved their profitability" UNCTAD World Investment Report. 1999 .Chapter III p.28.
10) "As many as 73,000 people were laid off in 1998 from companies involved in mergers and acquisitions in the United States, accounting for 11% of total job losses in that year." World Investment Report (above) p.27.

11) British Empires. The story of BP. Channel 4. 23/1/00

12) Quoted in When Corporations Rule the World (above) p.124. An interesting repeat of this came during the petrol crisis of 2000 when the oil companies were accused of conspiring with the tanker drivers' refusal to deliver fuel. The Daily Mail quoted a senior oil executive as saying "We resent being summoned to Downing Street as though we were just an outpost of government. We are not nationalised industries. We are global companies with, on the whole, more influence around the world than the British government." Daily Mail 17/9/00.

13) Joshua Karliner. The Corporate Planet. Sierra Club Books. 1997.

14) 'Feeding time for the bigger fish'. Global Investment Banking Survey. Financial Times. 26/1/01

15) Financial Times. 11/1/00

16) Financial Times 4/11/99

17) A Survey of Multinationals (above) p.17.

18) "As for capital mobility, UK capital flows between 1905 and 1914, were larger than for any industrial country, including Japan, in the 1980s and 1990s" Martin Wolf. Financial Times. 13/2/96

19) Quoted in Left Business Observer. Issue 72. April 1996. www.panix.com

20) Of the top 50 transnational companies ranked by the size of their foreign assets, exactly half still have the majority of their assets in their country of origin. World Investment Report (above) p.3

21) Tim Burt. Financial Times. 31/8/99

22) David Pilling. Financial Times 17/1/00

23) Unquenchable Thirst. John Willman. Financial Times. 30/4/99

24) The transnational world is a fairly static one. Giants are rarely toppled. 85 of the world's top 100 have been in the table for the last five years

and many are using strategic alliances amongst themselves to expand their foreign activities. UNCTAD World Investment Report (above).

25) See the OECD International Investment Statistics Yearbook. Also 'Investment stereotypes can mislead'. Chris Giles. Financial Times. 6/7/00. Counting take-overs as inward investment has interesting results. The purchase of Orange by Mannesman in 2000 counted as £20bn inward investment. When Orange was sold again a year later, this time by Vodafone, to French Telecom, it again registers as inward investment!

26) Arthur McEwan. Neo Liberalism or Democracy. Zed Books. 1999. p.39.

27) Examples can be found on numerous web sites. Corporate Watch, Friends of the Earth (World Trade Organisation Watch) and Labour Start are three to try (listed at the back). See also Global Warning. Bill Hopwood and Martin Cock. Militant Publications. 1996. or Big Business, Poor Peoples. John Madeley. Zed Books. 2000.

28) Yorkshire Post. Business Week. 5/11/96

29) 'British companies soaring profits outpace many rivals' Financial Times. 20/1/00 . Also 'International comparisons of company profitability'. Economic Trends No. 565. Dec. 2000

30) 'Growth Matters'. Stephanie Flanders. Financial Times. 25/9/95

31) The cost of capital, and so the rate of return required, was found in a study by the accountants Coopers and Lybrand in the early 1990s to be 20% a year in Britain and closer to 15% in the US, Germany and Japan. The State We're In (above) pp.150 & 163.

32) 1998 Capex Scoreboard. DTI Innovation Unit. Reported in Financial Times 9/11/98

33) Between 1989 and 1996 the gross operating surplus (gross profits

plus rental income) of non-financial UK companies rose from £103bn. to £158bn. while investment (gross fixed capital formation) hardly moved. ONS Profitability Bulletin 10/11/99 plus www.statistics.gov.uk/statbase/tsdataset2.asp

34) Manufacturing investment fell by 13% in 1998 largely as a result of competitive conditions and the strong pound. Investment in private sector services rose 27% in the one year, but in 1999 dropped back to an annual growth rate of 7%. Barclays Economic Review. 4th Qtr. 1999. p.5.

35) Lex column. Financial Times.20/1/00

36) Observer. 11/4/99. The phenomenon is particularly noticeable in the US stock market. In the boom conditions at the end of the 1980s companies took advantage of the rising market to issue new shares. The position was completely reversed in the 1990s boom. In the year to Sept. 1999 US companies 'retired' (mostly bought back) $158bn. worth of shares. They just did not want to use the money. '10,001: a stock odyssey'. Richard Waters. Financial Times. 17/3/99

37) British dividend levels as a proportion of profits are four times as large as in Japan and twice as large as in the US. The State We're In (above) p.160.

38) In the 18 months to June 1999 British companies were involved in 8 of the world's largest 20 merger and acquisitions. The deals brought into being companies with a stock market value of $227bn. As a minimum the premium to shareholders in these deals must have come to $20bn., the equivalent of twenty times the annual urban regeneration budget for Britain. UNCTAD World Investment Report (above) Ch.3 p.23.

39) 'Tesco knocks Sainsbury off No.1 perch' Guardian 5/5/98.

40) For discussion see for instance 'Selling to the sated'. Richard Tomkins. Financial Times. 22/3/00.

41) Naomi Klein. No Logo. Harper Collins. 2000. p.23.

42) No Logo (above). 'The global teen' p.119.

43) United Nations. Report on the World Social Situation. 1993. p48.

44) Business Wire. 22/2/99.

45) Business Services as a whole employed 2.1m. people in 1971. By 1997 that had risen to 4.5m. Although employment in banking and insurance fell slightly in the 1990s, employment in the rest of the sector continued to surge ahead with an additional 449,000 employed between 1991and 1996. DFEE . Prospects and Skills Needs in the Banking, Finance and Insurance Sectors. 22/9/99. www.dfee.gov.uk//skillsforce/papers/9f_2.htm.

46) 'It's an ad ad ad ad world'. Richard Tomkins. Financial Times. 21/7/00 and 'Trust me I'm a drug salesman'. David Pelling. Financial Times. 24/10/00.

BIG MONEY

1) Financial Times 27/1/95

2) J. Maynard Keynes. General Theory of Employment, Interest and Money. Macmillan. 1973. p.164.

3) This will be pursued further in the section on the stock market, but one measure of the bloated nature of stock markets is to examine the growth in their value compared to the growth of the real economy or Gross Domestic Product (GDP). The growth is overwhelmingly a result of the increase in share prices and not an increase in the number of shares. Below is the market value of domestic shares as a percentage of GDP:

	1980	1990	1996
Germany	9	22	28
Japan	36	99	66
UK	38	87	142
USA	50	60	114

As can be seen the UK stock market has been particularly effervescent. OECD. Financial Market Trends. Feb. 1998.

4) Initial Public Offerings (IPOs), that is money raised by newly listed companies on the U.S. stock market between 1989 and 1999, amounted to $350bn. Over that same period the value of shares traded between shareholders in the U.S. technology sector alone, rose by $4,200bn. 'Rebuilt by Wall St.' David Hale. Financial Times. 25/1/00

5) The growth in managed equity funds (funds invested largely in shares) is not confined to the Anglo Saxon countries. The growth in such funds across Europe is averaging about 20% a year. 'Changing family fortunes'. Jane Martinson. Financial Times. 27/4/99.

6) www.statistics.gov.uk/stats/ukinfigs/economy.htm . Also 'Pension funds urged to switch assets'. Simon Targett. Financial Times. 14/2/00. The growth in this form of fund has been even more phenomenal in America. In 1980 the mutuals had assets of $58bn, by 1994 the assets were $1,550bn and by 1997 they had reached $3,500bn. The growth of the mutuals has in part been at the expense of the Thrift Banks that historically have not invested savers money in shares (Risk and Reward

in Mutual Funds. Financial Times. 14/8/95 and also John Authers. Financial Times 22/1/97).

7) Mergers between the major fund managers continue and 20-25 are expected to dominate the entire industry in a few years. The globalisation of these funds is demonstrated by the value of pension funds being invested abroad rising from $302bn. in 1989 to $790bn. in 1994. Kavaljit Singh. Globalisation of Finance. Zed Books. 1999. p.25. Some argue (for instance US economist Paul Krugman) that falling saving ratios in countries like the US and UK, indicate a fall in the value of savings internationally, not an increase. This is possibly true in the recent past for the US, though an interesting study was recently produced in Canada showing how financial assets can rise while savings ratios fall (www.vifamily.ca/cft/sauve/sauve2). What is undeniable is the increase in the amount of savings that are internationally mobile and are being invested in shares. Deregulation of European pension funds for example has led to massive purchases of foreign bonds and shares (£28bn net outflow in Jan 2001 alone), that partly explains the low level of the Euro. Another indication is that foreign ownership of UK stock market shares rose from 12% to 27% in the decade up to 1999. 'Policy makers unconcerned at Euro's slide'. Chris Swann. Financial Times. 2/4/01. 'A judicious shake up'. John Plender. Financial Times. 7/3/01.

8) In the seventies, UK fixed interest bonds and property accounted for about 45% of pension fund investment. By 1996 they made up only 11%. Almost 80% of the funds were in shares by this time. Pension Fund Investment Supplement. Financial Times. 9/5/97.

9) 'Sick as a parrot'. Jane Martinson. Financial Times. 13/10/97

10) www.hm-treasury.gov.uk/pub/html/top/top8/an2.html.

11) 'Pension funds show second best results in ten years'. Simon Targett. Financial Times. 11/1/00

12) 'Blair urges pension funds to support new businesses'. David Wighton. Financial Times. 7/7/99

13) When Corporations Rule the World (above) p.200.

14) Dow Jones index was 717 at its low point in 1982. By February 2000 it was 10,500. The various figures come from '10,001: a stock odyssey'. Richard Waters. Financial Times 17/3/99 and 'Walking on troubled waters'. Martin Wolf. Financial Times. Jan 2000.

15) Equities are 39% of US personal sector net wealth, compared with 8% in Germany and 13% in France. 'Averting a free fall'. Philip Coggan. Financial Times. 2/9/98

16) By contrast the IT sector represents only 5.1% of stock market capitalisation in Germany, 9.4% in France and 4.9% in Britain. 'Rebuilt by Wall St.' David Hale. Financial Times. 25/1/00

17) 'Sparkling debuts'. Andrew Hill. Financial Times. 21/12/99. Details of Boo.com come from Caroline Daniel. 'How not to survive on $135m. a year'. Financial Times. 20/6/00.

18) 'Bears on the Prowl'. David Schwartz. Financial Times. 25/9/99

19) The market value of Microsoft in early 2000 was $535bn. The company's property, plant and equipment were valued at just $1.5bn. All the rest of the value comes from shareholder belief that there are sufficient skills in the company to guarantee future profits. As another example America Online has a larger market value than the whole American transportation industry (railways, trucking and airways). 'Unbearable lightness of being'. John Plender. Financial Times. 8/12/98.

20) During the 1990s the US equity market produced a total return of 18.4% a year. Over the same period profits increased 8.4% a year

and this during an exceptionally favourable period. The remorseless long-term logic is that dividend growth (for our purposes the same as profits growth) must come into line with share value growth if it is to be based on anything but dreams. 'The US cycle theory'. David Hale. Financial Times. 17/2/99.

21) Sam Brittan. Financial Times. 20/1/00

22) Susan Strange. Mad Money. Manchester University Press. 1999. p.55

23) Financial Times 21/12/99 (above)

24) The effect of a stock market decline is devastating for a place like New York City. Almost a third of all wages are earned by people working in the banking and securities sectors (though concentrated amongst a small number! In 1999 $13bn. was paid out to Wall St. bankers in bonuses). This is up from 22% at the beginning of the 1990s. In the 1987 stock market fall, even though it was not a permanent feature, the decline in trading caused a 40,000-drop in those employed in Wall St. New York Property. Financial Times Survey. 17/12/99

25) Financial Times 8/12/98 (above)

26) Kavaljit Singh. Globalisation of Finance. Zed Books. 1999. p.7.

27) Quoted in Frank Portnoy. FIASCO. Profile Books. 1997. p.89.

28) W. Greider. One World Ready or Not. Simon and Schuster. 1997. p.263.

29) As an expression of instability it is worth noting that the Asian Tigers saw an inflow of funds of $93bn. in 1995 turn to an outflow of $12bn. two years later. A turnaround equivalent to 10% of their combined GDP. Figures from Kavaljit Singh (above) and Korean Herald 24/12/97.

30) 'Financial Warfare'. Summary article to Michel Chossudovsky. The Globalisation of Poverty. Zed Books. 1997.

31) In 1995 the largest 26 economies accounted for outstanding derivatives of $47.5 trillion. All but two per cent were in currency or interest rate derivatives. Mad Money (above) p.30.

32) Frank Portnoy. FIASCO. Profile Books. 1997.

33) FIASCO (above) p.44

34) FIASCO (above) p.88

35) A UN estimate. Mad Money (above) p.127.

36) Bank for International Settlements. 69th Annual Report 1999. Intoduction: the darker side of the market process. p.8.

CHAPTER 3 – THE FAILURE OF CENTRAL PLANNING

1) Sotsialisticheskoe stroitel'stvo 1934

2) I. Babel. Izbrannoe. Moscow.1966. p.281

3) KPSS v rezolyutsiyakh Vol.9 1972 pp. 42, 49, 50. + 1986 statistical handbook.

4) A. Birman Novy mir, No.1 1967.

5) Is Market Socialism Possible? Debate between H. Ticktin and Prof. Brus. Critique 14 1981.

6) N. Barzin. Ekonomicheskaya Nauka. p.43. 1965

7) Izvestia 19/8/85. Also see for instance The Soviet Worker Ed. Leonard Schapiro. Macmillan. 1981

8) Pravda 23/3/72

9) Quoted in Ticktin - Towards a Political Economy of the USSR. Critique1 1973.

10) Trotsky. Soviet Economy in Danger 1932. Printed in Towards Socialism or Capitalism. New Park Publications. 1976. p.113.

11) Hungary - A Decade of Reforms. Ed. P. Hare. George Allen and Unwin 1981 p.28.

12) Cave and Hare. Alternative Approaches to Economic Planning. Macmillan 1981. pp20 & 50.

13) Peter Bihari. Reflections on Hungary's Social Revolution. Socialist Register 1991

14) Peter Rutland. The Myth of the Plan - Limits to Reform. Hutchinson 1985 p.200.

15) P. Hare (above) pp.3 & 49.

16) Statistics in this section are taken from either:
Milojko Drulovic. Self Management on Trial. Spokesman Books. 1978
or
Chris Prout. Market Socialism in Yugoslavia. Oxford University. 1985.

17) One of the distortions produced by enterprise power was that differentials were much greater between workers doing the same job at different enterprises than between all workers at the same workplace because of the relation to profitability.

18) Michele Lee. Labour Focus on Eastern Europe. Nov 1987.

19) Paul Hare. Planning the British Economy. Radical Economics. 1985. p39.

20) United Nations Development Programme. Transition 1999 - Europe and CIS Human Development Report.

21) China Survey. Financial Times. 27/6/96

22) John McNeill. What is happening in China? Socialism Today. Sept. 1999.

23) The Long March. Radio 4. 13/9/99

CHAPTER 4 – THE GREENING OF SOCIALISM

1) Details from Derek Wall. Red – Green or a new shade of grey? Red Pepper. February 2000. Derek Wall has been a member of the

Ecology Party / Greens since 1979 and is writing a history of the Green Party.

2) For instance 170,000 sq. km. of rainforest is cleared each year. Bill Hopwood and Martin Cock. Global Warning. Militant Publications. 1996.

3) Green Party General Election Manifesto 1997. See also www.greenparty.org.uk

4) Molly Scott Cato. Employment Spokesperson for the Green Party in 1999. Green Economics. Green Audit. 1999. p.39

5) Meghnad Desai. Paper written in June 1997. Available through Citizen's Income Study Centre. www.citizensincome.org

6) Richard Douthwaite. Short Circuit. Green Books. 1996. pp.31&32.

7) Molly Scott Cato. Green Economics (above) p.46.

8) For information on LETS www.letslinkuk.org

9) For information on Credit Unions www.abcul.org Association of British Credit Unions

10) For information on social enterprise www.sel.org.uk Social Enterprise London

11) For information on organics www.organics.uk.com

12) Victor Anderson. Can there be sensible economics? Green Economics. p.24.

13) Ian Hargreaves. New Mutualism. Co-operative Press. 1999

14) Paul Jones. Towards Sustainable Credit Union Development. Research paper from John Moores University. 1999

15) Short Circuit (above) pp.150-153.

16) Financial World Tonight. 1993. Quoted in Short Circuit (above) p.152

17) Short Circuit (above) p.368.

18) We wish "To devolve economic power to the lowest appropriate level, thereby rendering participants in the economy at all levels, less

vulnerable to the damaging effects of economic decisions made elsewhere and over which they have no control" page 1.

"Individual consumer choice can be exercised positively, in favour of environmentally and ethically sound products, and investment, including promotion of low interest loans; negatively as in consumer boycotts; or actively in favour of ethical investment and reduced overall consumption." page 2.

"In a decentralised economy, most taxation will be levied, most public services provided, and most expenditure decisions made at local level by local government....The revenue required should be raised locally, by local taxes which each local community selects from an agreed range of options, or be created by local community (or municipal) banks to fund capital expenditure" page 3

"Phased restrictions on the powers of commercial banks and other institutions to create money by credit can be introduced by such means as reserve asset ratio requirements, special deposits, personal credit controls, together with more directive guidance to banks and building societies to limit lending" page 6

"The damage caused by transnational corporations (TNCs) can be tackled through both economic and legal sanctions such as initiating research on TNC activities throughout the world; setting up national and international capital controls to ensure profits made by TNCs are reinvested in the countries of origin; legislation against transfer pricing activities; banning the export of environmentally damaging technologies and products; the acquisition of patents from TNCs to enable smaller companies to take over some of their activities" page 12

Manifesto for a Sustainable Society, Green Party
www.greenparty.org.uk/homepage/policy/mfss/economy.html Feb. 2000.

CHAPTER 5 – OUTLINES OF A SOCIALIST ECONOMY

1) 'Approval of big business at 30 year low'. Financial Times. 22/2/99. In similar vein a recent survey found only 11% of people in the USA, Europe and Australia trusted business to 'do the right thing'. Edelman Public Relations. Reported in Financial Times 6/12/00.

2) The Consumers Association, a member controlled charity, is a foretaste of what a fully-fledged consumer movement could look like. It has 600,000 members, an annual income of £50m. and 500 staff involved in research, advocacy and enquiry work. www.which.net

3) Vladimir Fisera. Worker's Councils in Czechoslovakia. Documents and essays 1968/9. Alison and Busby. 1978.

4) Remembering that the £800bn. in pension funds alone controls over one third of the UK stock market. Together with insurance companies the share is close to 60%. Simon Targett. Institutional Shareholders. Financial Times. 31/3/00

5) Beyond the Casino Economy (above) p.133

6) 'Putting Money to Work'. London Financial Strategy. GLC Industry and Employment Branch. 1985.

7) The position of the present Labour government towards business widening its responsibility beyond shareholders was made clear by the Trade Secretary Stephen Byers in response to a recent TUC request. He said it would be wrong to require companies to take equal account of the concerns of employees and customers along with shareholders. He suggested it would give directors an impossible task and damage their key focus on their company's success. Robert

Taylor. 'Byers rejects suggestion that companies become stakeholder enterprises'. Financial Times. 8/6/00.

8) National Institute for Economic and Social Research. April 2000

9) Ed Crooks. 'Lack of investment is enemy of business'. Financial Times. 6/4/00

10) The UK Skills Survey 1997 and other research studies indicate that some 30% of the workforce have more qualifications than they need to do their job. Francis Green. 'Overeducation – A tough nut to crack'. Centre Piece. London School of Economics. Spring 2000.

11) E.H. Carr. The Bolshevik Revolution. 1917 – 1923. Pelican Books. 1976. pp. 198 and 285.

12) Interestingly, as a punishment for their financial incompetencies, this is already happening in Taiwan. Since April 2001 banks have been forced to post detailed quarterly financial statements on the internet to prove to customers they are being well managed. Mure Dickie. 'Taiwan banks to put data on internet'. Financial Times. 19/1/01

13) E.Miles et al. The Future.org. in Long Range Planning No. 33. Pergamon 2000.

14) Peter Marsh. 'Profitable ideas that travel the globe'. Financial Times. 29/8/00

15) Richard Koch and Ian Godden. Managing Without Management. Nicholas Brealey Publishing. 1996.

16) Lex Column. Financial Times. 26/2/00

17) Richard Wise. Beyond the Exchange. The Future of B2B. Harvard Business Review. Dec 2000.

18) Uta Harnischfeger. 'The sale of German utilities stirs passions'. Financial Times. 5/3/01.

19) Carol Kennedy. Review of 'Managing without Management'. Financial Times. 23/8/96

20) Peter Marsh. 'Kaizen thinking fires productivity'. Financial Times. 23/11/99.

21) A wide ranging survey of available evidence on the efficiency of public and private companies produced the following summary comment "Neither finding (the effects of competition and regulation – CH) is inconsistent with the findings about the effect of ownership on costs – namely that, balancing the results of electricity and railroads against water, airlines and refuse collection, there is no general indication that private firms are more cost efficient than public firms" R.Millward. The Nationalised Industries in M. Artis and D. Cobham .Labour's Economic Policies '74-'79. Manchester University Press. 1991.

also   Total factor productivity (output divided by labour and capital) increased more in the UK from 1950 to 1985 than in the US in mining, gas, electricity, water, transport and communication while productivity growth in manufacturing as a whole was similar. M. Sawyer and K. McDonnell. A Future for Public Ownership. Lawrence and Wishart. 1999. p.26.

also   In a study of 12 privatised British companies in the four years before and four years after privatisation, half of them experienced falls in productivity even after allowing for the recession of the early 1980s. Martin and Parker. 'The impact on technical efficiency of the UK privatisation programme'. Applied Economics 1997. vol. 29 pp 297-310.

22) Figures derived from Financial Times Budget Special. 22/3/00.

23) James Robertson. Alternative Mansion House speech. Reported in New Economy. New Economics Foundation. Issue 14. July 2000.

CURRENCY AND TRADE CONTROL

1) J.M. Keynes. Pros and cons of tariffs. The Listener. 30th Nov. 1932. Reprinted in The Collective Writings of John Maynard Keynes (ed. D. Moggridge) Macmillan, London, 1982, vol. 21 pp. 204-210.
2) J.Stanford et al. Social Dumping under North American Free Trade. Canadian Centre for Policy Alternatives, Ottowa. Sept. 1993.
3) Graham Dunkley. The Free Trade Adventure. Zed Books. 2000. p.163
4) A fall of 1.3% in the value of exports over the first ten years was predicted for African, Caribbean and Pacific countries due to falling commodity prices. S.Page et al. The GATT Uruguay Round. Effects on Developing Countries. Overseas Development Institute. London. 1992.
5) J. Francois et al. Assessing the Uruguay Round. World Bank Conference Paper. 26/27 Jan 1995. Table 9.
6) Paul Krugman. The Age of Diminished Expectations. MIT Press. 1991. Ch.9.
7) Leon Trotsky. My Life. Penguin Books. 1975. p.257
8) Mike Crone. Local Sourcing by Multinational Enterprise Plants. Northern Ireland Economic Research Centre. Jan 2000.

CO-OPERATIVES

1) Ian Hargreaves. New Mutualism. The Co-operative Party. 1999. p.34
2) Richard Gourlay. 'Spreading the ESOP message'. Financial Times. 2/5/95
3) National Centre for Employee Ownership (USA). An overview of ESOPs. www.nceo.org/library/overview. 26/3/00.
4) Industrial Common Ownership Movement. 'Employee Ownership

Options'. New Sector. Issue 33. 1998.

5) Seikatsu Club Consumers Co-operative Union. http://iisd1.iisd.ca/50comm/commdb/desc/d08htm

6) New Co-operator. Issue 1. Vol.44. March 2001 and 'Ethics more important than money'. Financial Times. 22/8/00.

7) New Mutualism (above) p.15

8) CWS. A family of businesses. Delivering co-operative values. CWS. Sept. 1998. Also Annual Report 1997.

9) Food Crimes. A consumer perspective on the ethics of modern food production. CWS . May 2000.

10) Information on Mondragon was drawn from the following. Their web site www.mondragon.mcc.es .
Sharryn Kasmir. The Myth of Mondragon. Co-operatives, politics and working class life in a basque town. State University of New York Press. 1996.
Mark Lutz. The Mondragon co-operative complex. International Journal of Social Economics 1997 24(12), pp.1404-1421.
Howard Ehrlich. The Challenge of Mondragon. AK Press. 1996

11) In all parts of a socialised economy, the struggle to achieve a balance between meaningful democracy and effective management will be continuous. A short but instructive history on this score, can be found on the SUMA web site - a wholefood distribution co-operative of 70 employees. www.suma.co.uk/aboutus

PRIVATE ENTERPRISE

1) As an example, in a survey undertaken in 1994, 88% of firms with more than 500 employees had staff training plans. In firms with less than 25 employees this fell to just 17%. Employment Gazette. July

1994 p.231

2) Department of Trade and Industry (DTI), Small and Medium Enterprise (SME) statistics 1998 www.statistics.gov.uk/news/sme.htm , plus Labour Market Trends. Small and Medium Enterprises: their role in the economy. Oct. 1999.

3) Radio 4. 'Everybody has a dream'. 29/12/99

4) Nigel Meager. Institute of Employment. Sussex University. 1993.

5) Chris Adams. 'Venturers have more than one hill to climb'. Financial Times. 16/11/99

6) David Goodhart. 'Scepticism on jobs role of small business'. Financial Times 2/2/94.

7) Amar Bhide. The Origin and Evolution of New Business. Oxford University Press. 1999.

8) William Bygrave. 'How venture capitalists work out the odds'. Supplement - Mastering Enterprise 3. Financial Times. 1996.

9) Mark Atkinson. 'Challenge to ties that bind investment'. Guardian. 9/5/00

10) David Roche. 'The View from the Ivory Tower'. Forbes Global. 5/10/98

CHAPTER 6 - PROSPECTS FOR THE LEFT

1) In the 1928 election Hitler's party only received 2.6% of the vote. By 1932 that had risen to 37.3%. For an excellent review of the left in Germany after the First World War and beyond see Chris Harman. The Lost Revolution. Bookmarks. 1982.

2) Reduced voter participation is not an exclusively British phenomenon. In 18 of the world's 20 most industrialised countries turnout has decreased since the '50s - on average by 10%. Tom Bentley. It's

Democracy Stupid. Demos. 2000.

3) 'Roy's remarkable revolutionary call'. John McDonnell MP. Red Pepper. Aug 2001

4) Colin Ward. Anarchism. Red Pepper. March 2000.

5) PGA Bulletin No1. March '97. www.agp.org/agp/en/PGAInos/bulletin1

6) World Development Movement Report. Letter to the Financial Times 9/5/01.

7) The Socialist. 27/7/01.

8) Books by these activists include: The Economic Horror, Viviane Forrester, Polity Press, 1999. Fate Worse than Debt, Susan George, Pluto Press, 2000. No Logo, Naomi Klein, Flamingo, 2000. Global Finances, Walden Bello (Ed.), Zed Books, 2000.

9) The Global Conjuncture: Characteristics and Challenges, Walden Bello, Focus on Trade No.60, March 2001.

10) 'The polite face of anti-globalisation'. Alan Beattie. Financial Times. 6/4/01.

11) 'It's Democracy Stupid'. Demos (above).

12) System 3 poll for the Herald. Published 6/8/01.

13) In a study by Edinburgh University the number of Scottish voters describing themselves as 'left of the Labour Party', increased from 32 to 45% between 1997 and 2001. Scottish Socialist Voice. 10/4/01.

SOME USEFUL WEB SITES

Research into Social Conditions

www.sosig.ac.uk
The social science information gateway

www.jrf.org.uk
Joseph Rowntree Foundation. UK's largest independent social policy research charity

www.data-archive.ac.uk
The largest collection of social science data in the UK

www.ilo.org
International Labour Organisation. Employment information.

www.statistics.gov.uk
Official UK statistics site.

Economic stats and info

www.netec.mcc.ac.uk/WebEc
Free web resources for economic information

www.oecd.org
Organisation of Economic Co-operation and Development

www.imf.org
International Monetary Fund

www.worldbank.org
World Bank

www.hm-treasury.gov.uk
The Treasury

www.ifs.org.uk
Institute of Fiscal Studies. Info on tax and benefits

www.bankofengland.co.uk
Bank of England

www.niesr.ac.uk
National Institute of Economic and Social Research

www.europa.eu.int
Eurostat. Loads of European statistics

www.unctad.org

United Nations Conference on Trade and Development. Good for facts
on globalisation.

What's happening?

www.labourstart.org
Where trade unionists start their day on the net

www.corpwatch.org
Counters corporate led globalisation through education and activism

www.webdirectory.com
The world's biggest environment search engine

www.uk.indymedia.org
Useful anarchist inspired direct action news service

www.wtowatch.org
World Trade Organisation watch. Global information centre on trade and sustainable development.

www.oneworld.org
A wide ranging mainstream progressive site

www.zmag.org
Znet is a collecting point for US radical criticism and activism.

Who is making it happen in the UK?

www.leftdirect.co.uk
Comprehensive directory of all left, green and radical websites in the UK

www.socialistparty.org.uk
The Socialist Party looks to the future establishment of a broad-based workers party

www.worldsocialist-cwi.org
The socialist international that the Socialist Party is affiliated to.

www.scottishsocialistparty.org
The UK's fastest growing party!

www.socialistalliance.net
The site of the Socialist Alliance

All sites were active in August 2001.

BIOGRAPHICAL NOTE

Chris Hill was educated as an economist. He has spent most of his life working on development plans with private and socially owned businesses. After twenty years as an activist in the Labour Party, he was expelled in 1993 and is now a member of the Socialist Party.

He would welcome any comments on the book and can be contacted at chrishill.leeds@btinternet.com